Our
CEILING,
Your
FLOOR

Our CEILING, *Your* FLOOR

Thana Rolph

XULON PRESS

Xulon Press
2301 Lucien Way #415
Maitland, FL 32751
407.339.4217
www.xulonpress.com

Printed in the United States of America

Paperback ISBN-13: 978-1-6628-0194-5
Ebook ISBN-13: 978-1-6628-0195-2

In loving memory of Dick,
my husband, best friend, prayer partner, prod (kick in the pants),
and the one with whom I was incredibly blessed to
share sixty years of life

TABLE OF CONTENTS

INTRODUCTION

⟋

IN 2008, MY HUSBAND DICK AND I WERE LOOKING
forward to our fiftieth wedding anniversary. Our daughters had
arranged for a family gathering in Whistler, Canada, to celebrate.
Dick had been bugging me for a long time to write the story of our
life's adventures to share with our grandchildren. This seemed like
the appropriate time. But, if I was going to have their attention,
the teacher in me said I needed to give them more than our story.
I needed to give them the keys to replicate it and go beyond it. I
wanted to show them how to make our ceiling their floor. With
every chapter from our life's story, I included a Bible study and a
guideline for application. I also included an appendix with some
how-to information and a section with scripture I'd gathered over
the years under topics like family, fear, worry, friendship, love,
protection, provision, etc. I had the results printed, and we gave a
copy to each family member at our anniversary celebration.

I also gave a copy to a few friends. I'd only printed fifty copies.
Some of those friends passed them on to their friends, and I got
some very positive feedback over the years. Yesterday, when I
called one of those friends to ask if she thought I should include
the topical scripture section this time, she said, "Absolutely, I'll
buy a copy for each of my kids. This generation doesn't study the
Bible like we did. They need to be able to find what they need."

Through the years, I've had a number of people who wanted to
buy a copy, but I didn't have any more copies. Last year, on what
would have been our sixty-first wedding anniversary, I celebrated
it alone by rereading the story parts of the book over again. It was
still a wonderful story, and I thought, "I should get more copies

printed." Then I went on about my business. Since the coronavirus hit, all God's kids have had some time to reflect on what's important in life. I sensed the Lord telling me that a lot of His family need to read the story I wrote for mine and that He would like for me to finish it. So, I added four more chapters to conclude the story of a woman (me) who spent her life trying to figure out who she is and where she fits in life. This book records that success story. I hope you not only enjoy my journey, but that it helps YOU make Our Ceiling, Your Floor.

Chapter 1

HOW DID I END UP
WHERE I WASN'T GOING?

―

IT WAS JULY 5, 1966. DICK'S BOSS, WHO LIVED RIGHT across the street, stood in the doorway. He looked uncomfortable, apologetic, and was measuring his words carefully. There had been an accident. The plane had crashed. Everyone was alive, but we needed to get there as soon as possible. "There" was a small town some eighty miles east of Rapid City, South Dakota.

I was bewildered. I didn't know what to do or how to respond. I looked at my three little girls. Cindy, the oldest, was not quite seven. Dick was in a hospital someplace, and they "thought he'd live." What on earth did that mean? ...Get my things. They would wait for us.

The ride took forever. When we finally got there, I found my husband with multiple breaks in his back and chest and his front teeth knocked out, but, no, he wasn't paralyzed, and, yes, he would live. The small private plane, piloted by the boss' son, had tried to land on a short landing strip. The first try didn't work, so he had pulled it up. The second time, when he tried to pull back up, he was too close to powers lines, which caught the wheels and flipped the plane. Later Dick told me he had found himself lying on a wing. He didn't know how he had gotten there, but he remembered thinking, "I'm really hurt. I'm really hurt bad."

1

The next six weeks were a blur. They moved Dick back to Rapid City, which was home, in just a few days. But everything else took an eternity. Dick's brother, Neal, and his wife, Janice, were also living in Rapid City, and his folks got there as fast as they could.

When the day finally came that I could take Dick home, the nurses must have had a party. My man, who didn't even like sitting still for very long, was not happy flat on his back. Being home was better, but there was still a body cast that kept his activity down to doing some crafts and trying his hand at painting.

Dick had been a man on a mission. His goal had been to be a millionaire by the time he was forty, and he was on his way. But there's something about a brush with death and months of being incapacitated that rearranges values. During the time we were trying to figure out our next step, Dick received a call to work for a Fortune 500 company in Chicago. Earlier he had had an opportunity for a position as a chemical engineer in an oil refinery in Houston. Either would have been a step up the millionaire ladder, but he didn't want to raise our girls in Houston, and he thought Chicago would be even worse. He was ready to go home to Kansas, and his new goal became to own a hog farm and raise the girls in the country.

Dick had been in church all his life, and I had been since sixth grade. We were both born again, but we didn't either one really know the Lord. We knew religion, and we did our best to live by what we knew, but we didn't KNOW Jesus. We didn't know how to war over our circumstances in those days. We didn't even know how to pray for God's direction for our next step, but we went home to Kansas, taking a huge cut in pay and drastically changing the course of our lives, and whether we knew it or not, God was in the middle of all of it.

Three decades later, while living in Austin, Dick was driving past the oil refineries in Houston. The thought crossed his mind, "I wonder how things would have been different if I'd taken that job in Houston. I wonder if we'd be where we are in our relationship with God." The thought had only just entered his mind when he heard God say, "It wouldn't have made any difference. I'd have gotten you where I wanted you anyway."

What an interesting thought! Our trail had led through the County Extension Service in Salina, the hog farm near Delphos, ten years of my teaching high school English, Youth with a Mission, the mission field in Mexico, and a church staff in Austin, among other things. We had forfeited a secure retirement, not to mention the million dollars, but we gained the One who meets all our needs. We've never regretted our choice to leave the corporate world, but it's comforting to know that God is big enough to take whatever choice we might have made and work it for our good if we set our hearts to know Him.

God wants relationship. He wants to be known.

Just like you want to be known and loved for who you really are, He wants us to know Him and love Him for who He really is. He doesn't want us to obey out of fear, nor does He want us to draw close only because of what He can do for us. He doesn't just want to do things **for** us. He wants to do things **with** us. He wants friends and lovers and partners with whom He can share destiny.

Our destiny is encoded in our DNA. King David called it the "desires of your heart." *Psalm 37:4 Delight yourself also in the LORD, and He shall give you the desires of your heart.* That verse doesn't mean that if you're good you'll get what you want. It means that the deepest desires of your heart were placed within you by God Himself. He put them there because he has exciting and meaningful things for you to do, things that matter, but they are so great that you will only be able to do them with His enabling.

Most of us have made a great mistake in thinking God wants us to do things for Him. He wants us to do them with Him. He delights in your ideas and your creativity. He delights in your discovering great truths and attempting great feats. He delights in a baby's first steps. He delights in a football player's first solid hit. He delights in anything that makes us realize we are more than we thought we were, and we can do more than what we thought we could do. He delights most of all when we attempt the thing we know we can't do unless He helps us, and we step out in the faith that He'll show up. We delight ourselves in the Lord when we take that step of faith into something that will take all we have to give plus the Lord's enabling. There is nothing so satisfying in the world as knowing you gave your all, and God showed up to give the little extra to put you over.

Think about the deepest desires of your heart—the ones you scarcely dare to dream. What would they look like if you put feet to them? What would be the first step? Don't expect it to be easy. God gives you a vision that you will have to grow into. If you don't have to grow into it, the vision is too small. If you wouldn't need His supernatural enablement to do it, you haven't dreamed big enough. But what if you knew that even if you failed, God would still get you where He wants you? Great men and women dream great dreams. A setback is not a failure; it's simply a place of adjustment where you press back into God to allow Him to make the necessary changes so that you can grow into your destiny. Remember, God's values are eternal. He cares more about your character than your accomplishment. Battles and setbacks are simply the fertile ground where character grows.

Dare to dream big, and when problems come, just look at them as a retooling to prepare to go higher.

I WANT TO KNOW MORE - 1
Nehemiah, Man of Destiny

Deep in the soil of Nehemiah's heart were buried seeds of passion for a place he had never seen. More than a century before he was even born, his ancestors had been taken from their homeland

and led into captivity in Babylon. Nehemiah knew nothing of Jerusalem except from the stories that had been passed down from generation to generation of the place God had given as a homeland to the Jewish people. He probably didn't even know anyone who had actually been there, and yet, there was a hunger within that stirred every time he heard about the place. There was an empty place that nothing seemed to satisfy.

Based on the world's standards, he should have been satisfied. His position as cupbearer to the King was one of great authority and prestige, but there was something inside, like a call from somewhere beyond time that simply had to be answered.

> ➤ Read the first chapter of Nehemiah. What do you see in the passage that tells you that Nehemiah's heart for his people and his land didn't start with this report about Jerusalem?

> ➤ What things did he pray that tell you that Nehemiah already closely identified with the history of his people?

> ➤ What shows you that Nehemiah's relationship with God was personal and real?

The month of Chisley, mentioned in verse 1, corresponds with our months of November/December. In verse one of chapter 2, we have passed to the month of Nisan, which would be March/April. So, the prayer we read in chapter one wasn't something Nehemiah came up with on the spur of the moment. It was the culmination of around four months of fasting and praying and seeking God.

I imagine that the first part of those four months was spent in crying out to God over the situation in Jerusalem. You don't weep and fast and pray for many days unless there is a heavy burden in your heart. How do you think that burden got there? That deep desire to help a people and a city he'd never seen was born out of the seeds of destiny planted in Nehemiah's heart before he was even born. He was God's chosen man to do a very important job, and the empty place in his heart was designed to connect with the purpose God had for his life.

> ➢ Do you sense a place like that in your own heart that seems to beckon to something greater or more significant than anything you actually know? Can you identify anything that seems to touch that place and stir it up? If so, record what you sense in the last section of this lesson, or just get a spiral notebook to record thoughts that are meaningful to you.

Somewhere during that four months, Nehemiah received a certainty in his heart that he was to go and rebuild the walls of Jerusalem. Then he had to take up with God the logistics of the thing. How would he do it? How would he get permission to leave his responsibility to the king? How would he get the materials he needed to do the job? Those were all issues to be worked through in the presence of God's wisdom and guidance.

God didn't just plant a deep desire in Nehemiah's heart. He had obviously gifted him with administrative abilities to do the job he was called to do. God had also placed Nehemiah in the position to have access to the authority and resources he would need to do the job.

When you are seeking your destiny, there needs to be an alignment of several things. There is a desire or passion in your heart. You will have the gifts to do the job, and opportunity will present itself. However, the time between uncovering the desire and the opportunity to fully do it will be a lot longer than four months. It took four months for Nehemiah to pray through the specific course of action. It had taken a lifetime to get him to the place of actually being able to answer his call.

Life is made up of seasons. <u>Your purpose in life doesn't change, but your assignments do.</u> Your purpose is connected to the desire of your heart. For example, my purpose has to do with helping other people discover and go after their purpose. I'm sixty-eight years old, and I'm still try to define my purpose clearly, but I've always had a deep desire to understand who I am, who others are, and how life works so that we can be who we really are. I have had a lot of seemingly unrelated assignments geared to develop my character, hone my skills, and free me from my bondages. Nehemiah had those too. We get just glimpses of them in the prayer we have recorded, and we see more of them throughout his book, but it was all that God had already deposited in him plus the passion of his heart plus the specific direction and help from God that led to the results of that time of prayer.

➤ Read verses 1 through 5 of chapter two. Imagine yourself in Nehemiah's place. Why would he be so afraid?

➤ What risk was he taking?

➤ What indication do you see that he was partnering with and depending on God as he made his request?

➤ What can you learn about partnering with God in the adventure of life from Nehemiah's story?

As you continue to read chapter two, you see that not only does Nehemiah ask permission to go, he also asks for the resources he will need to do the job. Verse 8 says, *"And the king granted them to me according to the good hand of my God upon me."*

We'll study more about Nehemiah in another chapter. He's an amazing example of how a man, who has learned to partner with God, runs his life. Nehemiah not only teaches us to seek for God's direction in all things, he also gives a really good picture of how to handle the schemes of the enemy. You can use the following page to record the things God shows you about how to live your life in a strong and effective way. Simply ask God to reveal to you what He wants you to see through Nehemiah's story. Then record the ideas and insights that come to you as you read. Take time to meditate on passages that seem important and ask God for further understanding. The Bible is a living book. You aren't limited to what other people say it means. There are messages hidden within it that are just for you. One of the jobs of the Holy Spirit is to reveal the treasures that God has hidden there especially for you to discover.

Nehemiah was a destiny builder. So are you. Do the section called "I Want to Go Higher" to gain more insight into the desires and callings of your own heart.

I WANT TO CLIMB HIGHER - 1
Uncovering the Desires of Your Heart

Consider the following questions. You don't have to answer each of the questions individually. Just use them in the way that works best for you to do a heart search, and write about your real desires, as you currently perceive them. For this exercise, step outside of all the limitations that would rise up to hinder you. Just turn them off. You have God's permission to dream.

What is the desire of your heart?

What do you dream about?

What do you care most about?

What ideas or topics light your jets?

If money, age, education, time, family connections were not an issue, what would you really like to do?

What would you do if God said, "I give you permission to dream a great dream and do what is the desire of your heart"? What would you do with your life if you could do anything?

What one thing would you like to change if you could change one thing in the world?

What types of characters in movies or novels call forth the most identification in desire?

Why do you like that type of character?

Talk to God about what you see from your answers concerning your real heart's desire. Right now, it doesn't matter if the thing you see seems impossible. Just write out the desire or desires of your heart as clearly as you can define them at this point. Remember, this isn't written in stone. You can revise it as you see it more clearly.

Chapter 2

IDENTITY

———

My father was a good man. He was hardworking, honest, and well respected in the community. He was a good man, but that didn't necessarily make him a good father. Don't get me wrong; he wasn't a bad father. He protected me, provided for me, taught me to be responsible, and many other things that a father should do. He just didn't help me discover who I am. Children draw their identities from their fathers more than from anyone else. As they grow, they look into the mirror their parents, especially their fathers, hold before them to discover what sort of person they are to be. A really good father looks for the gifts and aptitudes that God has placed within his children and calls them forth. He encourages his children to pursue activities that will help them discover who they were created to be. In a perfect world an earthly father would reflect the character of the Heavenly Father, but this isn't a perfect world. I don't think it ever occurred to my father that I might have been created to be different from him. If it had occurred to him, he wouldn't have known what to do with that information.

He worked hard. Everyone should work hard. He didn't like parties or neighborhood gatherings. Why should anyone want to waste time that way? He didn't like cities. Why would we ever want to go to one? He liked asparagus, so I got a spanking every time I refused to eat it. I loved to read, but I felt guilty every time he found me lying on the living room floor with a novel. I don't remember him ever saying that I was wasting time, and I know he wanted me to learn, but nevertheless, the reflection I got from my dad-mirror said I would do better to be doing something more productive. My dad had spent his early manhood in the grips of the Great Depression. He had taken it upon himself to save his parents from bankruptcy. It was such a responsible and admirable thing to do, but the effects of that season had put an eternal warp in his mirror.

The reflections we get from our parents define what we believe life should be and how we should fit into it. My problem was that the desires God had placed in my heart, and the gifts He had given me, didn't align with what my dad-mirror said should be there. That has left me with a lifelong struggle to find and understand my own identity.

Dick's dad, on the other hand, put his children's welfare above all else. He didn't spoil them; he simply loved them well. Dick remembers working in the field from the time he was twelve years old. When he looked in his dad-mirror, he saw respect. He saw that he was capable. He also saw his parents in the stands at every football game, every basketball game, and every baseball game. They encouraged and supported all the things that were important to him. They worked hard together, and they played hard together. Dick never questioned his identity. He was a man while he was still a boy, and he believed that he could do anything he really wanted to do.

Dick remembers a couple of incidents that have impacted his life. One day he and his dad were plowing a triangular shaped field. The old tractor Dick was driving was really hard to turn. If the wheels turned too far and got locked, it would just go around in circles. He was in front of his dad and the wheels locked on one of those sharp turns. The tractor took him in two circles before he could break it loose. He remembers his dad coming up to his tractor with tears rolling down his cheeks. He felt so badly that his twelve-year-old son had to do a man's work before he had a man's strength. Dick's heart recorded two truths. His dad really needed him, or he wouldn't be having him do this work, so he was really important to the family. Secondly, his dad loved him deeply and had compassion for Dick's struggles.

The second incident showed a level of trust that Dick was determined to live up to. In rural Kansas at that time, a child could get a restricted driver's license when he or she turned fourteen. When Dick turned fourteen, his folks gave him a 1937 Ford, and his dad told him that he wasn't going to give him a curfew. He said he knew Dick was responsible and had a good head on his shoulders. He didn't think he would need a curfew. Dick's dad-mirror said he was trustworthy; he never failed to live up to that reflection.

I think one of the main reasons I was attracted to Dick was that he was strong and knew who he was. I needed what he had, but I didn't realize that I had to find it by following my own heart to my true identity. Instead, I tried to draw it from the acceptance of others. I worked hard, I tried to do everything right, to meet every standard, but that didn't bring the results I wanted. People didn't adore me for my efforts. It didn't make them need me. They were still more interested in their own lives than in mine. They respected me, but I needed more than respect. I needed to know that I was loved for who I really was, and I didn't know who that was. When I did get recognition, it was like dropping a thimble of water in an ocean of need, and to make it worse, I couldn't receive it well or believe that I deserved it.

Dick really didn't understand my insecurity. He didn't have any basis for understanding. He was always on his own quest for something — to become the best salesman, or to create the best hog farm, or to solve the next problem. It wasn't because he needed the recognition for identity. He simply loved a challenge. Life was all about challenge to him. He still tries to figure out the stoplights so he can hit them all on green. He's a competitor and a winner. He isn't trying to prove he is; he knows he is.

That created more problems for me. His pressing into greater challenges and his competence at achieving them simply told me that he was self-sufficient. I didn't think he needed me, and I desperately needed to be needed. I desperately needed to see myself as important, at least to someone.

Things culminated when I was teaching English at Glasco High School. Glasco was a small town north and west of Delphos that had a reputation for driving off teachers. From my current perspective, I can look back at how much my Heavenly Father loved me and believed in me to throw me into that pit with the lions. God doesn't put us in tough places to punish us or torment us; He puts us there to force us to deal with our bondages and take back the ground of our lives from the enemy.

I didn't have my current perspective in 1973.

The Glasco kids really weren't that bad. They were just kids who had not been taught the value of honor. It wasn't the external battles that got me. It was the raging storm within that told me I was worthless. Guilt, shame, and condemnation were my constant companions—not for what I did, but for what I thought about doing; not because I failed in my responsibilities, but because I should have done so much better in fulfilling them.

I knew I needed help, but I didn't know where to find it. The logical place seemed to be a pastor, but the pastors I knew didn't expect people to have the thoughts I had. I was pretty sure they couldn't help me, so I didn't give them a chance.

I still believed the answer should be found in church. I'd been in the pew of a Methodist church almost every Sunday since I first asked Mama to take me when I was in sixth grade. I had gotten there in time for the classes one takes to profess their faith in Jesus, get sprinkled, and join the church. I had also gone forward in a "revival" meeting at my friend's Baptist Church and had done so to receive Jesus at her urging. I was pretty much convinced I had already done that with the Methodists, but I didn't think it would hurt anything, so I made her happy. I'd been in church most of my life, but I didn't KNOW Jesus.

I don't remember why our local Methodist Church was having a midweek service. They usually didn't, but this was something extra, and I decided to go. Dick and the girls stayed home. There were very few people there, and I certainly didn't get any answers. What I got was simply more desperate. By the time I got home, everyone was asleep. The house was dark, and I had never felt so alone. I fell down on my knees in the middle of our dark living room and cried out through my tears, "God, if you're real, please come into my life and help me."

It was getting about time for teachers to sign their contracts for the next school year. I decided I couldn't take another year at Glasco, so instead of signing a new contract, I turned in my resignation. Then the assault on my mind began. A barrage of thoughts said the only good I did in the world was what little I helped the kids I taught. They said I would have absolutely no meaning in life if I resigned.

My response was a unique one for me. I prayed. I actually sat down and talked to God like I'd talk to anyone else. I said, "God, I'm putting this in your hands. I'm going to go back in tomorrow and tell the superintendent I want to keep my job. If You want me to teach, You have the job still open. If not, have it filled." It was that simple.

The next day I was in front of the superintendent's door before it was unlocked. When he arrived, I told him what I wanted. He told me he had filled the position the evening before. So that was that. The timing was just too perfect. <u>I knew in my heart that God had heard me and answered my prayer.</u>

The next August, as the girls were preparing to return to school, I was feeling pretty empty. I had thought of applying at other schools, but something inside me wouldn't let me. No, I had given the thing to God, and if He wanted me to teach, He would bring the job to me. I don't even know if I realized how totally illogical that was, but I'd made up my mind.

A couple of weeks after school started, the principal of the school in Delphos came to see me. He was looking for someone to work about half a day, to oversee the girls' locker room and one hour of study hall. There was no way that I considered that a teaching job, but it had come to me, so I took the job.

The Delphos Attendance Center went from kindergarten through 9th grade. The high school kids went to Minneapolis, a slightly larger town about fourteen miles south of our hog farm. That year Cheri was in 9th grade, so it was her class that I was overseeing. I enjoyed her class. There weren't any real troublemakers, and the kids were fun. It certainly wasn't a teaching job, but I really believed God had given it to me. Then He outdid Himself. .

The same principal, for whom I was now working, came into the study hall one day to sit down and talk with me. He said that the sophomore English teacher at Minneapolis had resigned after only six weeks of school. Would I be interested in interviewing for that position? Would I ever! I drove home KNOWING that God had brought the job to me and knowing I would get it.

The main thing I KNEW was that my Heavenly Father knew ME. He had heard me that night in our dark living room. He was real, and He wanted me to know He was real. He cared about me personally and wanted to be involved in my life. He knew about my problems and my search for identity, and He wanted to be the mirror I looked into. There were a whole lot of things that I still didn't know, but now I did know that I was significant to God. I still had a long way to go in knowing who God is and who I am, but I would never be really alone again. I had found the hand of my Heavenly Father.

I WANT TO KNOW MORE - 2
God's Plan for Man

From before time God had a purpose and plan for mankind. Read Genesis 1:26-28.

Genesis 1:26-28 Then God said, "Let Us make man in Our image, according to Our likeness; let them have dominion over the fish of the sea, over the birds of the air, and over the cattle, over all the earth and over every creeping thing that creeps on the earth." 27 So God created man in His own image; in the image of God He created him; male and female He created them. 28 Then God blessed them, and God said to them, "Be fruitful and multiply; fill the earth and subdue it; have dominion over the fish of the sea, over the birds of the air, and over every living thing that moves on the earth."

> ➢ God said, "Let Us make man in Our image, according to Our likeness." What does that mean to you? What is God like?

> ➢ What specific aspect of His own character does He emphasize in verse 26?

> ➢ What does it mean to have dominion over something?

> ➢ Now think a little bit about the things they were to have dominion over. Practically, what would that look like?

When we were in Mexico, once a week we would set out trash and garbage in plastic bags for the garbage collectors to pick up. Every week the dogs that roamed the neighborhood would tear into our trash bags and scatter their contents all over the yard. I got really tired of picking up after them, so tired that I finally marched around our yard and declared into the heavens that Genesis 1:28 said that I have dominion over everything that moves on the earth, and that I was taking my dominion over the neighborhood dogs. They were not to cross over the line where my feet had walked. You may not believe this—to be honest, I found it hard to believe—but the dogs never touched our trash again all the time we were there.

One time the Lord impressed me to look up the meanings of the Hebrew words from which these things we have dominion over were translated. Birds refers to birds, the word for cattle actually means any large four-legged beast, but the word for "creeping thing" was the one that caught my attention. NIV translates it "creatures that move along the ground." The Hebrew word is *remes,* which means: "a reptile or any other rapidly moving animal."

"A reptile? Reptile as in a serpent? Could you give me a little more info on that one, Lord?" I like to have the Bible define and back up what I read in other parts of the Bible. Check out Luke 10:18-20. Jesus told His disciples, *"I saw Satan fall like lightning from heaven. 19 Behold, I give you the authority to trample on serpents and scorpions, and over all the power of the enemy, and nothing shall by any means hurt you. 20 Nevertheless do not rejoice in this, that the spirits are subject to you, but rather rejoice because your names are written in heaven."*

That's clear enough. The Lord's plan for man is, and always has been, for us to take dominion over the devil and move him off our part of the planet.

So, what happened? Before we get to that, let's take a short detour through Genesis chapter 2. In chapter one we see that God made man in His image. Chapter two shows how He did it. *Genesis 2:7 And the LORD God formed man of the dust of the ground and breathed into his nostrils the breath of life; and man became a living being.*

At first glance that might not mean much to you, but let's look at it. The "dust of the ground" can also mean clay. God gathered up a handful of dirt and formed it into the shape of the human body.

He gave the creature physical attributes, including a nose, and then breathed into it His own breath, which carried life. With the entrance of that life, later referred to as spirit, man became a living soul. The life, or spirit, brought with it the soul attributes of mind, will and emotion, which make up the human soul. 1 Thessalonians 5:23 says, *"Now may the God of peace Himself sanctify you completely; and may your whole spirit, soul, and body be preserved blameless at the coming of our Lord Jesus Christ."*

When God created man, He created a three part being made up of spirit, soul, and body. You'll see why that's important in a little while.

Now back to our story. Read the rest of Genesis 2.

> ➢ What two trees were in the center of the garden?

> ➢ Which one did God command Adam not to eat? Why?

Read Genesis 3:1-6. This little portion of scripture is absolutely vital. It holds the seeds for understanding almost all of mankind's problems. Read it very carefully.

If you have any question as to the identity of the serpent, check out Revelation 12:9. It tells you clearly. Notice that the first verse said he is cunning or crafty.

> ➢ How do you see that in the way he deals with Eve?

> ➢ Why do you think he starts with a question rather than a statement?

> ➢ What does he imply about the character of God?

> ➢ Think about your own life. What has the devil implied to you concerning the character of God?

As you try to understand that question, realize you are dealing with an invisible serpent that feeds ideas into your mind rather meeting you face to face. He disguises himself as your own thoughts. I once heard a speaker say, "The devil speaks in first person, singular." He often does. Any time your thoughts take a turn that says that God is holding out on you or that He doesn't care about you, beware. Those thoughts didn't originate with you. One of the major schemes of the enemy is to call to question God's character, His faithfulness, and His love.

His other major scheme is to attack your worth. Read verse 5 carefully, and consider it in the light of Genesis 1:26.

> ➤ What is the devil implying about Adam and Eve?

> ➤ What had God said about them? (Hint: Reread Genesis 1:26)

> ➤ What has the devil told you about you?

> ➤ In the last lesson you began to try to define the desires of your heart. What sorts of things seem to consistently come against the desires of your heart?

> ➤ Are there things that you believe about yourself that tell you that you could never really do the things you really want to do? If so, what are they?

If you can identify such things, try to identify where you first got those ideas. Write down here or in your journal incidents, events, attitudes of others, etc. that have created limitations that would hinder you in pursuing your dream.

Whenever you hear the implications that you lack value, that what you do is worthless, or that you'll never make it, guess who's talking. What does God say about you? I'll tell you how to find out what God says in the "I Want to Go Higher" section of this chapter. But before you go there, let's look at one more thing from this passage.

In Genesis 2:17 God said that <u>in the day</u> Adam ate of the tree of the knowledge of good and evil, he would die. Did he die that day? Did God lie?

> ➤ This is why I had you do the sidetrack on how man was created. What three parts does man have?

We know his body didn't die that day. He went and stuck some fig leaves together to cover it. Nor did his soul die that day. He could still think and be afraid. But Adam and Eve's spirits did die that day. They lost their direct connection with God, and that is spiritual death. God's life within them withdrew because of sin. That's the real loss due to the sin in the Garden of Eden. It isn't that God got mad, because of their disobedience, and said, "Well, I'll show you. I'll just send everyone to hell." No, God immediately set in the works a plan for redemption. He spoke it to Satan in verse 3:15.

Here's the real deal. God had given man dominion over the earth. Man had the deed, but he would only be able use it so long as he was connected to the supernatural ability of God. It was the power that came through his spirit that enabled him to rule. That was the source of the wisdom he needed. Adam and Eve, in choosing to obey the serpent rather than God, handed him their deed to planet earth. The devil has no authority unless we give him ours. We give him authority by agreeing with him.

So, when you agree with him that you can't do a thing, you've just handed him the authority to stop you. Adam and Eve agreed that they weren't like God, and that agreement handed the devil the authority to cut their God line, and made them live like mere human beings, the kind of creature that has only his body, mind, emotions and will to depend on.

But don't despair. God knew that snake was in the garden. He had given Adam and Eve authority over it. All they had to do was to refuse to listen and to tell it to be gone. But God no doubt knew they would mess up. That's why the Bible speaks of the Lamb that was slain <u>before the foundation of the earth</u>. God had a Plan B, or maybe it was just the less obvious part of Plan A. In any case, the entire Old Testament is the story of how God worked with men and women, who would obey Him, to bring about the time and place where another Man could be born, a second Adam. Man had turned over his deed to the earth to Satan. A Man would have to take it back. It had to be a sinless man whose death wouldn't have to pay for His own sin but could serve to pay for the sin of all mankind. Jesus was born to a human woman, so He was truly man. But His Father was God, so He was also without sin. God sent Jesus to pay the price for sin and take back the deed to planet earth.

You became a beneficiary of what He did the minute you received Jesus as your Lord and Savior. In the event that you have not yet done that, you can learn how by reading "How to Receive Jesus" in the Appendix.

I WANT TO GO HIGHER – 2
Who God Says I Am

When God looks at us, He sees the person He created us to be. He sees us in Jesus. While our friends and family see us one way and judge us by the things we say and do, our Heavenly Father sees us clothed in Jesus and bursting with potential. <u>We have a choice of which mirror we are going to look into</u>. We can choose to see ourselves as the world says we are and as the devil says we are, or we can choose to believe what God says about us. We will become what we choose to believe. The whole New Testament tells us who we are and what we have in Jesus. For this exercise, read the book of Ephesians. As you read it, watch for the verses that tell who you are or what you have "in Jesus," "in Christ," or "in Him." Record everything you see that belongs to you because you belong to Him.

For example: Ephesians 1:3 says, *"Blessed be the God and Father of our Lord Jesus Christ, who has blessed us with every spiritual blessing in the heavenly places in Christ."* After recording "every spiritual blessing in heavenly places," you could spend a while just researching what that might mean. If you go on, verse 6 says you are accepted, verse 7 says you are redeemed and forgiven, verse 11 says you have an inheritance, and so on. Make your list from the whole book of Ephesians, and then begin declaring who you are in Jesus:

"I am accepted, redeemed and forgiven. I no longer need to fear rejection. I no longer need to carry guilt." As you declare what God says about you, choose to put your faith in what you are saying. Meditate on what it looks and feels like to be forgiven. Choose to line up your thoughts and your behavior with what God says about you. When you hear a thought in your mind saying that there is something wrong with you because of what so-and-so said, simply reject it. Don't argue with it; just turn it off.

Imagine you have a receptionist at the gate of your mind. The receptionist's job is to protect your mind from deception. She has two primary questions: Does the thought agree with what the Bible says about God? And does the thought agree with what the Bible says about you? When such a thought comes, your receptionist will stop it at the gate and say, "Does this thought agree with what God says about me?" If it doesn't, she says, "You do not have an appointment here. We cannot receive you today." Then force yourself to think about something else.

Doing that isn't easy. Our minds are accustomed to playing the recording of our fears and concerns over and over, of examining them from every direction. We will talk more about how to deal with that, but for now, just learn to do what Jesus did when Satan came to tempt Him. He said, "It is written," and then quoted God's word. Take your list of who God says you are. When the devil tells you who you are, simply say, "No, I don't receive that lie. God says I'm _____ (forgiven, accepted, etc.)" Then force yourself to think about something else.

Remember, reading, understanding, and agreeing with what I have said, or even with what the Bible says, does not change your life. Doing it and experiencing God's power to back you up will.

Chapter 3

HIDE AND SEEK

———

The '70's: Delphos, Kansas.

My mother was concerned. We were sitting by
the kitchen table at my parents' ranch, as she confided in me that
my Aunt Vera was into something strange. She was "speaking in
tongues." Did I know anything about that?

Well, I'd read the Bible, and speaking in tongues was in there, so
that's what I told Mama. I didn't share her concern. My Uncle
Forrest and Aunt Vera were some of the best people I knew. They
were in church all the time, and Uncle Forrest had given me the
best explanation I'd ever heard of the time issues in the creation
story. I figured whatever they were into was probably okay. So, I
tabled that issue and pretty much forgot about it for a year or so.

I suppose that must have been around 1974. Several months
or maybe even a year later, I was reading a book on the power
of praise when I ran into a chapter that talked about praying in
tongues. The book implied that there was power in that. I was
teaching high school English at the time, dealing with some kids
with issues, and I really needed power, so I asked our Evangelical
pastor about that chapter. He suggested I not read that book. It was
too late; I'd already read it, and I had to know more.

I went to Salina to the Christian bookstore. Way back amid the
stacks of books, I almost whispered when I asked the clerk if she
knew of any good books on "speaking in tongues." She smiled,

24

and it just so happened that she did. She recommended something called *They Speak with Other Tongues*. I bought it and hid it, but when I had time to myself I would dig it out and read it. The author seemed quite rational, the book didn't seem especially radical, and I was totally fascinated. A hunger was stirring within me. The book had told me enough to know that tongues came with the baptism of the Holy Spirit, and that could be received through prayer. But I didn't know anyone who had the baptism of the Holy Spirit, so I didn't have a clue how to find someone to pray for me.

Then I remembered that random conversation with my mother. My Aunt Vera would know! I couldn't go see her because she lived in Dodge City, half a state away, so I called her. She was extremely helpful. She sent me two books to read and told me that if I wanted to receive the baptism of the Holy Spirit, I should go to a Women's Aglow meeting. She even found the name and phone number of the person in charge of the Salina chapter of Aglow. I read the books, called the lady, and attended the next Aglow meeting. I got what I went for.

That was the spring of 1976. I attended one more Aglow meeting, but I made the mistake of having the girls drop me off while they went shopping. They came back earlier than I'd expected and came and looked in the door at a rather wild moment during the meeting. I had to answer a lot of questions from three daughters who were concerned about what I might be "getting into," so I continued my search for further understanding of the Holy Spirit on my own.

And yet, I wasn't on my own. I never had been. The God who hides things <u>for</u> us was leaving His trail all along the way. The conversations I have, the books I choose to read, the things I notice in nature, my dreams, can all be ways that God is dropping clues for me to follow that will lead to the next thing He wants me to discover.

Bill Johnson says, "<u>God doesn't hide things from us; He hides things for us</u>."

God doesn't teach like we teach in our Western culture. He teaches by discovery. If we want to find Him, if we want to know His ways, we have to seek Him. We have to want what He has to offer. That's why He hides things <u>for</u> us. We have to want the thing enough to really seek it. We have to want it enough to allow God to change our thinking to where we have the capacity to receive it. I would never have received the baptism of the Holy Spirit if someone had told me about it and tried to push me into it when I first had that conversation with Mama. I had to be led to "discover" it in my way and in my time.

> ➢ What's God hiding for you?

> ➢ What do you want badly enough to dig to get it?

> ➢ What have you caught glimpses of that seems to connect with someplace deep within?

Whatever it is, no one else can give it to you. You will have to discover it for yourself. As parents we try to hand our children and grandchildren all sorts of things—our belief system, our faith, our values, our dreams for their lives. Some of it rubs off and takes hold, but when push comes to shove, if it hasn't been proved true by their own discovery, it won't stand. That's why, as parents, we do well to watch for what our children are ready to learn and then give them a means to discover it rather than trying to hand them ready-made answers.

> ➢ Can you think of a discovery trail God has taken you over?

It wasn't until August of 1980 that Dick received the baptism of the Holy Spirit. I had remained an undercover tongues pray-er out of cowardly fear that he wouldn't understand. While he was secretly seeking for something more, I was secretly withholding the information he needed. But God had a right time for Dick.

It came at a Lay Witness retreat held in a Catholic Convent during a foot washing service. Talk about a strange place to hide something! At the time Dick was asking God for all that the Lord had for him. He experienced a huge download of love and was dramatically changed. However, he didn't speak in tongues at that time, because he didn't know anything about tongues. After that experience I began to share with him the books I'd read. Several months later, driving home from a basketball game, in which Debra had scored the winning shot, Dick was singing. All at once he realized he wasn't singing in English! The God who hides things for us had once again revealed Himself in the way and the timing that was right for Dick.

Your experience with God doesn't have to be like anyone else's. Just tell God what you are ready for. If you don't really know, tell Him you want what He has for you. Then just be alert for the next series of events, and be willing to see things from a different perspective.

I WANT TO KNOW MORE – 3
Seeking Truth

➢ Let's look again at Genesis 2:9,16 and 17 and Genesis 3:1-7. What trees were in the midst of the garden?

➢ Before Adam and Eve listened to the serpent, was there any rule against eating of the tree of life?

In Genesis 3:24 the way to the tree of life was guarded, so they could not eat of it. One of the things we need to understand is what was so bad about the tree of the knowledge of good and evil. We know that the choice to obey the devil rather than God was wrong and that it cut off man's spirit from being able to communicate with God. Equally important is that it changed the way mankind thought and understood. Mankind could no longer function in the image of God because they no longer could think like God thinks. They were stuck with what they could understand through their five senses. Humanity has been programmed to function by our five senses ever since. People who have the life of Christ inside no longer have that limitation, but because that is the way they have been programmed to think and to learn, it is hard to take advantage of the new knowledge resident in their spirits. We aren't trained to listen to what the spirit is saying. Our mind and our emotions are so dominating that we can't hear the spirit. So one of the things we are going to try to do with this study is to get your spiritual ears and spiritual eyes open so we can get to know God better, so you can understand how He speaks to you, and so you can better understand your own potential.

> ➢ The world has programmed us to learn from the outside in. We are taught that seeing is believing. We draw our information from what our senses perceive. Can you see any problems with that?

> ➢ If you and I see the same accident, will we necessarily have the same understanding of what happened?

> ➢ If someone says to you, "I love you," would it always be interpreted to mean the same thing?

> ➢ What factors would contribute to your understanding and interpretation?

> ➢ How much do you believe the commercials you "see" and "hear" on television?

> ➢ So, I can tell you the truth, but you may not believe it. Or someplace between my mouth and your heart it may get distorted. What sort of things could cause you to hear something different than what I intended to say?

28

God values an understanding heart over a knowledgeable head. So, while people are interested in educating your head, God is more interested in dealing with your heart, in training the place of deep knowing within you with truth that cannot be shaken.

Let's look at how He does that.
Read Isaiah 55:8-11.

> *8 "For My thoughts are not your thoughts,*
> *Nor are your ways My ways," says the LORD.*
> *9 "For as the heavens are higher than the earth,*
> *So are My ways higher than your ways,*
> *And My thoughts than your thoughts.*
>
> *10 "For as the rain comes down, and the snow from heaven,*
> *And do not return there,*
> *But water the earth,*
> *And make it bring forth and bud,*
> *That it may give seed to the sower*
> *And bread to the eater,*
> *11 So shall My word be that goes forth from My mouth;*
> *It shall not return to Me void,*
> *But it shall accomplish what I please,*
> *And it shall prosper in the thing for which I sent it.*

➢ To what does the Lord compare His word?

➢ What do you think He means by that? What does it tell you about His word?

Read John 17:15-19 and John 8:31,32.

John 17:15-19 I do not pray that You should take them out of the world, but that You should keep them from the evil one. 16 They are not of the world, just as I am not of the world. 17 Sanctify them by Your truth. Your word is truth. 18 As You sent Me into the world, I also have sent them into the world. 19 And for their sakes I sanctify Myself, that they also may be sanctified by the truth.

John 8:31-32 Then Jesus said to those Jews who believed Him, "If you abide in My word, you are My disciples indeed. 32 And you shall know the truth, and the truth shall make you free."

> ➢ What purposes do you see for the word of God?

> ➢ What does it mean to be "sanctified"?

> ➢ What do you understand about the truth setting you free?

> ➢ Have you ever experienced that? What would it look like (give an example)?

> ➢ Read Matthew 13:1-23. To what is the word compared?

> ➢ From this passage, what hindrances do you see to the truth setting you free?

> ➢ Take each hindrance and give an example of what that would look like translated into your life or the life of someone you know?

> ➢ Where are those hindrances found?

We are after heart knowledge more than head knowledge. <u>Heart knowledge isn't taught. It's discovered.</u> Your heart doesn't know a thing just because your head says it's so. Your heart demands proof that goes beyond facts. Your heart lives by revelation knowledge (that which is revealed internally) not by sense knowledge (that which is received through your five senses). Revelation knowledge is something that you just know is true. Something deep within you simply "knows." Have you ever simply known that someone was lying to you, or that something was wrong, even though everything looked and sounded good? Some people call it a gut feeling.

> How would you explain the difference between sense knowledge and revelation knowledge?

As we approach the word of God, which is recorded in the Bible, we want to approach it with a heart set on discovery. <u>We care about what the word says and what it means, but we care even more about what the living God wants to say to us personally through His word</u>. You will find that what He says to one person through a particular verse will not always be the same thing He is saying to another person AND BOTH THINGS CAN BE TRUE. I am more concerned with connecting your heart with His heart than I am with connecting your mind with the words written on the page. The Bible is a living book. The same passage can express truth on many levels. If your heart is set to receive the truth the Lord wants to show you, the Holy Spirit may take the passage and show you one truth today and a deeper truth the next time you meditate on it. One of the ways your heart can be stony is to be so set on what you already believe about a portion of the Bible, or about anything else in life, that you close your mind to other possibilities.

Having our minds set a certain way can also be the reason we don't understand in the first place. Another reason we don't understand can be that we are too lazy to dig. If you don't understand something, instead of just skipping over it, consider it an invitation to a treasure hunt with the Holy Spirit. Read cross-references to the verse or passage. Ask the Holy Spirit for revelation, and then meditate on what is going on around the part you don't understand. Envision yourself in the passage, and imagine the scene from various perspectives. You'll be surprised at what will be revealed to you.

When you begin to read the Bible or study a lesson, ask the Holy Spirit to speak to you through the word and to reveal the truth to you that you need right now. Record in your journal anything that gives you revelation.

Read Hebrews 4:12. *"For the word of God is living and powerful, and sharper than any two-edged sword, piercing even to the division of soul and spirit, and of joints and marrow, and is a discerner of the thoughts and intents of the heart."*

➤ What's that mean to you?

Read John 6:63. *"It is the Spirit who gives life; the flesh profits nothing. The words that I speak to you are spirit, and they are life."*

➤ What is this verse saying?

Also, remember to be alert to what is happening in your life. Look for ways the Lord uses circumstances to relate to something you read. When you write in your journal, ask the Holy Spirit to bring to your memory things He wants to use to illustrate what He is teaching you.

This is the lesson I felt led to put with this story. However, I have included an extensive lesson on the baptism of the Holy Spirit in the appendix.

I WANT TO GO HIGHER–3
Stepping into God's Word

I have chosen just one chapter of the Bible for you to "step into." You could do this with most any passage. It's exciting to discover things hidden in God's word. The Holy Spirit takes pleasure in being your personal guide and revealing secrets to you. As you prepare to read the chapter, ask the Holy Spirit to draw your attention to any verses He wants to use to speak to you. Record in your journal anything that really gets your attention. Ask Him what He wants you to understand about those verses. If He shows you something He wants you to do, do it.

I'm also suggesting that you meditate on the verses found in this lesson. This isn't like Eastern meditation. I just want you to read the verses slowly and thoughtfully. On the verses you are assigned to meditate, ask the Lord to reveal the truth He wants you to see in them. Read them over and over. If you have more than one translation of the Bible, read them in different translations. Emphasize different words to see if you get different understanding. If you receive understanding or new ideas, record it in your journal. If some of the verses seem to be more significant to you, meditate on them for more than one day. Continue until you feel like the Lord has spoken all He wants to on that verse for now. Remember, it may say something really different to you when you meditate on it at some other time.

Read Luke 7. Choose the person with whom you most identify in this chapter. There is a man who understands authority, a woman who has lost a son, a man who has served well and feels deserted, a woman who has been forgiven of great sin, and a self-righteous man who judged that woman. Look at Jesus from the perspective of that person and listen for what He would say to that person and what He would say to you personally.

Meditate on John 8:31-32, John 17:15-19, Isaiah 55:8-11, Hebrews 4:12. Don't do them all in one sitting. Just do one or two a day.

Chapter 4

THE HOG FARM

—

IT WAS A BITTER COLD WINTER DAY ON THE HOG FARM. Sheets of ice covered everything, including the roads. No one would be driving for hours. There was no chance that our hired man would be able to come help with chores. Even we would not be able to drive the quarter mile down to the hog farm. We'd have to walk. I didn't normally help with chores, but I would be needed this day, so we bundled up in layers of sweatshirts and insulated coveralls and headed toward our hungry sows.

When we got to the farrowing house where new babies were arriving daily, we were met with a sight that's a hog farmer's worst nightmare. Litter after litter of newborns were dead or dying from a fast-spreading disease. We fed the sows, cleaned out the dead pigs, and did what we could, which was precious little.

As we walked back toward the house, Dick's mood was somber. If the loss continued, we might not be able to meet our high interest payments. We stood a chance of losing the hog farm.

By the time we entered the house, the warrior in me was armed and ready. I reminded the Lord, the devil, and probably the neighbors, if they were listening, that our God meets our needs according to His riches in glory in Christ Jesus, that we're blessed in our barns and in the offspring of our beasts, that the devil is defeated and has no right to steal from us, and a number of other passages that rolled out of me. I sang and danced and praised God for His faithfulness. I praised and warred until my spirit arrived at a place of peace where I KNEW that my GOD is bigger than anything the devil could bring against us.

The loss of that cycle of pigs was devastating. We lost half of them, probably some 300 pigs. If we had chosen to focus on the problem, it was bad and much bigger than we were. It was hard, and we had to refocus many times, but we chose to focus on God's ability rather than our inability. With good management, Dick managed to keep the disease from moving into the next cycle. In mid-summer, when it was time to sell that group of pigs, we sold our normal number. That, of course, was not possible, but the hogs were there, and we got paid for them. How? We don't know, and we don't have to know. God is the Lord of the impossible. Would it have happened if we had accepted the circumstances as the final word? I don't think so. We had to choose to believe God's word and not let what we saw pull us off of it. When you're dealing with a set of circumstances that is larger than your capacity to handle, it is critical where you focus.

If you look at the circumstances, they will overwhelm you. If you look at your own ability and resources or lack of them, all you will see is the impossible. You must learn to bypass the way things look in the natural and find a way to get God's perspective. Lance Wallnau gives an excellent visual of what that looks like. The majority of us, if asked to break a board with our hand, would focus on the board, and if we were dumb enough to try it, would hit the board and stop there, a good way to break our hand rather than the board. A person trained in karate doesn't focus on the board, but rather on a point beyond the board. When his hand hits the board, it's in full thrust to its destination beyond the board, and the board must give. When we focus on God, on His purpose and ability, we are focusing on a point beyond the problem, so the problem doesn't stop us. God's ability trumps circumstances every time.

God doesn't look at things the way we do. His value system is based on eternal values. Temporal issues are best seen as means by which eternal ends can be accomplished. We would do well to view the circumstances in our lives as vehicles through which God will accomplish eternal purposes. Even circumstances perpetrated by the devil will produce good fruit in us and through us if we take them to God for His direction. When God allows us to be in such circumstances, He wants us to overcome, defeat the enemy, and take ground in that area of our lives or in the lives of those we touch.

Lance Wallnau says that an impossible situation is an invitation to go with the Lord to a whole new level of understanding. It's your invitation to press through to a place you have never accessed before. It forces you to press into God for a whole new paradigm because the paradigm you are in doesn't have the answer. If we seek God, He will turn those circumstances that the enemy is trying to use to destroy us into strength and blessing in our lives.

Romans 8:28 And we know that all things work together for good to those who love God, to those who are the called according to His purpose.

Take some time to talk to God about some of the difficult situations in your life. What have you learned from the hard places? How are you different because of something you suffered? Are you better or worse, stronger or weaker? If you are better and stronger, what was the key to your victory? What have you learned that would benefit those around you? If you feel the situation left you weak and wounded, there is still time to take it to God for His perspective. It's never too late for God to work a thing for good.

I WANT TO KNOW MORE – 4
Discerning the Source

At the point where the Bible picks up on Nehemiah's life, we see a man who already had a firm grip on his identity. He was not easily shaken. His story provides us with a wonderful opportunity to see how the devil operates and how one, who is secure in his identity, can overcome the enemy's schemes.

I am just going to pick up on parts of the story. It might help you to read the rest of the story if you aren't very familiar with it.

Read chapter 2, verses 19-20. Sanballat, Tobiah, and Geshem, in the natural represent other Semitic people who opposed Israel. However, they also represent spiritual forces that want to destroy God's people in any age.

> ➢ What method do they use in verse 19 to try to stop Nehemiah and his people from building the wall?

> ➢ Have you experienced that tool of the enemy in use against you?

> ➢ If so, what channel did the enemy use? How did you deal with it?

> ➢ What was Nehemiah's response?

> ➢ Read Nehemiah 4. What methods does the devil use in verses 1-3?

Sometimes the enemy wants people to see themselves as rubbish. I believe burned stones are an apt description of some people who have suffered a lot of destruction or painful places in their lives. The enemy wants them to believe they are useless.

> ➢ What might that look like in the lives of people you know or even in your own life?

> ➢ Explore Nehemiah's response in verses 4-6. What do you see in the way he handled the situation that we can use in dealing with the devil?

In verses 8-12 we find three very familiar enemies. The first, confusion, is clearly named. The others you have to discern by the reactions they cause.

> ➢ What are the enemies?

Notice, they don't all come from Sanballat and Tobiah. Some come from people who are friends to the cause. The enemy can use your friends and loved ones. That is even harder to discern, because those people don't mean to harm you. Usually, their intent is to help you. That's why Paul warns in Ephesians 6: *"For we do not wrestle against flesh and blood, but against principalities, against powers, against the rulers of the darkness of this age, against spiritual hosts of wickedness in the heavenly places."* When people say or do things that bring confusion, discouragement or fear into your life, remember who your enemy is. It isn't people. Don't get angry and strike back at your friends. Take the thing to God and ask for the Spirit of Truth to reveal truth in the situation. Sometimes we run into roadblocks because we are on the wrong road, so when people we love try to warn us, we need to be willing to take it to God for the truth test. If you find peace you are on track, so ask God for how to deal with criticism. If you have taken a wrong path, it doesn't mean you are a bad person. God used the burned stones. It's simply time to say, "What are you doing, Lord? How do I need to shift my position and thinking to join you? Or, what do I need to learn from this to make me better able to line up my future with my destiny?"

> ➢ How did Nehemiah deal with each problem?

> ➢ In chapter 6 we find a much more subtle enemy. What do you see as the scheme in verse 2?

> ➢ Are you ever tempted to get off course by other things to do? What might that look like for you?

> ➢ What is the scheme in Sanballat's letter?

➢ How would that one look in your life?

➢ Note Nehemiah's answer.

The last one, verses 10-14, is really a hard one. The warning was from people Nehemiah trusted. Notice that Nehemiah had to act on the basis of <u>who he knew himself to be</u> BEFORE he received the revelation of what was really going on.

That's why it is so very important that you discover who God really is and who He says you are. The enemy's attacks on your identity and your destiny come in a wide range, from the very overt and obvious, to the very subtle and sneaky. As you seek God's guidance, He will help you recognize where you have believed lies. As you learn the truth, the truth will set you free.

➢ Be sure and read verses 15 and 16. What were the results? Who was responsible for those results?

If you answered the last question "God," you would be only half right. Nehemiah is a wonderful example of how we co-labor with God. If we don't do our part, God won't show up to do His. If we think we can do it all in our strength, we'll break under the burden. But if we learn to do all we can and continually seek God for how to do the next thing, He will show us, teach us, and provide the supernatural edge we need to complete the thing. It's an incredibly exciting way to live.

I WANT TO CLIMB HIGHER – 4
Uncovering the Schemes Against Your Life

You are a human being, destined to take dominion over the enemy. That's enough to put a target on your back. You are incredibly important to God, and He has special plans for your life. That makes you important to the devil as well, and he also has plans for your life. God's plans are full of life, hope, and victory. The devil's plans are to kill, steal and destroy (John 10:10). While God values and respects your personal will and chooses to win your cooperation through love and goodness, the enemy doesn't value you at all. He'll use any sneaky and cruel scheme he can to keep you from knowing how valuable you are, and he doesn't play fair. He begins his attacks before you can walk. He places circumstances in your life that are especially designed to cripple your emotions and foul up the way you think. He lashes you to the tree of the knowledge of good and evil and continually shows you just how evil you are. He corrupts your identity and blames it all on you. He does it by the significant emotional events in your life. They can be huge things, or they can be something seemingly irrelevant, but they form the basis for what you believe about yourself. Wise and godly parents can help you interpret emotional events in a positive way, but that doesn't always happen, and parents aren't always wise and godly. The purpose of this exercise is to expose the lies the enemy has used to keep you from being all that you were created to be. So let's take a journey through your past and see if we can pinpoint the significant emotional events of your life and how they have affected you.

Think of the three strongest emotional event memories, positive or negative, the first ones that come to your mind. List them here:

Positive	Negative

Consider the following areas of life, and add to the significant events that have impacted you emotionally:

Family history: growing up, relationships with family members positive and negative.

Positive	Negative

Consider relationships in general: love life, dating, friendships, associates, people you could trust, people you couldn't trust, memories about your best friend, memories about your biggest betrayal, biggest heart break.

School and/or professional life: happiest moment, disappoint-
ments, failures, embarrassment

List emotional spiritual experiences

> When you grew closer to God

> When you were drawn away from God

Go back through your lists and star the ones that you feel carried
the strongest emotional impact, good or bad.

Two questions that may add to your insight:

What was it that you wanted to get from your father that you
didn't get?

What was it that you got that you didn't want?

Now, you are going to plot your emotional experiences on the
chart on the next page. The line through the middle separates
the positive experiences from the negative experiences. The hor-
izontal line represents your age at the time of the event. The ver-
tical line indicates the intensity of the experience. Put a dot for
the experiences with less intensity closest to the line across the
middle and the events that most impacted your life the farthest
from the line. Put them in age order, so you end up with a graph
of significant emotional events plotted in the timeline.

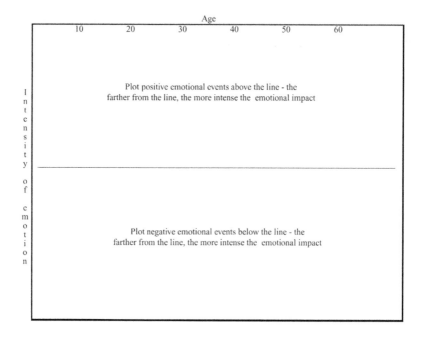

Those are the events that have shaped your identity.

(When I first heard Lance Wallnau teach this material[1], I didn't want to do this exercise. I didn't want to go back and look at old thought patterns again because God has already helped me see and deal with so much of those things in my life. But I realized as I did it that the lowest points were places where, in desperation, I gave more of me to God, turned loose of more control, and found, not only more freedom, but also more of the goodness and faithfulness of God. From the time I invited God to come in and take over in the living room that night, every really low point has had a really high point that corresponds with truth breaking through.)

Pick the clearest, most positive one on your timeline and ask yourself: As a result of that experience, what did I begin to believe about myself or about others or about God?

---

[1] Lance Wallnau, *"Doing Business Supernaturally 101"* CD series, (Lance Wallnau Ministries), www.lancewallnau.com.

The power of those good experiences is that they produce positive belief systems.

Take the strongest negative one. When that happened, what did you begin to believe about yourself or others or God?

If you don't know, that's all right. Just know that <u>circumstances lead to belief systems</u>. They reinforce them or they challenge them. Where you recognize that negative beliefs have been established in your life because of negative emotional experiences, there is a way to renew your mind and correct your belief system. Here's what you do:

The Real Way to Repent

When you realize your thinking is wrong, even if you can't see why it's wrong or how to change it, you repent. <u>Bill Johnson says to "repent" means to return to the penthouse</u>.

- You set your heart and your mind to turn from your old thought patterns and to agree with God even if you don't know what that looks like.
- You choose to repent for agreeing with the enemy concerning your life or who God is or wherever you know you are thinking wrongly. For example, the events of my life told me that I was ignored or overlooked because I was unimportant. I couldn't see any reason in the natural to believe otherwise, but I knew that God was not in agreement with that, and that it contradicted what His word said about me. So, I chose to repent for listening to the lies of the enemy concerning my value. I repented for allowing the circumstances of my life to define my identity.
- To do this, tell God out loud: "Lord, I repent for agreeing with the enemy and believing his lies about my significance..."
- The second part of this is to ask the Lord to reveal truth to you. You don't overcome an emotional experience with another emotional experience. You overcome it with

revelation knowledge down in your spirit—a knowing in
your knower. You can't make that happen. You simply tell
God you want and need His revelation, and then you wait
and watch and listen. Over the next few days or weeks,
God will find a way to drop truth into your spirit, and the
truth will set you free.

I have sought and received healing from old wounds in many ways
over the years. I have forgiven those who wounded me (which,
by the way, is essential). I have received deliverance and inner
healing. I have made choices based on the word of God. All of
those things have been good and brought a greater measure of
freedom, but the greatest freedom comes from uncovering the lies,
realizing they are lies, and receiving a revelation of the truth. It is
the truth that sets you free.

Chapter 5

SEEDS OF DESTINY

Early 1980's.

WE WERE AT THE LEAN-TO. OUR SEARCH FOR A church body, where we could fit, had led us along a strange path. We had both grown up in the Methodist Church. When we really got hungry for more of God, we tried the Wesleyan Methodist Church and then the Community Bible Church. The former didn't contribute much to our quest; the latter taught us a lot about the word of God. However, after we both had received the baptism of the Holy Spirit, we found we didn't fit.

The only Spirit-filled "church" short of driving forty miles to Salina was the Lean-to. The Lean-to wasn't a church exactly. It was actually a small group of folks like us who had received the baptism of the Holy Spirit and no longer fit. Most of them had been Catholic. We met in a large room shaped like a lean-to, built on the side of a mobile home. (A lean-to is a structure built on the side of a shed or barn that "leans" on the other building).

This particular day we had a guest speaker, Dick Paige, who was a pastor from a small church up near the Nebraska border and the brother of one of the members of our group. Dick was pretty prophetic, and his words into our lives have been significant. One evening he prophesied over my Dick that he was to prepare to have someone else run the hog farm, because we were going to the mission field. That was startling news.

We did what we had learned to do with prophecies. We put it on a shelf and waited to see what would happen. We didn't have to wait long. The next morning, our hired man, Jack Parrish, came to work and said that the night before the Lord had told him he needed to learn to run the hog farm, because we were going to be leaving.

That was seed sown for quite a destiny adventure, but that isn't the story of this chapter. The particular sermon that morning at Lean-to concerned using what we'd been given, but the only part I really remember was a point in the sermon where Dick asked forcefully, "What do you have in your hand?" I looked down. I had been taking notes. I had a pen in my hand. I knew that Dick didn't mean literally at that moment, but I also knew that God did. It was a prophetic moment that said I'm a writer. God called to my attention something that I already knew at some subliminal level, but it had never hit my radar so clearly.

I've always loved to write. Sometimes when I write, something takes hold within me, and I find ideas flowing out of me that I didn't know were in there. <u>When you're doing something you're good at and the Holy Spirit adds His touch to it, that's called anointing</u>. You know it's better than you can do, wiser than you can be. That's a place of incredible satisfaction. <u>It puts the stamp of God's favor on the essence of who you are</u>. It settles the question of significance and worth.

That incident at the Lean-to seems like a very small thing, something that could easily have been overlooked or dismissed. But it's an example of the kind of revelatory moment that God uses to direct our lives. It's not a random thing; it's by design. *Psalm 139:13 For you created my inmost being; you knit me together in my mother's womb.* (NIV) <u>The essence of my being, and yours— our true identity—was created or designed in the birthing place of God's heart.</u> You are a one of a kind original. There's not now, nor will there ever be another person just like you. What's unique about you? What's the God-ordained desire seeded into your heart?

I believe there are things that God plants in our DNA while we are still only a vision in His heart. The destiny He has for us was written into the fiber and substance of our being. Our hearts are ever in search of the fulfillment of that destiny we sense within. Our greatest fulfillment is experienced when we shape our lives in agreement with that design.

God plants the vision like seed within us. Then He sends forth His word to us to connect with the seed he has already planted within us. It can come through the words of a parent or a friend. It can come through a movie or a dream. God can use a sermon, as He did with me, or He can use any number of other ways to touch that place that cries out to be discovered. The word quickens and calls forth that latent seed so that it can begin to grow. From time to time more water of the word comes to nourish the little plant until the roots become strong and eventually it grows to a place of fruitfulness.

When God gives us a vision of who we are to be, He already sees us complete and fruitful because He operates by the faith that calls things which don't exist into being. Our part is to stay close to Him so that he can guide us through the labyrinth of life that forms our character and makes us into the vessel that can carry the vision. From God's side, He already sees us as what we are to become. From our side, we have to receive the vision and then grow into it. We cling to it, allow it to call us forth, and conform us until we become the person we are meant to be. The seeds of our destiny are like the minas given to the servants (Luke 19). We are to do something with them here. We are to invest them for the sake of the kingdom.

I WANT TO KNOW MORE − 5
In Control

To discover and fulfill our own destiny, we must be free from the tangle of hindrances that would block it. We tend to see the circumstances of our lives as being our hindrances. If others would just recognize my ability or listen to my ideas... If I just had the money or the education or the time...

In truth, it is never the circumstances of our lives that stop us; it's how we view those circumstances. Our success depends on whether we allow circumstances to govern our life, or whether we choose to use them as a ladder to climb higher.

Mankind was created for dominion, but before we can take dominion in the world out there, we must learn to take it in the world within. We are looking for a way to exercise self-control, but not the type of self-control that comes out of our soul's authority. I'm not looking for a way to put more rules, regulations and law on my life. That comes straight from the Tree of the Knowledge of Good and Evil. If all my legalism fails, I come under condemnation because I wasn't strong enough, smart enough, or good enough. If I manage to pull it off, my pride and arrogance jump up, and I expect everyone else to be able to do what I did. I become the devil's helper in spreading condemnation and inadequacy. That sort of thing is what a religious spirit is made of.

So, what do we get if we go to the Tree of Life? Jesus said, *"I have come that they might have life, and that they may have it more abundantly."* (John 10:10) In Romans 8 Paul goes to great lengths to contrast living by the Spirit to living by the Law. In Galatians 5:18 he goes so far as to say, *"If you are led by the Spirit, you are not under the law."* If we are led by the Spirit of God, there is no need for law.

The Lord once gave me an interesting analogy as I watched some of my grandchildren pressing the behavior line. They knew the rule—the "law" if you will—and they pressed just as close to the limit as possible. They were full of their "rights." As long as they didn't step over the line, they were "right" even if they were driving everyone crazy. If they stepped over just a little, that shouldn't arouse much opposition, as long as it was just a little.

Of course, it they weren't stopped there, they had just managed to move the line. Then the process began anew, and they were never satisfied or at peace because they were always on a quest to see just how far they could go. The Lord showed me that this children's game is a perfect picture of living by the law.

Then He asked me how it would be different if the children so adored and respected their father that the desire of their heart was to emulate him and please him. I quickly saw that there would be no need for the line.

The problem is where we focus. Like children, we tend to focus on <u>our</u> needs and <u>our</u> wants and <u>our</u> desire to be in control of the circumstances around us, to bend them to our will. The challenge is to learn to trust the Lord so completely that you can be at peace walking with Him regardless of the circumstances. That can only happen by spending time with Him and getting to know Him. That, of course, is a process. It requires some major shifts in our thinking regarding who God is and who we are. Just like making a trusted friend, it takes time. But there are things we can learn and do to help the process.

We must start by seeing ourselves as we really are. That means we must be able to stand aside and look at ourselves honestly — to recognize what we are really doing, including our motivation for doing it.

In his wonderful series *In a Heartbeat*, Lance Wallnau says: "Circumstances do not create your emotional state. They will only magnify the emotional state you already live with."[1]

> ➤ Meditate on that statement, and write down what it means to you.

---

[1] Wallnau, Lance. *In a Heartbeat*, (Cranston, RI: Lance Learning), CD 1.

Here's his next nugget of truth: "I must take 100% responsibility for the state that I'm in.

My emotional stability is my responsibility."[1]

Let's analyze this a little bit. Is he saying that other people have no blame or that they are never at fault? No.

> What is he saying?

Let's look at a situation. Let's say you worked hard most of the afternoon to fix your husband's favorite meal. Dinnertime comes, but he doesn't. You try to keep it warm. He still doesn't show. At 9:30, well after the food has been dried out and ruined, he walks in and tells you he had dinner with the boss. Oh, did he forget to call you?

> Think about it for a minute. How would you respond?

> What would your emotions be saying?

> Was he wrong not to have called you? Absolutely. But who is responsible for your reaction, internal and external?

Okay. So, the guys are saying, "What's the big deal?" So, let's do another one. You have a deadline to meet, and there's way too much to do to meet it, so you pull a couple of all-nighters to get it done. You get to work, hand in the project, only to have the boss say, "Oh, didn't I tell you we are scrapping that project? We have to get the Jones job done by Friday."

> Okay, guys, how do you respond? Not just how do you respond on the outside—what do you do with the knot in your stomach?

In this day and age, there may be more gals that identify with the last one than the first one, but whichever example touches you, what is the real issue behind the offense? Isn't it the lack of value that someone else put on your time and therefore on you as a person?

> Whenever you are offended or hurt, it has less to do with the actions of the other person and more to do with what you perceive their actions to say about your value or lack of it.
> ➢ Examine that statement. Is it true or isn't it? Defend your answer.

You can't change what other people do, but you can change how you allow it to affect you. The point is that you aren't responsible for the dumb or thoughtless things that other people do, but you are 100% responsible for the way you react—for what you let it do inside you. If you don't take responsibility for what happens in your mind and emotions, your internal life and well-being will be at the mercy of whoever makes you feel devalued, every time they fail to act responsibly. Do you want other people to control your life?

So, what is the truth? Can you step outside yourself and understand why a given situation affected you as it did? Usually, a new offense causes the reaction it causes because it hits an old wound or it reinforces an old lie concerning your identity.

➢ Make a list of the things that offend you.

Now think about why those particular things offend you. Do some of the things have the same motivation? For example, people changing the subject when I'm talking, being overlooked in any form, and having my ideas ignored, all hit an old wound left over from childhood that said I wasn't important.

➢ How about the things that offend you—do they have a common root?

If there are areas of your life where you are frequently offended, look back over your significant emotion chart, and see if you can identify the old event this type of offense is hitting. If you find it, ask God for truth about the lie it attached to your identity. Use the 'repent and ask for revelation' method, and I'm going to give you some other tools for this sort of situation. We bring our emotions and our mental processes back into line by what we see or focus on, what we say, and what we do. We'll talk about those things in future lessons.

When you have discovered and dealt with the lie, you will no longer be offended—inconvenienced maybe—but it won't torment you or affect how you see yourself. So quit blaming others for your emotional highs and lows. You are 100% responsible for your emotional state. As you take the responsibility that is yours, you will experience the freedom that comes with it.

I WANT TO CLIMB HIGHER – 5
Words of Life

Find a comfortable place where you can relax in the presence of the Lord. Consciously turn loose of your current cares and responsibilities. See yourself putting them into God's hands and ask Him to take care of them for a while. Receive peace and a quiet mind from Him.

This exercise might help. It comes from a wonderful book called *Celebration of Discipline* by Richard J. Foster. This exercise is on page 24 of my ancient copy.

Palms down, palms up

"Begin by placing your palms down as a symbolic indication of your desire to turn over any concerns you may have to God. Inwardly you may pray, 'Lord, I give You my anger toward John. I release

my fear of my dentist appointment this morning. I
release my frustration over trying to find a baby-
sitter for tonight.' Whatever it is that weighs on
your mind or is a concern to you, just say, 'palms
down.' Release it. You may even feel a certain sense
of release in your hands. After several moments
of surrender, turn your palms up as a symbol of
your desire to receive from the Lord. Perhaps you
will pray silently: 'Lord, I receive your love for
John, Your peace about the dentist appointment,
Your patience, Your joy.' Whatever you need, you
simply receive. Having centered down, spend the
remaining moments in complete silence. Do no
ask for anything. Allow the Lord to commune with
your spirit, to love you. If impressions or directions
come, fine; if not, fine."[1]

Take time to do this every morning before you start your day. You
may also want to do it last thing before you go to bed. If you do
receive any impressions from God, record them in your journal
and date them. If you don't receive anything, don't worry about
it. The main purpose is simply to begin to learn to just relax and
be at peace in God's presence. You don't even have to sense His
presence for this to be successful. It's our starting place.

On a day when you do feel quieted and at peace, ask the Lord to
take you on a trip back through time. Ask Him to bring to your
memory words and experiences that have been your seeds of destiny. Simply allow Him to lead you. Later, record in your journal
the things He shows you.

If you don't receive anything, don't worry about it. Just enjoy the
peace of God's presence. Learning to recognize and experience
that place of peace is as important as anything you can do.

---

[1] Richard J. Foster, *Celebration of Discipline,* (San Francisco,
California: Harper and Row, Publishers, 1978), p. 24.

Chapter 6

SHINE

—

1979 to 1980

BILL TAUGHT SCIENCE DOWN THE NEXT HALL FROM MY classroom. The sophomores would sometimes come to my class all riled up from a hot discussion of evolution. Bill delighted in challenging the students' belief systems. He and I would sometimes exchange friendly barbs at the teachers' lunch table.

A couple of years earlier, Bill had married a woman quite a bit younger than himself, and they had a baby boy. I noticed a softening in him, but then I realized things weren't going well. He lost a lot of weight, and the hollowness in his eyes reflected what was happening in his heart. Then his wife asked for a divorce. Although Bill had never been one of my favorite people, I found compassion rising up in me.

One morning, as I was praying for him, the Lord told me to take him Catherine Marshall's book *Something More*. It was the book that had transformed my life several years before when I realized I needed to make Jesus my LORD, not just my Savior. I balked. That wasn't a book for an intellectual like Bill. He'd laugh at me. I made some more plausible suggestions to the Lord, but He wasn't negotiating. Was I going to obey Him or not?

As soon as I got to school, I headed for Bill's classroom, trying to rehearse what I'd say. I finally simply told him that he might think me crazy, but God had told me to give him that book. I also told him which chapter had meant so much to me. He thanked me graciously, saying that he needed something. Amazed and delighted by his response, I went back to prepare for my day.

That afternoon, during my free period, Bill came to my room and asked if he could talk to me. I said sure, and to my surprise, he closed the door. He proceeded to tell me that he had been planning to commit suicide that night. He had read the chapter I recommended while his chemistry class was studying. It didn't mean anything to him, but as he finished it, the title of the next chapter caught his attention. It had to do with recognizing the devil's schemes. As he began to read, he was aware that Jesus was standing right beside him. He didn't turn to look because he was afraid to, but he felt His presence. The dam inside was about to burst. He went to the janitor's closet and cried and cried.

He told me that as a kid, he had grown up in a Pentecostal church. He had sought the baptism of the Holy Spirit, but he didn't receive it. He had decided that God didn't care about him, so he left the church and gave up on God. He had gotten into some occult stuff that had opened the door for the enemy. As he read that chapter, he realized that God had never given up on him. He could feel the deep love and acceptance permeating from the Lord's presence.

I spent several days in awe that God had used me to save Bill's life, and in holy fear, realizing how close I had come to being disobedient.

Another thing Bill had said that touched me deeply was that for years he had been uncomfortable at lunch when I was there. He said the spirit in him didn't like the Spirit in me. I thought about all the times that I had represented the Lord badly, all the weaknesses in my own life. But that wasn't the issue. Though a very imperfect vessel, I carried a perfect God, and the enemy knew it even if I didn't.

2 Corinthians 4:6-7 For it is the God who commanded light to shine out of darkness, who has shone in our hearts to give the light of the knowledge of the glory of God in the face of Jesus Christ. But we have this treasure in earthen vessels, that the excellence of the power may be of God and not of us.

It wasn't until years later that I began to comprehend this concept. One day I was reading in Colossians about the mystery that had been hidden from ages and generations, but now was revealed to the saints. What was that mystery? "Christ in you, the hope of glory." (Colossians 1:27) I love Philippians and Colossians. I had to have my Bible rebound because those pages were coming out, but no matter how many times I'd read it, I'd never really gotten it.

What makes Christianity different from all other religions? Not only did God Himself pay for our sins, He actually came and took up residence within us in the form of the Holy Spirit.

Almighty God actually lives in me. I'm a Christ carrier. So are you.

Even when we feel weak, stupid, and inadequate, there is a force radiating within us that the devil recognizes. He lives in dread that we will realize what we carry and begin to release it. When the Body of Christ realizes the power resident within, the devil will be toast. That's why he works so hard to make us believe we are insignificant and worthless.

The devil is defeated. In Matthew 28:18 Jesus said, *"All authority has been given to Me in heaven and on earth."* If all authority has been given to Jesus, how much does that leave for the devil? He has no authority of his own. When he creates problems for you, he isn't operating out of **his** authority; he's operating from **your** authority. In the next verse in Matthew, Jesus said, *"Go therefore and make disciples of all the nations, baptizing them in the name of the Father and of the Son and of the Holy Spirit, teaching them to observe all things that I have commanded you; and lo, I am with* *you always, even to the end of the age."* <u>Jesus has appointed us to be the designated vessels through which He releases His authority</u>.

The key is to learn to go to the power source. Because of the mind-set of our society and the way we have been trained, when problems arise, we concentrate on the problem and try to figure out how we can resolve it. We rehearse the circumstances. We fret over things beyond our control. Some of us are so adept at the process that we not only stew over our own issues, but we also feel responsible to solve everyone else's problems as well. We've been trained to order our lives by the logic and reasoning of our minds, but the mind is not the part that communicates with God.

<u>The trouble is that our minds don't have the answers</u>. We've been trained to order our lives by the logic and reasoning of our minds, but the mind is not the part that communicates with God. God is spirit and we must learn to communicate with Him through our spirits. When Adam and Eve sinned, it was their spirits that died. Their spirits were disconnected from God through the sin. <u>When we receive Jesus as our Savior, our spirits are reborn. They come alive, and the very life of God takes up residence within our human spirit</u>.

A new control center
The minute He moves in, He establishes a new control center within us. It's like He plugs us into heaven's Internet with a full connection to the throne and the heart of God. But until we learn how to go to the Internet connection, we use our computer as a word processor only. Instead of connecting to the power of the universe, we are stuck with what we have programmed in through our human resources. We are limited to what we've seen, heard, and discovered through our five senses. You can't access the Internet through a word processor. So, if you want to know God, you have to learn to close down your word processor mind and risk stepping outside of that which you can control. If God has to limit Himself to what you understand—to your ways—to communicate with you, you will never know God as He really is, and you'll be stuck

searching for answers within your own mind. I frequently tell my mind to be quiet. I remind it that if it had the answers, I would already know them.

<u>I change my focus. Instead of focusing on the problem, I focus on the One who has all the answers</u>. I give Him the issue I'm dealing with and set my heart on His ability to make good out of any situation. Sometimes, I just worship Him. Sometimes, I recall the many ways He has been faithful to help me in the past. Sometimes, I just go for a walk and look with awe upon endless variety of nature. I'm reminded of His infinite creativity and relax into the security that if He doesn't have a solution to my problem, He can create one. Bill Johnson says that God can win with any hand, even a pair of deuces.

<u>Faith is the commodity of heaven</u>. Worry and fear are an invitation to the enemy to act in our situation. Faith opens the door to God. The more we concentrate on the problem, the more we invite the enemy to make us fearful. When we concentrate on the One with the answers, faith arises, and we open the channel to heaven's Internet. <u>When the power and creativity of God begin to flow through that channel, we become conduits to release light into even the darkest situations</u>.

I WANT TO KNOW MORE – 6
Body Language

1 Thessalonians 5:23-24 Now may the God of peace Himself sanctify you completely; and may your whole spirit, soul, and body be preserved blameless at the coming of our Lord Jesus Christ. He who calls you is faithful, who also will do it.

Some of us have been prone to see our bodies as the enemy. After all that's the part of us that whines for food when we are dieting, wants to sleep in when we need to get our day started, and rebels when it's time to exercise. BUT, the above scripture seems to indicate that our bodies can also be sanctified and, better yet, that God will do it! So how do we cooperate with that process?

I once heard Jerry Savelle, one of the Word and Faith teachers we enjoyed in the 80's, telling the story of trying to develop the practice of getting up for a quiet time. I don't have the tape anymore, but the abbreviated version went something like this:

> "I set my alarm for 7:00 am, excited to begin spending time with God in the morning. When my alarm went off, my body said, 'I'm not ready to get up. I'm tired.' My soul agreed, so I turned over and went back to sleep. When I finally woke up, I was full of condemnation, totally disgusted with myself for being such a lazy slob.

> "The next night I was determined I would get up. The alarm went off. My body and soul were in agreement again. I said, 'Oh, no you don't. I'm not listening to you. I'm getting up.' So, I stumbled out the bedroom door, paused, and decided to pray in the guest room. I lay down on the bed – and woke up an hour later, up to my ears in condemnation.

> "The third morning I prayed, 'Lord, you have to help me.' I pried myself out of bed. I looked in the guest room, and told my soul and body that I wasn't falling for that one again. I stumbled around the house, looking for a place where I wouldn't go back to sleep. Finally, I chose the bathroom. I climbed up and planted my feet firmly on the side of the tub. 'Body,' I declared, 'we are going to stay awake and pray. If you fall asleep, you die.'"

After a couple of days of that, Jerry found he could stay awake and pray in a chair quite nicely. Savelle is also the one who taught us to say, "I'm not moved by what I see; I'm not moved by what I feel;

I'm moved by what I believe. I believe the word of God." Dick used that almost every day at the hog farm when he had to overcome physical pain from the damage caused by the plane crash.

So, in sanctifying the body, our part is to commit to a thing, and to ask for God's help to do it. Then we take the faith steps in actual physical action toward its completion. The Holy Spirit provides the enablement.

The Discipline Process

There is a process of bring the body under discipline. The discipline starts with making a choice to obey God in something that He is impressing you to do. It is followed by asking for His enabling. The Lord has used various and assorted types of fasting to help me learn to bring my body under discipline. The body will learn rather quickly that, if it can do without food, it can do without a lot of the comforts it thinks are indispensable. But here again, fasting can be a legalistic club. When I was teaching, I decided to fast one day a week for a year. I didn't eat any kind of food, and the only liquid I allowed myself was water. And, I didn't just do it for 24 hours. I would eat my evening meal on Monday night and not eat again until breakfast on Wednesday. That may sound pretty spiritual, but it wasn't. It was legalistic hogwash that I made up to try to be spiritual and to try to coerce God into doing what I wanted done. Mostly, what I got out of it was hungry.

<u>I have learned to only fast when I feel prompted by the Holy Spirit to fast. Then I do the kind of fast He shows me and for the purpose He gives me</u>. The most powerful of these for me was several years ago. I had been praying about a situation in the family for several months. I had already felt impressed to give up soft drinks and sweets until it was resolved. In the fall the Lord told me to do a Daniel fast for twenty-one days.

Scripture isn't very specific on what Daniel fasted except it says he ate no desirable food and no meat or wine. So, I interpreted a

Daniel fast to mean I would drink juice in the morning and evening and eat only vegetables at noon.

As the days passed, I discovered a number of things that God was doing. First, I realized that He was reordering my eating habits for a healthier lifestyle. He set me free from a sugar dependence during that time. It brought my body into levels of obedience I hadn't experienced before, and it wasn't that hard. I learned that if I concentrated on God and His purposes, He would be faithful to give me the grace and enablement. Dick and I both discovered that God was calling us to new levels of prayer and warfare, not just for our family but also for many other things. While the situation eventually did change in our family, we realized that God was using something we cared for enough to sacrifice for to bring us to a new level of commitment and sacrifice that we hadn't considered before. And we discovered that God's kind of sacrifice is a blessing rather than a burden. It was so neat to discover He wanted to partner with us and enable us.

So far I have talked about ways to discipline the body, but that's not the main message of this lesson. A sanctified body is a spiritual weapon. It can actually be used to bring our souls into alignment. It can help with our emotional states. Lance Wallnau says:

> "God has so marvelously made your body that He has wired it neurologically so that what you do with your body sends a direct relay message to your brain in terms of the emotional state you're in. If you smile, your brain receives a message that says, 'Something's up.' If you frown your brain senses, 'Something's down.' What you do with your body affects your emotional state. Your body doesn't lie. Your body is so wired to your soul and your spirit that what you do physically connects with a neurological system that supports or contradicts what is going on in your soul and spirit. If you want your body to be on the same

page with your soul and spirit, you have to take control, not just the stuff you eat, but also of how you manage your physiology. People who have mastered what their body speaks attract people to them because strength is being communicated by what they're doing."[1]

In other words, you can use your body to change your emotional state. I did that before I had ever heard the principle. In the of 2001, Dick was diagnosed with prostrate cancer. He had a supernatural peace the whole time, but I had to fight the fear of losing him. What I discovered to do was this: When the fear would begin to rise up, I would put on a Glory of Zion CD and dance to it. Their music is strong and lively, full of faith and warfare. I would dance until the faith and warfare filled my soul and spirit. The strength of my moves and the faith in their words changed my focus from the fear of what the devil could do to my husband to the ability of my God to handle anything that came our way. I used that method to keep me up emotionally and mentally for several months until the surgery was done and recovery was complete.

After hearing Lance teach the concept, I had a better understanding of why my dancing had worked. I decided to put it to work in daily life. One day I woke up from a nap just feeling useless. I had to go to the grocery store, so I couldn't sit and mope. As I started down the aisle of the store, I thought, 'What would I look like if I was feeling strong and capable?' I remembered a time I had felt that way. I lifted my head and put a bounce in my step. I began to sing a happy song under my breath. Everything in and around me began to look different. By the time I left the store, I was back on top and filled with excitement about the new weapon I had just added to my arsenal.

When circumstances are closing in on you, begin to choose how you want to feel. Think of times you have felt like you want to

---

[1] Wallnau, In a Heartbeat CD series.

feel, or think about how someone else acts when they project the confidence you want, and then just make your body line up with what that looks like.

There is one caution here. I suppose for anything that God has for us, the enemy has some sort of counterfeit. I'm not suggesting that you put on a façade that merely covers your pain so that you can make other people think you're okay. When there is deep stuff there, it needs to be uncovered and dealt with. That's what we've been talking about in the last two lessons. <u>This isn't meant to hide something. It's meant to change something</u>. It is one of the keys used to bring your whole body, soul, and spirit into alignment with the truth of who God says you are. It's only one piece, but it is a helpful one. Learn to make your body line up with the truth, and that will help bring your soul along.

I WANT TO CLIMB HIGHER – 6
Praying in the Spirit

If you haven't yet received the baptism of the Holy Spirit, you will need to go to the Appendix and receive before you will be able to do this exercise. Every day, for at least a week, pray aloud in tongues for at least fifteen minutes each day. You can do that while driving or cooking dinner or whenever you can get fifteen minutes alone. When Dick is driving along, he automatically begins praying in the spirit. After praying in tongues for a while, be quiet and listen deep within. Record in your journal anything you "hear." Hearing refers to impressions that just seem to drop in or float up from within. It isn't something you hear with your natural ears. It is more like a knowing within—a revelation that you now have that you weren't aware of before. Don't be discouraged or concerned if you don't "hear" anything. Just give God your undivided attention and the opportunity to speak to you. It may take some time to recognize that He is speaking or to be able to quiet yourself enough to listen. The exciting thing is that with the baptism of the Holy Spirit, you now have a whole new capacity to hear. It will come.

In the meantime, also work on making your body line up with the attitude you want to have. If you are meeting to discuss these lessons with a small group, record body language experiences that you can share with others.

Chapter 7

BIRTH OF A WARRIOR

—

AN EVANGELIST BY THE NAME OF LARRY JONES CAME
to hold a crusade in the gym of the high school where I taught in
Minneapolis, Kansas. I have no idea who pulled that off, but it was
an amazing thing. The local churches worked together, and the
event was a great success. It stirred up some of the youth and made
them hungry for more, so we started a Bible study in our home.

While he was there, Larry was promoting a mission trip he would
be leading into Haiti in a few months. Dick and a couple of other
local people decided to go. Dick thought he was just going as
an observer, but shortly before time to go, Larry's organization
informed him that he would be preaching in a church while he was
there. He had never done anything like that. Pretty much all that
either of us had done was lead the little Bible study for the youth.
I always wrote the lessons, and then Dick would add whatever he
wanted to. Usually, I wrote the meat of the thing, then Dick would
say it was dry and boring, so he would add stories from our experiences to give it life. But preach? Well, let's just say it would be
a challenge. I wrote some lessons for him to take. He readapted
them to fit his style.

We hadn't been out of the United States except for an across the
border tourist visit one afternoon into Nogales, Mexico. Nothing
Dick had ever seen or experienced prepared him for the sights and
smells of Haiti. The stench of open sewers met him as they left the
airport. The poverty jolted him, and the hotels encircled with high
walls topped with broken glass gave him a different perspective on

what life might be like there. But Dick loves different cultures, so he thoroughly enjoyed seeing women carrying large loads on their heads, boys scurrying up coconut trees to throw down their fruit, and the throngs of people in colorful clothing that filled the streets.

He discovered quickly that the Haitians in the local churches were hungry. The twenty to thirty-minute messages we had prepared were just warm-up for them. They told him they wanted more food than that. They wanted him to preach for at least an hour. So, he would spend time during the day working to add to what he had to say. The good thing was, they appreciated everything, and since he was from far away, he was automatically an expert, and they would listen intently to whatever he presented.

One night, when Dick had planned to teach on spiritual warfare, there was a violent storm. Heavy rain pelted the tin roof of the church, making it impossible to hear anything. He finally got to deliver the message, but he realized that if you were going to teach on spiritual warfare in a place where witchcraft was a major religion, you'd better practice what you preached before you got there.

The pastor of the church where Dick was preaching invited him to accompany him to a church dedication out in a mountainous region several hours from Port-au-Prince. Dick checked with the leaders of his trip, and they said it would be okay, so a couple of days later he found himself in a pickup-like vehicle which served as a bus, loaded with thirty Haitians. He was the only white man, and he had a place of honor, which meant a seat to himself beside the driver. Every other inch of the vehicle, including the top, had black bodies crowded against one another to get everyone aboard.

The trip was fascinating. They drove on little dirt roads until there were no more roads, and then they drove up through dry riverbeds the rest of the way. Sometimes they would have to stop so men could jump out and move rocks out of the way before they could continue.

Their destination was a village partway up the mountain. Pigs and chickens wandered amidst the people. Children, who had never seen a white man before, would come up and touch Dick's skin to see if it felt different from their own. When it was time to eat, Dick ate what was placed before him and didn't ask any questions. He really didn't want to know what he was eating. He kept in mind the Lord's promise that if you eat any deadly thing, it will not harm you. It was a strange atmosphere, but they treated him with such honor, as if he were a king.

As it began to get dark and near time for the service, Dick could see spots of light moving down the mountain from above as people from other villages walked for miles to join them. The people sang and danced and praised God with more emotional intensity than Dick had ever experienced in church. At one point they sang that those who loved God the most would jump the highest, and Dick was amazed at how high they could jump, especially in a room that was so crowded that people were hanging out the windows.

The biggest surprise came when he gave his message. He had not much more than started when people began coming to the altar. Dick didn't know why they were coming. There hadn't been any kind of altar call, so he just kept preaching, and the pastor would gather those people to one side, and more would come. Later Dick found out that the people were coming forward under the conviction that they needed Jesus, and the pastor was taking them aside to minister salvation to them. Then more would come. Dick wasn't even preaching a salvation message. That night was an incredible picture of what God can do with a messenger that is willing to just show up. A number of people received Jesus, and Dick knew that God was sovereignly in charge. It really touched his heart and changed his life as he understood that God could use him, unprepared and inexperienced as he was—still God wanted to use him.

After the service ended at about 2:30 in the morning, Dick was given a room of his own for his quarters in a little three-room house. The phrase "of his own" is only somewhat accurate. He was the only one who slept in the room, and he actually had a cot to sleep on; however, the door to his room, which opened to the outside, was a cloth hanging down, and his room was an entry-way to the rest of the house, so everyone and everything, including the pigs and chickens, passed through.

There was activity outside all night, so he didn't get much sleep, and in the morning he woke up to the sound of people singing.

One thing that had interested Dick the day before was watching the women washing clothes in a stream. He was amazed at how clean they got the clothes. This morning he saw the completed results of their efforts as women, and especially teenage girls, appeared in glistening white dresses, perfectly pressed. He couldn't get over how perfectly white the dresses were.

The reason for the white dresses was a special baptism service at which around twenty people were baptized in the stream. After the baptism service, they loaded the "bus" and headed back to Port-au-Prince.

That trip to Haiti was a destiny experience for Dick. The deepest impression was that, even though he was not equipped, God used him. It gave him a hunger to be used more. The other thing that touched him deeply was his awareness of the demonic. Dick was not especially aware of his prophetic gifting at the time, so it was a new experience for him when he saw demons on a young woman that sang at one of the church services. He could see it, but he didn't know how to do anything about it. He saw part of a voodoo service and was repulsed by what the devil does to people.

Perhaps the warrior in Dick came alive in Haiti. Whether or not that's true, the Haitian experience was certainly one of those calls to destiny that God drops into our lives. It planted the desire to see the devil defeated and to set people free that has been a hallmark in Dick's life ever since.

I WANT TO LEARN MORE – 7
The Power of Words

For good or for evil, the words you speak carry great power, especially if they truly reflect what is in your heart.

Look up the following verses and check out the power of the spoken word.

> ➤ Hebrews 11:1-3 and Genesis 1:1-19. What ingredients functioned together to create the world?

> ➤ Romans 10:8-10. What two ingredients function together for a person to be saved?

Speaking God's Word Builds Faith
God creates by forming a faith picture in His heart and then declaring it into being with His mouth. We are capable of creating the same way. In fact, it's pretty clear in scripture that God intends for us to take part in His creative process with the words of our mouths.

Isaiah 51:16 And I have put My words in your mouth; I have covered you with the shadow of My hand, that I may plant the heavens, lay the foundations of the earth, and say to Zion, 'You are My people.'"

Jeremiah 1:9-10 "Behold, I have put My words in your mouth. See, I have this day set you over the nations and over the kingdoms, to root out and to pull down, to destroy and to throw down, to build and to plant."

> ➤ According to these verses, what sort of things does God do through the power of a human being choosing to set his heart in agreement with God's heart and speak the words God speaks?

➢ Are there things that you know you are supposed to be speaking over your life or over situations you touch?

➢ If not, how are you going to know what you are to speak?

You can start with general things, like statements of who you are and what you have in Jesus that you found in Ephesians. There is a lot of power in simply declaring what God says in the Bible. When you find promises that meet your needs, keep track of them and declare them. In the Appendix you will find a single page confession called "Our Confession" that Dick and I declared over our lives every morning at the breakfast table for years. It is all directly from the word of God. Sometimes I would read though my tears when the promise seemed so far from reality that I felt like I was lying. But I wasn't lying. I was saying what God said and doing what God does. Like Abraham of old, we declared those things that were not until they conformed our lives to the truth of God's word and came into being.

Romans 4:16-18 Therefore, the promise comes by faith, so that it may be by grace and may be guaranteed to all Abraham's offspring-not only to those who are of the law but also to those who are of the faith of Abraham. He is the father of us all. 17 As it is written: "I have made you a father of many nations." He is our father in the sight of God, in whom he believed-<u>the God who gives life to the dead and calls things that are not as though they were</u>.

18 Against all hope, Abraham in hope believed and so became the father of many nations, just as it had been said to him, "So shall your offspring be."
(from New International Version)

2 Corinthians 4:18 while we do not look at the things which are seen, but at the things which are not seen. For the things which are seen are temporary, but the things which are not seen are eternal.

For Dick and me, things didn't change very quickly. Back then, I thought that just because I said it, it should happen. Over the years, I've learned that saying it, meditating on it, choosing to act upon what the Bible says, whether it makes sense or not, are the faith tools that God uses to paint the faith picture in our hearts.

It is with the heart we believe and with the mouth we confess. At some point the believing becomes strong and immovable enough that, when we speak, it calls the heavens into action on our behalf. Until we are unshakable on the inside, our God-ordained declarations work to build the faith we need. They begin to break us loose from old negative mindsets and form new patterns of thought that more closely resemble the way God thinks.

God's word is frequently compared to seed:

Isaiah 55:10-11 "For as the rain comes down, and the snow from heaven, and do not return there, but water the earth, and make it bring forth and bud, that it may give seed to the sower and bread to the eater, so shall My word be that goes forth from My mouth; it shall not return to Me void, but it shall accomplish what I please, and it shall prosper in the thing for which I sent it.

Isaiah 61:11 For as the earth brings forth its bud, as the garden causes the things that are sown in it to spring forth, so the Lord GOD will cause righteousness and praise to spring forth before all the nations.

> ➤ How does seed grow?

Mark 4:26-28 And He said, "The kingdom of God is as if a man should scatter seed on the ground, and should sleep by night and rise by day, and the seed should sprout and grow, he himself does not know how. 28 For the earth yields crops by itself: first the blade, then the head, after that the full grain in the head.

It takes time for seed to produce fruit. We can't bypass the growth stage, but sometimes God puts extra grace on just to bless us.

So, we speak God's word, not just what is written in the Bible, but also what He has spoken over our lives. <u>Prophetic words and words God has given to you in your personal prayer, and scripture that has come alive to you, are powerful things to declare over your own life.</u>

Your Words Are Weapons—For You or Against You

1 Timothy 1:18-19 This charge I commit to you, son Timothy, according to the prophecies previously made concerning you, that by them you may wage the good warfare.

➢ What do you think Paul is telling Timothy to do?

In Ephesians 6, one of the weapons of our armor, in fact, the only offensive weapon listed is the sword of the Spirit. We can wield God's word, written or spoken, as a weapon against the enemy. What better weapon against his tools of lies and deception than truth? Not only does it set the record straight, but also God watches over His word to perform it. *Jeremiah 1:12 Then the LORD said to me, "You have seen well, for I am watching over My word to perform it."* (NASU)

So, when you speak what God says, He acts on it, but there is another side to this that you also need to understand. <u>When you speak what the devil says, he also acts on it.</u> When you agree with the enemy, you have handed him authority in your life to do the thing you say! SO, LEARN TO GUARD YOUR MOUTH. A lot of what you believe to be harmless chatter or even funny remarks should never be spoken. "If anything bad can happen, it will happen to me." "If it can be messed up, I'll find the way." "No one in this house ever listens to me." "I always get a cold this time of year." Just listen to what you are saying. If it doesn't agree with what God says, keep your mouth closed. Learning to simply be quiet is a tremendous discipline.

➢ Read James, chapter 3. What's the most significant thing you see in that chapter? (Remember, it won't be the same for everyone. The Holy Spirit draws your attention to what you need to see.)

So remember, we are on a quest to take 100% responsibility for how we feel and for our reactions—for our emotional condition. One of the keys was bringing your physical reactions into line with the state you want to be in. Another is to bring your mouth into agreement with the mental and emotional place where you want to dwell.

Begin listening to yourself. Ask the Lord to put a red flag on the negative things you say. He will begin by causing you to hear it after you've said it. That's the first step. If you simply repent, turn your mind to agree with God, you will soon begin to hear it right before you say it, and you can close your mouth.

It works the way Dick learned to quit running stop signs. We lived in the country in a flat part of Kansas. When you pulled up to a stop sign you could usually see a half-mile down the road both directions. So, Dick would slow down and look and then roll on through.

Then Cindy took driver's education. Her teacher was a friend of ours, and one day he mentioned to Dick that Cindy didn't stop at stop signs. He had finally started banging his hand on top of the car every time she ran one. Dick was immediately convicted. He was setting a bad example for his children. So, he determined to stop at stop signs, even if the road was clear for miles.

That was easier said than done. Old habits are heard to break. He would run the stop sign and be several yards down the road, when he'd sense the nudge of the Holy Spirit that he'd done it again. So instead of going on, he'd stop, right in the middle of the road however far he had driven. Since there was so little traffic, that wasn't a hazard, but it didn't have to happen very many times before those red octagons actually told him to stop <u>before</u> he passed them.

Proverbs 18:21 Death and life are in the power of the tongue, and those who love it will eat its fruit.

I WANT TO CLIMB HIGHER – 7
Praying Scripture

These exercises come from *Experiencing the Depths of Jesus Christ* by Madam Jeanne Guyon, a book I highly recommend for growing in your ability to hear God. "Praying the Scripture" comes from pages 7-8. Before you do the exercise, find a quiet place where you can be comfortable and relaxed. Ask the Holy Spirit to be your guide as you walk into this passage. Then just trust that He will.

Praying the Scripture
Choose a passage of scripture. You could choose any number of passages. For this exercise you might choose Matthew 6:25-34. Come to the Lord quietly and humbly. Before Him, read a small portion of the passage you have chosen. Take in fully, gently and carefully what you are reading. Taste it and digest it as you read. Don't read quickly or look for the main point. Chew on it and sense the very heart of what you are reading. You may want to turn that portion into a prayer. When you sense that the essence of that portion has been extracted and all the deeper sense of it is gone, then, very slowly, gently, calmly begin to read the next section. Let the Holy Spirit speak to you through the deeper sense of what is being taken in.[1]

---

[1] Jeanne Guyon, *Experiencing the Depths of Jesus Christ,* pp. 7-8.

Chapter 8

THE DESTINY PUZZLE

―

Summer 1981

DICK AND I WERE IN THE AUDIENCE AT CHRIST FOR the Nations, Dallas, listening to a man called Cecil Pumphrey from Melodyland Church in the Los Angeles area. He was talking about his experiences smuggling Bibles into places closed to the gospel. As he talked about his plans to take a group to smuggle Bibles into China in the fall, I knew what Dick was going to say. Sure enough, he turned to me and said, "We're supposed to go with him. My stomach's about to explode."

I didn't want to hear that. Communist China was not on my list of places to visit. The doors to tourist travel in China had opened only months before. It wasn't safe, and it wasn't within our budget. But there it was: God had spoken to Dick, and I knew in my heart that it was God speaking. So budget, safety, nor my desire had anything to do with it—we were going to China.

When it came close to the time that we had to submit our first deposit, Dick got a phone call from the buyer where we sold our hogs. He announced that we had failed to cash a check for hogs we had sold a couple of years before. He had a check for us.

Us, not cash a hog check? Not likely. Them, discover that after two years and decide to give us another? What are the probabilities of that happening? But there it was—our deposit to go to China.

The hog buyer asked Dick what he thought of that. Dick simply said, "I think I'm blessed."

That trip changed our lives in many ways. First we spent a few days with Cecil in L.A. He took us to visit the Crystal Cathedral, which felt like a tourist attraction, and followed that by a visit to Chuck Smith's church called Calvary Chapel, where the presence of God was so strong that we felt like we should whisper. Just walking into those two churches gave us a clear revelation of the difference between religion, managed by a man's charisma, and relationship covered by the presence of God Himself. We also attended a morning service at Melodyland where we experienced our first clear view of the supernatural power of God to heal. A man with a bad leg went down under the power of the Spirit. As the pastor prayed over him, his body was jolted like he was receiving a shock treatment, and he got up running! That made our hearts say, "Wow! There's more of God to be experienced than we realized."

One evening we visited Trinity Broadcasting which led us to invest in a huge satellite dish, which was in our back yard, and which allowed us to tape messages and teachings that just didn't exist in rural Kansas at the time. We distributed those among our spirit filled friends, and they planted the seeds that eventually led to a Spirit-filled church in Delphos, Kansas. That's another story.

After an endless flight, we landed in Hong Kong, which was still a British protectorate at the time. We purchased some canvass bags which had an expandable bottom. The height of the bag could be adjusted by unzipping a zipper to release more of the canvass. Then we packed our luggage in such a way that sleeves and pants legs were filled with Bibles. Some of the "Bibles" were just the Gospel of Luke and the Book of Acts written in English on one side of the page and Chinese on the other. Lots of Chinese people wanted to learn English, so they would take the book to learn. We also had some New Testaments in Chinese and a few whole Bibles which were meant for the Underground Church.

Our particular tour was a strange mix of people. There were eight or ten denominational people, whose sole purpose for the trip was to sightsee in China, and six of us who were Spirit-filled radicals bent on getting God's word into the hands of the Chinese. The denominational people didn't want to have anything to do with smuggling Bibles, nor did they want to have anything to do with us when we crossed the border. So, Cecil made arrangements for them to go into Canton by train, while we went in by hover-craft—a boat that actually skims above the water.

Our route was up the Pearl River. We stopped at the border for the Red Guard to get on board. They stood in the middle of the boat with large guns strapped over their shoulders. I took one look at the soldiers, and a strange thing happened in me. The Spirit of God rose up in me like a warrior. I wasn't afraid. I was taking authority, and I prayed in tongues under my breath all the rest of the trip and into customs.

Customs was a "trip" all its own. Everyone in the group was on separate visas, except for Dick and me, so we could all go through individually. That way if anyone got caught, it wouldn't incriminate the others. Dick and I prayed to get the right inspector, and we prayed the Brother Andrew prayer that seeing eyes would be made blind to the contents of our bags. Dick wanted a certain young woman, and that's where they sent us. As she inspected our luggage, we could see Bibles that had shifted and were showing in any number of places, but she didn't see them. We passed on through and joined the others outside. One of our men didn't show up. Time passed, and he still didn't show up. Dick and Cecil got nervous and decided we'd better move on to the bus for fear they would call the rest of us back. They didn't. Our man finally came. They had found the Bibles in one of his bags. They put a seal on it and sent him on. While in Canton, Cecil found someone from the underground church who translated the seal for us. It said, "This bag contains Bibles and must be taken from the country." The men opened the zipper extension on the lower part of the bag, carefully made a slit in the canvass inside and removed most of the

Bibles. Then they closed the zipper, leaving just five of the Luke/ Acts "Bibles," so that it would still meet the customs requirements on the way out. When we did leave China, that man was passed through customs, and none of his baggage was checked. It was as if they didn't even see him.

We experienced a lot of interesting things in China. There was the day in Beijing when Dick and Cecil rode around in an embassy vehicle for hours before their contact felt it was safe to transfer the Bibles from our bags to theirs. That was the main drop for the underground church.

There were the mornings we got up early in Shanghai to be on the streets to hand out Bibles while the people were all out in the parks to take part in the required exercise drills. People would flock around to get a copy of the English/Chinese version of Luke and Acts. Especially the young people wanted to learn English. They wanted us to arrange for them to go to the States to study. A few older people, who had learned English in a missionary school, would want to talk. They wanted to know the truth about Taiwan and other things. Most people didn't try to talk very long.

Dick's most incredible experience came when he was praying about to whom to give a whole Bible. We didn't have many of those to hand out. He moved away from the crowds where the Red Guardsmen were leading drills and headed down a side street. He felt the Lord direct him to give it to an old Chinese man. He handed the man the Bible and moved on. All of a sudden, he realized the man was chasing him down the street, shouting to him. Dick didn't know whether to stop or to run. When he turned to meet the man, there were tears streaming down the old man's cheeks. He said he was a Christian. His Bible had been taken from him and burned during the Cultural Revolution. He had been praying for another Bible ever since. You could say Dick had traveled all the way to China to answer the prayers of that old man.

But there were so many other reasons, the greatest being direction for our next step. While in China, Cecil shared with us about Youth With a Mission (YWAM). Before the trip was over, we knew we were to attend a Discipleship Training School (DTS) with YWAM.

It's kind of like the design of our lives is a big three-dimensional puzzle, with thousands of pieces, and some of them connect to other people's puzzles. Or maybe it's all one big puzzle, and we just have a part in the overall design. Either way, we look at the pieces and can't see where to begin, but God has the cover to the box. He knows exactly how the sum total is to fit together to create a beautiful picture. Instead of giving us the cover to the box and making us struggle alone, He gives us a piece here and a few pieces there. That way, instead of getting our focus on trying to manage all those mystery pieces by ourselves, God has designed the process in such a way that we must keep our eyes on Him and on fitting in the pieces He gives us. I believe He does it that way because He wants to partner with us in the process of life. If the puzzle is to be complete, some of the pieces will be our pieces, and some will be His. Some will be fitted to the very particular and special way He made us, including our gifts, passions, and talents, and some will have to do with the unique anointing that He puts on our abilities to enable us to do what would be far beyond our capacity apart from His touch.

I think for most people the puzzle remains a puzzle. They get part of it together, but they feel like something is missing, and they don't know where their pieces connect to the grand scheme of things. It seems to me that very few people actually know who they really are and have connected with the purpose for which they were designed.

Most of us live in the midst of a battlefield within our own beings, suppressing desires that never really go away, but which we see no possibility of fulfilling. Some of us are reluctant to even pull up our desires to look at them, because we don't want to be disappointed again. <u>But our desires are connected to our passion.</u> <u>If we stuff them, we lose our passion for life, and we just go</u> <u>through the motions.</u>

The eternal struggle within is rooted in identity. Until we can understand and accept who we are, we cannot have real peace. Most of us believe we have to do certain things and avoid other things to earn God's approval. <u>The truth is you have had God's</u> <u>approval since the time you were only an idea in His heart.</u> He made you to be the person you are. He built into you an amazing potential for greatness—a wonderful mix of gifts, passions, values, and desires—that, brought into harmony, not only define your true identity, but also will lead to your greatest fulfillment. You carry something that other people need, that you were designed to give as no one else can. Discovering and yielding to that imprint, which is built into your DNA, is the key to peace and fulfillment.

I WANT TO KNOW MORE – 8
Focus

One of the very important things in life is to learn to focus on God and His ability rather than on you and your inability. When the circumstances of life are impossible, that's the time to get excited, because that's when the God of the impossible is at His best. That's the time to expect Him to show up.

Some evenings in Mexico, as we headed to a church where we were ministering, I would feel absolutely no anointing. Everything in me would be telling me that I had not prepared well, that I had nothing to give. One such evening, I remember praying, "Lord, Your word says that Your strength is made perfect in my weakness (2 Corinthians 12:9). I am very weak tonight, so I am putting my trust in Your strength." He heard me, He showed up, and better things happened in the lives of people than if I had felt strong and capable. I have prayed that prayer many times over the years, and I have learned that coming to the end of my rope is not a bad

The Destiny Puzzle

thing. When I change my focus from my ability to God's ability, He extends, not just His rope, but also His hand to help me.

> ➢ Can you think of examples in your life when God showed up at the point of your helplessness?

> ➢ If that's happened to you various times, can you see anything in your experiences that would give you clues as to how God operates—to God's ways?

Lance Wallnau says an impossible situation is an invitation to go with the Lord to a whole new level of understanding. It's your invitation to press through to a place you have never accessed before. It forces you to press into God for a whole new paradigm because the paradigm you are in doesn't have the answer. I know of no way that we honor the Lord more than when we can turn to Him, with peace in our hearts, the midst of an impossible situation, knowing that no matter how bad it looks, He is not only capable of working it for good, that's His desire and His way.

> ➢ Why do you think it is that sometimes we have to get to the end of our ways before God can bring the needed answer?

Bill Johnson says God doesn't allow us to be placed in a tough situation unless He has already placed within us the capacity to win. He says we are in that place for the purpose of winning and taking ground from the enemy. Sometimes the victory comes in the form of external things where mountains move on our behalf. Sometimes things change rapidly like a dramatic healing or a financial gift that arrives at just the right time. More often, things change slowly, and it's less obvious that it's God at work.

> ➢ Ask God to help you remember times in your life where negative situations have been turned into victory for you. Pick out a couple of such times and record what you learned, about you, about God, and about how life functions.

Usually, God is doing more than one thing in the process. He's a great multi-tasker. While He changes our situation, He is also changing our hearts and attitudes. Frequently, He doesn't change the outward circumstance until He's brought about the inward renewal. I very frequently pray, "Spirit of Truth, please lead me into truth in this situation."

The thing we are trying to do is to learn to change perspective. Instead of looking at circumstances through the eyes of our logic and sense knowledge, we choose to look at them through the eyes of God and what He is doing in the midst of the storm. Jesus taught His disciples to pray, "Thy kingdom come, Thy will be done on earth as it is in heaven." So how would the situation we are focusing on be managed in heaven? The question to ask is, "What are You doing in the midst of this situation, Lord, and how do You want me to join in what You're doing?" Another helpful question is: "What does the Father want me to learn from this that will make me more effective as a believer?"

The best way to change your focus is to move from your mind to your spirit.

Praying in tongues pulls the shift lever from your mind to your spirit. *1 Corinthians 14:14 For if I pray in a tongue, my spirit prays, but my mind is unfruitful.* (NIV) Allowing your spirit to pray without the interference of the logic and reasoning of your mind, opens the way to spiritual understanding that gives you God's perspective.

As I pray in tongues, I listen for the mood of the prayer. If it comes strong and forceful, I know that Holy Spirit and I are doing warfare. I just continue until the tongue changes and until I sense peace. Many times, I find that if I will sing in tongues, I will begin to sense the Holy Spirit's attitude or mood. One time when I was quite concerned about a situation, the Lord told me to "dance it." I got up and started making rather mechanical moves out of obedience. Then, much to my surprise, both my song and my movements became light and joyful. I quickly sensed that the Lord was not concerned about the situation. As I sang and danced, I knew I was releasing victory over the thing. I have learned that if the Lord isn't concerned about a situation, I don't need to be. If He has it in control, then I can just look for how He is going to work it for good.

I WANT TO CLIMB HIGHER – 8
Quieting Your Soul

In order to be able to focus on and receive direction from God, you must learn to quiet your mind and emotions. In 1 Kings 19 we find Elijah hiding from Jezebel on the mountain of God. He is alone and full of fear. All the circumstances of his life are yelling doom and destruction in his ear. Verses 11 and 12 are very interesting and instructive. He faces a great destructive wind, but the Lord was not in the wind. Then there was an earthquake, but the Lord was not in the earthquake; and after the earthquake a fire, but the Lord was not in the fire. Then there came a still small voice.

As long as our mind and emotions are impressed with the storms of life, we can't hear the still small voice – the one that comes like a quiet impression from the depths of our being. The question is how do we turn off our mind and emotions in the midst of the battle, so that we can hear God. It's best to learn how to quiet yourself when the storm isn't raging. Try to find time each day to be quiet before God. To begin with, this seems like a waste of time, because we are so accustomed to accomplishing something that we can see. Just remember, you are working at learning to operate in a kingdom that doesn't run by earth rules and that measures accomplishment in terms of relationship with the Lord.

Exercise: "Beholding the Lord" comes from pages 9-13 of *Experiencing the Depths of Jesus Christ,* where Jeanne Guyon goes into a lot more depth to guide you than I have done here.

Beholding the Lord (or entering into His presence)

In this exercise you are using scripture to quiet your mind and help you focus on the Lord rather than focusing on the passage. As we wait on the Lord to move us into His presence, the hardest thing to deal with is our mind's tendency to stray away. The use of scripture is to help you quiet your mind. Again, you could use many passages. For starters use the 23rd Psalm. Come to the Lord quietly. Turn your heart to His presence by faith. Simply choose to believe that you have come to the presence of God. Begin to read the passage. As you read, pause. The pause should be quite gentle. You have paused to set your mind inward on the Spirit of Christ down deep in your spirit. Consider your spirit to be housed somewhere deep down in the area of your womb (if you're a man, down in the seat of your procreative organs.) Don't look to your mind. The Lord is found only within your spirit, in the recesses of your being. He will meet you in your spirit.

Remember you are not seeking understanding of the passage. You are seeking the presence of God within you. Focus inward. Don't let your mind wander. If it does, don't become frustrated. Simply draw it gently back to the passage and back inward.

"Once your heart has been turned inwardly to the Lord, you will have an impression of His presence. You will be able to notice His presence more acutely because your outer senses have now become very calm and quiet. Your attention is no longer on outward things or on the surface thoughts of your mind; instead, sweetly and silently, your mind becomes occupied with what you have read and by the touch of His presence." In this very peaceful state, swallow what you have tasted. Simply receive what is there. You may receive some word. You may only sense His peace. Receive whatever you sense, knowing that God is doing a work within you whether you know what it is or not.

Don't let your unruly mind discourage you. It has had years of operating almost exclusively from sense knowledge. It takes the same patient training that it takes to teach your fingers to type, to teach your mind and body to cooperate to run while dribbling a basketball, or any other thing that involves mental and bodily skill. With practice this becomes easier. In time the mind will form a habit of drawing deep within. By faith, bring yourself to His presence daily, simply trusting God to enable this, and He will.[1]

---

[1] Guyon, *Experiencing the Depths of Jesus Christ,* pp. 9-13.

Chapter 9

YOUTH WITH A MISSION

—

Fall 1982

DICK WAS ATTENDING HIS SMALL GROUP PRAYER FOR the first time on the Youth With a Mission base near Tyler, Texas. At that time Dick didn't know he was called to be an intercessor, but God went out of His way to give him and his fellow group members an object lesson in prayer that they wouldn't forget. There were five or six people in the group. The leader explained how one person might get part of the information for prayer and others would get other pieces. They were to stick with one topic until the Lord showed them they were finished.

It didn't take long to get into it. One person saw a wide river. One saw a white baby and another a dark baby. Somebody had a name. Someone saw an angry mob and another saw rain. As they put their parts together, they realized they were praying for the brother of a man who was on staff on the base. They sensed that he and his family were in a desperate situation. A week or so later the brother on base got a letter from his brother in the Amazon. The couple, who already had a baby of their own, was trying to adopt a native baby who had been abandoned. Apparently, that flew in the face of native custom, and a mob had gathered. The couple was in real danger at the time the small prayer group was piecing together the information they were receiving through the spirit. A handful of people in Texas were used to save the lives of a missionary family in the Amazon that they didn't even know.

From that point on, Dick was very impressed with the power of prayer, and it was the starting point of his becoming an intercessor.

We learned to pray at an entirely different level at YWAM. That training became the foundation for praying in a Spirit-filled church in Delphos. I know that God had us do the Discipleship Training School (DTS) with YWAM to learn to pray, but that wasn't the only reason He sent us there.

At the time we drove onto the YWAM base, we were deeply entrenched in the Word and Faith movement. We were driving a brand-new custom van. We believed in prosperity, in positive confession, and in a powerful God who met our needs. I am eternally grateful for everything we learned from that movement. The solid faith we gained in the word of God has taken us through a lot of hard places. But there is another side to faith that we didn't know much about. We knew a lot about getting OUR needs met, but we had little to no experience at taking Jesus into the hard places where other people are suffering in sin and poverty. We looked at the world through white America's middle-class lenses, and I guess that underneath it all, we pretty much believed that if everyone else could just see what we saw, everything would be all right.

Among the leadership on the YWAM base, pretty much no one saw what we saw. They were looking through an entirely different set of glasses. They weren't looking to get their needs met; they were looking for a place to lay down their lives for Jesus. We soon found that the staff couldn't believe God for toothpaste, and their confession was that the buses would break down and things would be hard. Sure enough, we got what they believed for. From our perspective, it looked like a poverty spirit. From their perspective it looked like dedication to Jesus. I suspect from God's perspective that we were part of the provision to get that DTS through. Our prosperity van became a backup to go for parts, to provide a warm place for those who got sick during a road trip in January (the bus wasn't heated), and to act as an emergency vehicle when a girl broke her leg.

Also, from God's perspective, there were things we needed worked in our lives that would never have happened in Kansas. We learned that we could sleep on the floor, survive without meat, and forego many "necessities" on behalf of touching lives with the love of God. We trudged through littered streets in poverty areas of Juarez, and we prayed through the drunken crowds at Mardi Gras. We helped tare away parts of an old house, so that it could be prepared for the use of the black church where we were staying in New Orleans. We got a first-hand look at black culture living in a 7' square room off the sanctuary of that church. We had to see the world through different lenses to explain why the black pastor came down on our DTS kids so hard. Life in a ghetto is just different. That tough-spoken, big-hearted man was the best one to talk straight with the daughter of one of our DTS women, who had come to visit her mom and had disappeared for most of the night in the French Quarter.

We learned to honor authority, even when we believed they were wrong or inadequate, and to place our trust in God instead of in men. Now, mind you, we didn't learn that lesson the easy way. Dick was invited to go to breakfast with our male leaders several times, so they could adjust our attitudes. One time it was to inform Dick to make sure I didn't look upset in class when I didn't like the teaching. And, of course, after the reaming, Dick got to pick up the tab for breakfast, because they didn't have any money. We were indignant, and we sharpened our prayer skills by praying for God to straighten up the leadership issues on base. That got us in trouble too. I'm not sure how they knew we were doing that. But the bottom line is that regardless of who was right or wrong, God was dealing with our arrogance and pride, and broadening our perspective on life.

I can look back and see what God was doing. I couldn't see it at the time, but one of the biggest things that happened was that God made big-time headway in teaching us to honor authority, keep our mouths shut, and pray. He also made great strides in teaching us to put our trust in Him in all situations. He proved Himself faithful at every turn—not necessarily to make things happen as we thought they should happen, but to make the situation come out to produce the ultimate good.

Our stint with Youth with a Mission was one of the most difficult seasons of my life up to that point. It took my belief system and shook it like a puppy shakes an old sock. It sent me to my Bible countless times to see what God had to say about things that were being taught and done. Some things I believed were proven as gold through fire. I still hold onto those truths. Some things I had to turn loose of, and doing so actually brought greater freedom. In most cases, I just learned that there was another perspective. In those cases, it didn't mean I was wrong. It just meant that life is bigger and more complex than I had realized, and that I needed to make room for a bigger picture.

Youth with a Mission laid the groundwork for the next couple of steps on the Holy Spirit's timetable for our lives. The first was starting Living Cornerstone Church, which I'll discuss in the next chapter. The second was our six years on the mission field in Mexico. I believe YWAM planted the seeds for that during our outreach in Juarez. Dick loved the Mexican people. He was frustrated by not being able to communicate with them. He vowed, "Someday I'm going to learn Spanish." I thought, "Yeah, sure," but little did I know about what Jehovah Sneaky had up His sleeve.

I WANT TO LEARN MORE - 9
Under Authority

Michelangelo quotes:

"I saw the angel in the marble and carved until I set him free."

"In every block of marble, I see a statue as plain as though it stood before me, shaped and perfect in attitude and action. I have to hew away the rough walls that imprison the lovely apparition to reveal it to the other eyes as mine see it."[1]

I believe the above quotes are an apt reflection of how God deals with us. He sees within us the person He created us to be, but that person is hidden in the stone that has encrusted itself upon lies concerning our identity and capabilities or lack thereof, upon misconceptions of who God is and how He deals with us, and upon religious systems created to explain the things mankind doesn't understand.

The Master Sculptor is capable of using all sorts of tools to chisel away the stone that imprisons us. Some of His most useful tools are the authorities He places over us as we move along life's journey—pleasant authorities...and also, the parent or grandparent with unreasonable expectations, the teacher who doesn't understand you, the boss who ignores your abilities and potential, the pastor who doesn't see your need.

The issue here isn't the ability or lack of it in the authority we are under. It isn't whether or not they deserve respect and honor. The issue is that we are to honor and respect the authorities that God places in our lives. We are to submit to His authority through their authority. Why? Because God uses those in authority, good and bad, to form our character and prepare us to be able to carry His authority.

Matthew 8:8-11 The centurion answered and said, "Lord, I am not worthy that You should come under my roof. But only speak a word, and my servant will be healed. 9 For I also am a man under authority, having soldiers under me. And I say to this one, 'Go,' and he goes; and to another, 'Come,' and he comes; and to my servant, 'Do this,' and he does it."

---

[1] http://thinkexist.com/quotes/Michelangelo

10 When Jesus heard it, He marveled, and said to those who followed, "Assuredly, I say to you, I have not found such great faith, not even in Israel!

> ➤ Why was the Roman Centurion capable of such great faith? What do you think he understood about authority?

> ➤ What did he mean, "I also am a man under authority"?

I still remember the impact it had on me when I realized that when I am under God's authority, I carry His authority. It's His authority, not mine, so He's the one who is responsible to back it up.

If the United States Army sends a lieutenant and his platoon out to take a hill, and the lieutenant sees he needs air support, he can call it in because he is carrying out orders from a higher command. If one morning the lieutenant wakes up and just decides on his own he'll take his men out to take a hill, what happens if he needs air support? If he makes it back alive, he shouldn't look for his captain's bars anytime soon. Why? Because he doesn't understand the chain of command. He acted out from under authority. There are certain things that God wants worked into our lives if we are going to carry His authority.

King David Is Our Best Example
of God's Leadership Training

The statue of David was one of Michelangelo's greatest masterpieces. The man David was one of God's greatest examples of one who carried authority well. He succeeded Saul, who was a man to whom the kingdom was simply handed without leadership training. Saul was rejected. David was the man after God's heart, who set the standard for every king after him. Let's look at a few of the chisels David encountered on his way to the throne.

> ➤ Read 1 Samuel 16:1-13. What criteria does the Lord look for in choosing a leader?

➤ What happened with the anointing of David, and why do you think it's important?

What God says is ours already belongs to us. Even so, we must possess it. Notice that when David was anointed to be the King of Israel, it was still many years before he took the throne. God called forth the image in the stone, but it would take time for others to see it and for David to conform to it.

When Joshua led the children of Israel into the Promised Land, the Lord said, "I have given you the land, possess it." It already belonged to them, but they had to fight for it. There are a lot of analogies we could use to illustrate this aspect of the way God operates. The thing you need to try to wrap your mind around is that God operates outside of time. He knows the end from the beginning. He called Abraham the father of many nations when he didn't have any hope for even one descendent. What God says is ours already belongs to us. It belongs to us right now. It is ordained in a realm that is much more powerful than the one we see and touch, but to move it from that realm into this one, we have to fight for it—not in the natural against flesh and blood—but in the realm of faith where we must allow God to change the way we look at things until we can see what He sees. That's something only God can do, but we can learn to cooperate with the process.

➤ I am listing below a number of passages where you can see this process in the life of David. If you have time to do the study, look for these things in each story:

1. The test or challenge that David faced
2. How the enemy wanted to use the situation
3. How God wanted to use the situation
4. How David dealt with the situation and what his response shows about his character
5. The quality for leadership that was tested or honed

You may not find a clear example for each one in every incident.

1 Samuel 17:1-37

1 Samuel 17:38-51

1 Samuel 18:5-16

1 Samuel 22:6-23 (Especially note verse 22. Note this isn't just affecting David and the men who chose to follow him anymore.)

1 Samuel 23:1-13

1 Samuel 24 (Meditate on verse 12. What does it teach you about how a man or woman of God is to seek retribution?)

1 Samuel 30:1-15

1 Samuel 30:16-25

2 Samuel 23:13-17

Summarize in your own words the key things God seems to want in His leaders.

I WANT TO CLIMB HIGHER − 9
Group Prayer

There are things you can learn about prayer in a group that you can't learn alone. It's exciting to experience how God functions among us corporately. I am including here our guidelines for group prayer. Try them out with your family or with a small group of friends.

Prayer Guidelines

Begin by asking for the Holy Spirit's guidance.
It's always good to spend time acknowledging who God is and submitting to His direction before you start addressing issues. A time of worship is appropriate.

Listen
- Listen to God for your topic and how to pray it.

  It's good to discuss things the group would like to pray for. God will probably have you pray on issues that are of concern to people within the group, but you need to let Him direct you to which issue. He may also bring something completely different to your hearts. You may only pray one or two needs at a given setting. Sometimes it takes time to pray through an issue when you are actually allowing God to lead you. You want to do what He is taking hold of and to do it His way. It's much better to pray a thing through until God says you win than it is to touch the surface of many things and resolve nothing.

- You are NOT here to pray our ideas or to tell God what He should do.
- You are here to get His guidance and wisdom and to pray and proclaim that.

- Listen inside yourself with your spiritual ears for impressions of what God is saying.

  May be a word or phrase
  May be an impression
  May be a picture

- Listen with your natural ears to what others are praying and let that register in your framework of what God is saying. Try to sense where your part fits in.

Share

- Share what you sense God is saying. Your part may be important to the whole.
- It's okay to step out of the prayer mode to talk about what you are sensing.
- Don't be afraid of sounding foolish or saying something wrong. It's okay.

Keep your praying as concise and to the point as possible.

- Don't pray long prayers and don't wander around over more than one topic.
- Don't use prayer to preach, not to God and not to the group.
- Pray what God gives you to pray.
- Stick to the topic – no popcorn praying. Popcorn praying is taking a scatter shot at a lot of things. You want to hone in on one thing and pray it clear through until you sense you've done what God wants on that topic. Then you can move to another topic if there's time.

Learn who to address when

- When you are talking to God, talk to God.
  Worship, supplication, searching for direction and understanding go to God.
  You remind God of His word and His promises, because He wants you to come to Him in faith.

- When you are talking to the enemy, talk <u>to the enemy</u> from a position of authority. Don't say, "God, I bind the spirit of rebellion." Get the fire of God in your heart and say, "Spirit of rebellion, I bind up your works against _____ in the name of Jesus."
  You declare truth to the enemy from the position of the authority you have in Jesus. Truth is light and it pushes back darkness.

- In prayer sessions it's okay to switch back and forth from talking to God and then talking to the enemy. In either case you are operating from <u>your authority in Jesus</u>. Jesus said to pray to the Father in His name. It is because of what He accomplished on the cross that you have the right to go to the Father at all. It is also from the position of the authority He took back from the devil that you have the right to address the enemy in His name. You are His legal representative just as long as you are truly representing His character and His will.

Chapter 10

LIVING CORNERSTONE

———

1983

THE DELPHOS COMMUNITY ALREADY THOUGHT WE were a little crazy. People in North Central Kansas didn't just go traipsing off to China or spend six months away from their business to do some unorthodox Christian thing. It just wasn't logical. Certainly, we confirmed their suspicions when be began to build a 30' by 30' room on the back of our house. Our kids were grown. Two of them were married. What on earth did two middle-aged folks need with a 30' by 30' room?

Well, the truth was, we didn't know. We had just arrived back from our stint with YWAM knowing we were supposed to build it. It was to have high ceilings and big sky lights, to fill the place with light, and a large banner like we had seen in a church in El Paso, that said, "And Jesus said, come to the water…" Truly, it didn't look like very good stewardship of God's resources, but we knew God wanted us to have it. It was reminiscent of the huge satellite dish we had put in our back yard after we returned from China. That extravagance plugged us into Trinity Broadcasting, and we taped tons of programs to share with hungry friends, as we all began to discover what God was doing outside our community's box.

As people talked, we smiled and said, "Good, that will take the pressure off some of the kids who usually sit on the gossip hot seat." The rumor was that we were going to start a church. We had no intention of starting a church. In fact, we had returned to the Methodist Church and were teaching faith concepts to a group of young adults. Sometimes the pastor would sit in on our class and get all excited as he took part in our discussions.

We were also having prayer meetings in our living room where we taught the same group what we had learned about group prayer at YWAM. We also got them all baptized in the Holy Spirit. It was in the prayer meetings that Jehovah Sneaky caught up with us again. We were praying for a spark of life in the Methodist Church among other things. It became clearer and clearer that Holy Spirit life wasn't going to happen there. Dick and some of the others were beginning to see it before I would even consider looking at it. I still cared what people thought of me, and I didn't want to make any more waves than we were already making in our little community. Then two things happened.

One Sunday I was very frustrated during a particularly faithless church service. I just happened to let the thought cross my mind in the Lord's direction, "Lord, what would you do in a service like this?" In less than a heartbeat, I heard, "I'd clear the temple."

That startled me and made me look at the whole situation much differently. In retrospect, I realize that the Lord was dealing with me, in a way I needed to be dealt with, much more than He was making a statement about the local church, but at the time it was the first real wake-up call that told my heart we'd have to leave the Methodist Church... again.

The second came on the way home from a Lay Witness Mission in Western Oklahoma. I don't remember anything at all about the weekend. All I remember is that on the way home Dick and I were talking about our little prayer group and what was to happen, when the Lord clearly said, "You can't put new wine in an old wineskin." That sealed it. No more trying to change the Methodist Church. We would have to take our new wine elsewhere. Where would we take it? Why, to a 30x30 room on the back of our house that was newly finished and waiting. The townspeople had prophesied it well before God let us in on the plan.

There were still months of prayer before Living Cornerstone Fellowship became an official body. We found a pastor and his wife from McPherson who came up every Sunday evening for several months to help form us into a church. Then we found Tim, a Rhema graduate with a young family, to take the helm.

The fledgling church moved to the meeting room in the bank basement and then built a building on the edge of town. As it grew, Tim asked Dick what position he wanted in the church. Dick said, "I don't know. I'll ask God."

He did, and God replied that he (Dick) didn't want any position, because He (God) was sending us to the mission field. Dick protested, "But Lord, we're two hundred and fifty thousand dollars in debt. We can't go to the mission field. We'll support missionaries and go when we get out of debt."

God informed Dick that He had lots of people to support missions. He needed people to go. "If you don't go, you won't get out of debt."

That was pretty clear, so we started making plans for the next chapter in our lives. We began to realize that life is a journey. What we believe to be a destination is often just a signpost that directs to the next stop. So, I began to prepare my heart to leave the house I loved so dearly, the great room where I had spent hours with God, travailing over the baby church that I would now have to leave in the hands of a young man, an outsider really. How could I do that, Lord?

At the time I was willing to go simply because I was more afraid to disobey God than I was to leave my sanctuary of security, but since then I've learned that God is my sanctuary. My only real security is in His presence.

I WANT TO KNOW MORE - 10
Forgiven and Forgiving

It is very important to understand that the basis for your forgiveness has nothing to do with you. You are forgiven because Jesus paid for your sin. Every mistake you've ever made, every unkind thing you've ever done, and every spiteful word you've ever spoken were paid for by the blood of Jesus. God deemed His death to be sufficient to pay for every sin you have ever committed or ever will commit. Look up the following verses and note what each one says about your forgiveness.

➤ Ephesians 1:7

➤ Colossians 1:13-14

➤ Colossians 2:9-15 (You might want to meditate on all the implications of this passage.)

➤ Read 1 John 1:5-2:2. Why do you think it is important to confess your sin?

➤ What do you think the phrase "cleanse us from all unrighteousness" in verse 9 means?

➤ What does it mean when it says that Jesus is the "propitiation" (NIV says "atoning sacrifice) for our sins?

The idea of receiving forgiveness, which has already been paid for, is another example of "I have given you the land. Possess it." Jesus paid the price for your sin in full. Once you confess the sin, there is nothing more you need to do or can do to be free from sin except to believe what Jesus did and receive it. All the blessings of God are like money placed in your account. They are yours. You don't have to earn them. To make a withdrawal, you simply have to write a faith check. <u>You do that by choosing to agree with what God has said (in both confessing the sin and in believing that it is</u>

already paid for), by declaring your agreement, and by acting on what you have chosen to believe. And the really good thing is that your head doesn't even have to be in agreement to start with. Faith is a choice and an act, not a belief in your mind. If you choose to put your trust in God no matter what the circumstances say, you will discover His faithfulness, and eventually even your doubting mind will come into agreement.

 ➤ Receive your forgiveness by faith, and you will discover that sin doesn't have any power over you anymore. Carefully read Romans 6:1-7. What does it say to you?

Faith is agreeing with God rather than agreeing with the lies of the enemy. Taking some concrete actions upon your choice to agree God strengthens your faith. Water baptism is a concrete action that gives you a visual hook to hang faith on. I am not going to go into that in this chapter, but if you have never been baptized in water, or if you have but you don't really understand the legal transaction that took place there, you'll find that information in the "I Want to Know More" section in Chapter 19.

Forgiveness is a coin with two sides. One beautiful side is that you are forgiven. Now let's look at the other side.

Read Matthew 6:12,14-15. Forgiveness was the only thing in this prayer that Jesus felt it was necessary to repeat. We must receive and give forgiveness in every situation.

There is a true story of a woman named Corrie TenBoom who lived in Holland during World War II. Corrie and her family were Christians, and they hid and protected many Jews in their home during the time of worsening persecution. But the Nazis found them and arrested the TenBoom family along with the Jews they sheltered. Corrie and her sister were taken to a concentration camp and were treated very badly. Because of the miserable conditions and cruel treatment, Corrie's sister died in the camp, and it was only by a miracle that Corrie was released shortly before she was to be executed.

Several years later, Corrie was giving her testimony to a group of Christians. After her massage a man came up to her and asked her forgiveness. Corrie recognized him as one of the guards who had beaten her and her sister. At first, the horrible memories rushed back, and Corrie couldn't forgive the man. She knew what the Bible said, but she couldn't bring herself to extend her hand in forgiveness. Then she thought of how Jesus had died on the cross so that she might be pardoned. She prayed within herself and, by an act of sheer obedience, extended her hand. With that step of faith, the Lord gave her the ability to forgive the man, and even to feel love for him. It wasn't the love of Corrie. It wasn't <u>humanly</u> possible to love someone who she had watched beat her sick sister and had felt his blows herself. But the love of God was shed in her heart, and with His love, it was possible. Our God is the God of the impossible.

Forgiveness doesn't depend on the other person deserving it. It doesn't even depend on them asking for it. In fact, forgiveness for another person doesn't depend on them any more than your forgiveness depends on you. We forgive because God does and because He says we must. But there's another very important reason why we must forgive.

The Cost of Unforgiveness Is too High to Pay

Look up each of the following passages and write down the price of unforgiveness that each one relates.

 ➤ Matthew 6:14,15 and Matthew 18:21-35

 ➤ The Matthew verses are related to a spiritual law. Check out Galatians 6:7 and Luke 6:35-38. What do they tell you about the principles of forgiveness?

102

> ➤ Mark 11:22-26

> ➤ Ephesians 4:26-27

Now, related to the Ephesians verse, read Genesis 4:3-8. Anger is an emotion. God created emotions. They have a place to bring color and excitement to our lives, if they are controlled and handled correctly. If not, they cause many problems.

> ➤ What did God tell Cain about his anger?

Cain was warned about the results of his anger. He chose not to listen to the warning. There is a place for anger in God's economy. It is incentive to correct the evil in the world, but if we allow the evil one to get hold of it, we, like Cain, become the evildoers.

> ➤ Hebrews 12:14-15. What problems are you aware of that have their root in bitterness?

When we were in Mexico, we ministered one day in a little home group. One of the ladies that came had to be almost carried because she suffered so severely from arthritis. During ministry time, we set a chair in the middle of the room, and I was ministering to this lady. Because I was aware that in many cases arthritis can be attributed to unforgiveness and bitterness, I asked her if there was anyone she had not forgiven. She said, no, not that she knew of. I asked her when the arthritis had started. She told me how many years before. I asked if anything unusual had happened about that time. She said her husband had left her that year. Bingo! We led her through forgiving her husband, then ordered the arthritis to leave, and she left walking on her own. It isn't always that obvious or that easy, but the point is that when you hold onto unforgiveness, it turns into a root of bitterness. If it isn't dealt with, it can contribute to things like headaches, heart disease, most anything that is stress related, and a number of other things. If you have any chronic illness in your life, ask God if there is a bitter root you are hanging onto. That may not be the cause, but it's worth checking out.

Besides, bitterness does other nasty things as well. It can cause depression. It can contribute to dissension in your family, your workplace or your church. It's the root of many mental and emotional problems as well as physical ones.

One of the big issues that people have with forgiving those who have hurt them has to do with a sense of justice. They feel it isn't fair for a person to do the things that person did and "get away with it." It's hard to release a wound when justice has not been served.

➢ Read Romans 12:19-21. What does that passage say to you?

Matthew 5:41 And whoever compels you to go one mile, go with him two.

There's a revelation in Matthew 5:41 that, if you really get hold of it, could revolutionize your life. Everything in the context around this verse seems to speak of yielding to being a victim, but I don't think the Lord ever intended for us to be victims or to have a victim mentality. Sometimes there are things we simply have to do. At the time Jesus wrote these words, it was common practice for a Roman soldier to come up beside a Jewish citizen and force him to carry his gear for a mile. Apparently, the Roman was not allowed to conscript the other person for more than one mile. The Jew had no choice as to whether to go that mile or not. But we all have a choice as to how we deal with such a circumstance. We can be sullen and resentful. We can let it gnaw at our guts. We can rehearse what we would do if we could. OR we can declare within, "You can conscript my body, but you can't have my soul." And to prove that, instead of being forced to walk a mile, I choose to walk two miles. Instead of being forced to clean our room or do the dishes, we choose to not only do what our parents ask but to scrub the kitchen floor as well.

➤ Think about the concept for a while. What can you do to go beyond the call of duty?

➤ If you do that, what would it do inside of you?

➤ What would it do in your relationship with the other person?

There is a little poem by Edwin Markham. I don't know the source anymore, but it says:

"He drew a circle that shut me out,
Heretic, rebel, a thing to flout.
But love and I had the wit to win;
We drew a circle that took him in."

At the best of being like Jesus, we turn those who wound us into our friends, but it isn't necessary to be able to do that to free yourself from the responsibility of bringing justice. All you have to do is to choose to release them into God's hands, and trust Him to deal with them in whatever way He sees fit. It is simply releasing the responsibility for something that we can't do anyway.

How to Forgive

Forgiveness is a road to freedom. When we hold onto grudges, they hold onto us. Our bitterness may not actually hurt the person who wronged us, but it will certainly harm us. So, here's what you do.

• Choose to forgive. It is important to understand the forgiveness is a decision, not an emotion. It is an act of obedience. You can forgive whether you feel forgiveness or not. Pray something like this, "Heavenly Father, in obedience to You, I choose to forgive _____ for _____. I ask that You also forgive him and set him free from any bondage that my unforgiveness has caused in his life"

- Release the person. You do that like this: "Now, Father, I release _____ from having to fulfill any obligation to me, and I put him in your hands for You to deal with him according to Your will. It isn't my responsibility. I declare that I am free from the need to change him and free from the things that hurt me. Lord, Your word says that Jesus bore my grief and sorrows. I receive that word for me, and I cast all my hurt over on to Him. I will not carry it anymore. Thank you, Father, because You free me from bitterness and unforgiveness. I declare I am free in Jesus name. Amen."

- Bless the person you forgave. That is like going to extra mile.

How to Forget and Be Healed

Forgiveness is an act. We can do it by faith. But forgetting is a process. If the offense was serious, it may take time to be truly free from the pain of it. You may find that you will have to forgive on various levels as you walk through the process. It will all happen much faster if you can separate the offense from what it caused you to believe about your identity. When the lie you received is clear, and when you have received the revelation that dispels that lie, healing should be almost instantaneous.

Ask the Lord to give you the revelation you need. Until it comes, make the right choices. The devil doesn't like forgiveness. He flourishes in the ambient of dissension, misunderstanding, and bitterness. He will do his best to bring back negative memories, bad thoughts, and depressing feelings. You must choose to close the door to those things. Here are some things that help:

- Throw away things that bring bad memories such as letters, photographs, certain CDs, etc.
- When negative thoughts come, say, "I have already forgiven that offense." Then ask God to bless the person. The

devil really doesn't like that type of a response. He'll quit bringing the bad thoughts if you respond with, "Oh, thank you, devil, for reminding me of him. I need to pray for him and ask God to bless him." Then do it.

- Put your mind on other things. Don't let the old thoughts to even start. Praise God and thank Him for the blessing in your life, or just focus on the activities of the day.

- Put the situation in God's hands again and trust Him for the revelation you need.

These steps will probably be enough if it is something that happened in the past and is over. But if you live or work with a person who hurts you day after day, try these things:

- Bind the negative spirits that are affecting the other person. Do that by speaking directly to the spirit (but not in the presence of the person) and telling it that it's bound in the name of Jesus. It works like this: "Spirit of _____ (pride, rebellion, etc.), I take authority over you in the name of the Lord Jesus Christ. According to the word of God, I use the authority that He has given me to use His name, and I bind you from working through _____ in the name of Jesus." One of the keys on this is that you have to discern the spirit you are dealing with. A lot of time you can tell by the behavior being manifested. You can also ask the Holy Spirit to show you what the spirit is. It helps you to be able to deal kindly with the person when you realize that your real enemy is the devil who is using the person to harass you. At the same time loose the opposite spirit. "I bind up anger and loose peace." Another key is to do it regularly, like every day. Binding a spirit isn't the same as casting it out. You can't cast it out if the other person doesn't want to get rid of it, but if you continue to bind it long enough, you will weaken its hold on the other person, so that they will be able to see the truth in time. In the meantime, it should lesson the spirit's ability to use the person against you.

- Choose to forgive every offense, every day. Just don't let it build into bitterness. Jesus told Peter to forgive seventy times seven times. That isn't easy, but it's easier when you remember that you are choosing obedience to Jesus and that the real enemy is the devil, not the person.*

- Don't judge. You don't know what causes the other person to do the things he does.

*This is not to say that you should stay in a truly abusive situation. Most of us find ourselves in situations that hurt and offend us, but as we truly find out who we are, we don't have to receive the offense. Some people are in situations where there is continual physical or sexual abuse. People in such situations should seek help. God doesn't ask us to stay in those places.

I WANT TO CLIMB HIGHER – 10
Forgiveness

Take a sheet of paper. In one side write out 1 John 1:9. On the other side, write Matthew 6:14,15.

Ask the Holy Spirit to bring to mind any sin in your life that you have not confessed and/or repented for. Write anything that He brings to mind on the 1 John 1:9 side of the paper. Once your list is complete, go through it prayerfully. Agree with God that sin is sin. Confess it and repent as I have instructed you to repent. If there is anything on the list that you feel led to confess to a person you may have hurt and ask for their forgiveness, do so. It really doesn't matter if they choose not to forgive you. That rarely happens, but the issue isn't their reaction; it's your obedience. If you need to make restitution, such as pay back something you stole, do that. Do whatever the Lord leads you to do. Then receive God's forgiveness and cleansing. You may or may not "feel" it. It doesn't matter. We do these things by faith, and God honors them whether we feel anything or not.

Now on the Matthew 6:14-15 side, write every offense that has brought pain to you. It doesn't matter how large or small, real or imagined. Just write whatever comes to mind. Consider authority figures you've had in your life, including parents, teachers, spouses, perhaps even God.

When you have finished making your list, go through and do the forgive, release, and bless steps that I've included in this chapter. It doesn't have to be just like I've written. Allow the Holy Spirit to guide you. His ways are tailored to each individual.

When you have finished forgiving and releasing other people, you may find you also need to forgive yourself. Should you have difficulty doing that, find a place alone with God and envision the cross. Envision what Colossians 2:14 says happened. See your sins nailed to the cross. See you cleansed by the blood of Jesus. When you leave the place of the cross, leave the sin behind.

When you are finished praying through both sides of the paper, find a fireplace or barbeque pit, or someplace you can have a fire, and burn the paper. As the paper disintegrates into smoke, release everything on it, and know that you are set free from everything you wrote on there. You don't have to revisit any of those things. You don't have to confess again anything that God has already forgiven, nor do you have go back to old wounds. Just consider them all dead and gone.

Chapter 11

LANGUAGE SCHOOL

—

DICK MADE A PHONE CALL TO A MISSIONARY WE HAD met at Christ for the Nations. The man had worked in Mexico for decades. He had connections all over the place, and Dick really respected and valued his opinion. In this case, however, his opinion was that we had no business in Mexico at all unless we could speak Spanish. We couldn't, but Dick had made that crazy vow that he was going to learn that language. Well, we did.

The fall of 1984 found us in language school at King's Way Missionary Institute in McAllen, in the part of Texas known as The Valley. We were really close to the Mexican border, and I was appalled that signs on businesses, menus, almost everything were as likely to be written in Spanish as English. In restaurants, conversations at adjoining tables would switch back and forth between English and Spanish in mid-sentence. "We're still in the United States, aren't we?" I complained. The answer was yes and not so much.

Dick and I had different problems at language school. Dick's was with the language. He went about learning it like he would learn chemistry, and most of the time he didn't have a clue how to put a sentence together. Well into our nine months, his conversation teacher told him he had the strongest English accent she'd ever heard. She didn't mean it as a compliment.

The language itself was not so much my problem as the concept of leaving my home and living in a foreign country. I was afraid

God was going to have us sell our home and go to Mexico forever. I wanted desperately to please God and be happy about our next assignment, but the battle within wasn't showing any signs of abating. Finally, out of desperation, I just surrendered. I went so far as to write to each of our daughters and tell them to think about what they might want from our home, because we might have to sell it, and we couldn't take all our stuff into Mexico. I remember thinking particularly about the Jesus-said-come-to-the-water banner and wondering if any of the girls would have room for it. Then I would cry again.

Shortly after I sent the letters, Dick and I attended an English-speaking church on Sunday. We were required to attend a Spanish service each week, so going to this church was a luxury. We could actually understand the sermon. But it wasn't the sermon that got my attention. During praise and worship there was a prophecy. It started out, "I don't want your sacrifice. I want your obedience, not your sacrifice. There are no hands clean enough to sacrifice to me…" I don't remember the rest. That was enough. God was speaking directly to me, and Dick and I both knew it. He wasn't asking us to sell our home. This time I cried from relief and gratitude.

I really didn't know God very well at that point. I knew His promises, I knew His commandments, I even knew His authority, but I didn't know His heart. I guess I saw Him as a rather stern Father who kept track of my good marks and my bad marks, and there could never really be enough good marks. I really believed I had to earn His acceptance, and no matter what I did, I couldn't believe it was enough. It was many years before I really came to understand that God adores me. He doesn't adore me because of who I am or what I can do. <u>He adores me because of who He is and what He can do</u>.

During language school we spent a lot of time with John and Debi Berger and their three kids. They became our new prayer partners. I remember one night stretched out on their living room floor crying out to God over the debt back in Kansas that wasn't getting paid. We were paying the interest payments but nothing on principal. That's pretty painful when you're paying interest on a quarter of a million dollars. I don't remember whether the revelation hit Dick first or me, but all at once, there in the Berger's living room, we knew that God would cover whatever payments we could believe for. We checked our faith level and decided we could believe for fifteen hundred dollars a month towards principal. We determined that this would be paid first, and we'd trust God to cover the bills and interest. He did—every month. So, in a few months, we increased the principal payment. It was probably a dozen years before the last of the debt was cleared, but God was faithful to His word. We went to the mission field, and He got us out of debt.

Faith isn't simply believing something is true. Faith is an act. I don't remember where we first heard this story, so I can't give credit to the source, but Dick loves to tell of the difference between faith and belief. The story goes that once a tightrope walker stretched a rope between two very tall buildings. People gathered on the street below to watch as the man pushed a wheelbarrow from building to building many stories above their heads. They believed he could do it, because they saw him do it. That's belief. Belief is agreeing with a concept. <u>Faith is when you get in the wheelbarrow.</u>

God wants us in His wheelbarrow. We aren't to be presumptuous and just do any old thing and expect God to back us up, but when He says, "I want you to go to the mission field," it's time to say, "When and where?" When He says, "Now," it's time to pack your bags even if you don't know the where part. When He says, "It's time to act like you believe I'll enable you to pay off your debt," it's time to start making payments.

In language school we learned some Spanish. We also began learning to minister to wounded hearts. Dick learned that it was time to quit playing football with the twenty somethings and turning cartwheels for the junior high girls. After pulling both hamstrings on the former escapade and dislocating a shoulder on the latter, the doctor said, "How old do you think you are anyway?" We learned quite a bit about God's love and faithfulness, and we learned the next step in life's journey.

Another couple at King's Way was Henry and Josie Zaragosa. They already spoke Spanish. They grew up in east Texas in Spanish-speaking homes, but they didn't think their Tex-Mex brand of Spanish was good enough for the work they planned to do in Monclova, Mexico. They only went one semester, but in that time, it was decided that we would join them in Monclova and help them start a church there as soon as we finished language school. It felt good to have a clear destination and reason for wading through eight Spanish verb tenses.

I WANT TO KNOW MORE – 11
Faith

Hebrews 11:1 Faith is the substance of things hoped for, the evidence of things not seen...3 By faith we understand that the worlds were framed by the word of God, so that the things which are seen were not made of things which are visible.

Faith is the commodity of the Kingdom of Heaven. It's the substance God builds with. It lays hold of that which God has spoken in the kingdom realm and brings it into manifestation in the natural realm. It's the force field that connects "I have given you the land" to the place of having the land in your possession so you can build your house on it.

Faith starts with the word of God.

Isaiah 55:10-11
10 "For as the rain comes down, and the snow from heaven,
And do not return there,

But water the earth,
And make it bring forth and bud,
That it may give seed to the sower
And bread to the eater,
11 So shall My word be that goes forth from My mouth;
It shall not return to Me void,
But it shall accomplish what I please,
And it shall prosper in the thing for which I sent it.

Matthew 17:20 I say to you, if you have faith as a mustard seed, you will say to this mountain, 'Move from here to there,' and it will move; and nothing will be impossible for you.

We start with a seed of God's word. A seed can lie dormant for a long time and still have life. It simply needs to be planted so that the elements in the earth can cause it to open up and bring forth life. We plant the seed by agreeing with it verbally.

Romans 10:8-11 But what does it say? "The word is near you, in your mouth and in your heart" (that is, the word of faith which we preach): 9 that if you confess with your mouth the Lord Jesus and believe in your heart that God has raised Him from the dead, you will be saved. 10 For with the heart one believes unto righteousness, and with the mouth confession is made unto salvation.

The principle that opens the door to God's kingdom in the first place is the same principle that opens the door to everything God has for us. We believe in our heart and confess with our mouth. The first thing you need to know is that believing with your heart is different from believing with your head. Your head will want to understand and see proof. The kingdom doesn't operate by sense knowledge. When you approach the word of God, whether it is written in your Bible or spoken to your heart, you simply **choose** to believe it. It isn't necessary for your mind to be in agreement. The way you choose to believe is to declare that what God says is true whether your mind agrees or not, and then act like it's true. That's the way you receive and plant the seed.

114

Read Mark 4:1-20 and Matthew 13:1-23, which is Matthew's account of the same parable. In verse 13 of the Mark version, Jesus essentially says that this parable holds the key to understanding all parables. So, let's look at it carefully.

In Matthew's version, the disciples ask why Jesus speaks to the people in parables. Read Jesus' response carefully.

➢ Why are some people capable of receiving kingdom principles while others are not?

➢ What do you think closed eyes symbolize?

➢ What things can you see that cause people to close their eyes? Another way of saying this might be: what mental blocks do people put up against truth?

➢ What would be the value of speaking in parables to someone who is closed to the truth?

➢ If you find an area in your life where you are not willing to listen to and consider what others are saying, what can you do about it?

I believe the category of people who represent the wayside are those who have chosen to close their minds. The word comes, but they can't understand it because they have closed their minds to kingdom thinking. Immediately, the devil comes to steal the word. It has no chance to grow and produce faith.

➢ How would you describe the stony ground people?

➢ In Ephesians 6 Paul says that the word of God is a sword. What should you do when tribulation and persecution arise "for the word's sake"?

You may rest assured that when you receive a new truth, the enemy will try to take it from you. His weapons are lies and deceptions. He likes it best when people are closed-minded and won't even receive the truth like the wayside people. The stony ground folks are willing to receive so long as it comes easy, but they don't have enough internal fortitude to take hold of the truth and turn it into a weapon. <u>Faith is choosing to believe the truth God has given you regardless of what the circumstances are saying.</u>

> ➤ Can you give an example of a time when you chose to believe God even though the circumstances looked like what God said couldn't be true?

> ➤ What happened?

This is the reason why declaring what God has said, out loud and with conviction, is important. <u>It's the way you wield your sword.</u> It's the way to fight back against the lies of the enemy. Declaring what God has said does three powerful things.

- It backs off the enemy. He has no authority in your life unless you give it to him by agreeing with him.
- It strengthens your soul. Hearing truth fortifies your ability to stand in the midst of the battle.
- It activates God's angels. The angels of God act upon the word of God. Indeed, speaking what God has said activates God Himself on your behalf.

Jeremiah 1:12 Then the LORD said to me, "You have seen well, for I am watching over My word to perform it." NASB

> ➤ What do you see as the problem with the thorny ground people?

It isn't only important to be on guard when you are going through a hard time, it's also important to be alert at the points of transition in your life. Getting married, a new job, having a baby are all joyous things, but if you aren't careful they can fill up your life and become your priority, crowding God into a corner where He no longer has the prime time He needs to keep you living by the Spirit. One day you wake up and find you've been operating in your own strength so long that you're mostly used up, and you can't find the refill connection.

Fruitful ground folks are the ones who hear the word, receive the word, and put it to work in their lives. They act upon it.

Faith sees. Faith speaks. Faith acts.

I WANT TO CLIMB HIGHER – 11
Sharpening Your Sword

Choose an area of your life where you desire to be stronger or more fruitful.

Do a Bible search to find out what the word of God says about that area. A resource you can use on-line is www.blueletterbible.org/. You can also use Strong's Concordance, if you have access to one, and cross-references in your Bible.

After you choose the verses that is most significant to you, you can simply declare what they say, or you can write it into a confession like the one below that Dick prays daily for our family:

Claiming Our Destiny
Lord, we declare that we are your children, Your own inheritance. You have known us from before time, and You have destined us to be conformed to the image of Your Son.

Your plan for us, Father, is not merely to receive salvation. Your plan for us is that we be disciples and that we make disciples. We declare that You have an inheritance in us. You have a calling for us. We lay hold of that for which you have laid hold of us. We lay hold of our inheritance. We receive Your power and Your authority to accomplish those things that we have been called to do.

We declare that there is an upward call of God on our lives. We are not destined to remain children, but to grow up individually and corporately into a mature man, to the measure of the stature of the fullness of Christ. We are called to be warriors and kingdom builders. We are seated with Christ in heavenly places

It is our desire and our destiny to KNOW You, Lord, to see You as You really are, and to know You to such a depth that we love You with all our hearts, with all our souls, with all our minds and with all our strength. It is our destiny to be like You, and that can only happen as You reveal Yourself to us as You really are.

We command that all the veils be lifted off our minds and understanding so that we may behold Your glory and be transformed from glory to glory by Your precious Spirit.

Below are the scriptures that make up that confession.

Romans 8:29	Ephesians 4:11-16
Matthew 28:19	2 Timothy 2:2-4
Ephesians 1:8	Ephesians 2:6
Philippians 3:12	1 John 3:2
Philippians 3:14	Matthew 22:37-38
2 Corinthians 4:4	2 Corinthians 3:18

Praying the word of God over your life doesn't change you instantly, but if you will be faithful to do it consistently, it will change your life.

Chapter 12

MONCLOVA–THE FUNERAL

MONCLOVA, COAHUILA, MEXICO IN 1985 WAS A DIF-
ferent world. For the first several months we lived in a fifth-
wheel trailer parked in the patio of a Mexican doctor and his wife,
Amilla. Amilla was a gift of God to us. She spoke English. I wrote
out every word of everything we taught for months, and Amilla
patiently checked and corrected my rough Spanish.

One day a young couple, from the church we were helping to start,
was coming for us to teach them about the baptism of the Holy
Spirit. Teaching from pre-written notes was one thing. Teaching
when you had to understand what the other person was asking
was quite another. Four years of college Spanish stuffed in nine
months at King's Way had still not enabled us to separate the
linking of Spanish words. Much of the time we still didn't know
if we were hearing one word or three. While we could say most
of what we wanted to say, understanding what was being spoken
to us was about forty percent mystery. That, plus the difference
in culture, created some interesting situations, like the time one of
our youth told us about her upcoming celebration of her fifteenth
birthday, a really big deal in Mexico. The day after her party, we
had to deal with a hurt and offended young lady. We were supposed to be there, but unfortunately, we didn't realize we were
invited. Then there was the time we had a couple of giggling
teenage girls riding with us. Dick had been teasing them, and he
innocently asked them if they were "embarazada." Someone had
told us that if you add an "o" or an "a" on the end of lots of English
words you get a Spanish equivalent. Not this time! The reaction

from the girls sent me to our English/Spanish dictionary. Instead of asking if they were embarrassed, it seems he had asked them if they were pregnant!

So, it was with some misgiving that we prepared to share with Rafael and Sonja about the baptism of the Holy Spirit. About ten minutes before they were to show up, Amilla dropped in to ask for a recipe for some muffins I had given them. We explained what was about to happen, so she stayed to interpret should we run into trouble, and all three of them received the baptism of the Holy Spirit that afternoon.

As the weeks passed, we became less and less surprised at the way things worked out. We'd have an interpreter when we really needed one, or we would supernaturally understand when it was really important, or the anointing would make up the difference. Then there was the time when Henry and Josie were in the States, and we were holding down the fort alone. We'd been doing okay until the day one of the women from our little congregation came to us all dressed up and extremely urgent. As we pieced the story together we learned she had a friend whose husband had been killed in a knife fight the night before. The body was at his parents' home. Our friend wanted us to go conduct some sort of service for him. None of the family were believers. Dick said okay, when did she want us to do it, thinking we would have a day or two to prepare. She said, "Right now."

Well...okay. We dug out a little pastor's handbook that had some appropriate scripture for a funeral, changed our clothes, and were on our way. The house was filled with very solemn looking folks. The body was in the first room in a glass-covered casket so that it was in full view. The lady we were with thought we should sing some songs, but the only songs we knew in Spanish were praise songs. One man knew of someone who had a Spanish hymnal, so he went to get it. As we mingled uncomfortably with the mourners, a man, who turned out to be the dead man's father, came in with his arm in a bandage. Apparently, he had gone to avenge his son.

Our friend sang a couple of hymns off key, and it was time for Dick to speak. Just as he was about to start, a young man came in the door. He asked Dick if it was okay if he said a few words. Glad for the reprieve, Dick said to go ahead. The man proceeded to share comforting words that we could actually understand. From time to time, he would ask Dick a question or politely draw him back in. Standing by the casket, he shared the truth about Jesus and even led in singing a song. He smoothly did everything that needed to be done, and then he just stepped out the door and disappeared, literally disappeared. No one seemed to know him or have any idea where he came from. He was not to be seen in the street outside. There were no known pastors in the area. That was the first of two times in our lives that we felt we had the help of an angel in disguise. We were incredibly grateful that he showed up.

Time and time again what we needed was provided. There have been so many times when we could not have done what had to be done in our own strength and resources. We just chose to do what we felt God was telling us to do, and God would enable us to actually do it. We really didn't understand back then about co-laboring with God. We still thought we were doing things for God. It was much, much later that we came to realize that He loves partnering with us. He loves to see us do our utmost and then reach beyond to draw on His resources. I think He loves it most of all as He feels us trusting Him no matter what the situation looks like. That's the commodity of faith that draws on the resources of heaven.

I WANT TO KNOW MORE – 12
Building a House of Faith

As we learn to be led by the Holy Spirit, we must learn to know His voice and trust His guidance. He communicates with us in many ways, but He doesn't use the logical reasoning processes of our mind to communicate. Frequently, He uses subtle impressions that just sort of float through. It's very easy to overlook those fleeting impressions and just pass them off as random thoughts.

As we begin to pick up on impressions from the spirit realm, we want to be able to sort out what is from the Holy Spirit, what is just our own thinking, and what comes from a negative source. Here are some guidelines that will help:

- **The Spirit of God will not contradict the word of God.**
  When I was teaching English, the families of two of my students were very close. They did everything together. When one of the students found her mother in bed with the father of the other student, the repercussions rattled the whole community. The erring couple said that God had told them they were to be together. I don't know if they really thought they were hearing God or if they were just making up an excuse, but whatever they heard, it wasn't God. He may tell you to do things that you don't find precedent for in the Bible, but He won't tell you to do something that His word tells you not to do.

- **The Holy Spirit will not have you do something against God's character.**
  There are times when the Lord will ask us to say hard things to people, but it will not be out of vengeance or a prideful attitude. When He asks us to share the hard things, we must be sure that we are actually feeling God's heart for them and His desire for their welfare. God doesn't call upon us to "straighten out" someone else. If the thing you are sensing isn't wrapped in love and humility, you'd better do some praying before you act on it.

- **Peace is the seal of the Holy Spirit.**
  If you have a sense of uneasiness down in your gut, that's a warning signal from the Holy Spirit that something is not right. That impression can warn you when you are about to make a mistake; however, it can also be a call to prayer for someone else. When you sense that uneasiness, stop. Don't make a major decision until you have peace inside.

If you are married, or if there is another Christian involved, wait until you both have peace.

I may need to bring a little more clarity on peace. It's really wonderful when all the parts of your being are in agreement and at peace. The fact is that it may take your logical mind a while to trust what is going on in your spirit. Your mind wants to understand before it receives peace. In time your mind will understand that it can trust the impressions of your spirit. Until then, the peace you are looking for is what you sense deep within. Philippians 4:7 calls it the peace that surpasses understanding.

- **Beware of pressure tactics.**
  This one is a little trickier because there are times when the Lord wants us to move NOW. But generally, it's the enemy who uses pressure tactics. The urgent pressure to act when you still don't have peace is the enemy's way. Especially on major decisions, God doesn't mind if you ask for several confirmations. When you sense urgency from God, it will generally come physically in the area of the womb or midsection. The enemy assails your mind.

There are things you can do to build a hedge of protection so that you can follow the Lord's leading without fear:

- **Worship—declare who God is in your life.**
  Declaring who God is to you sets everything straight in the heavenlies. It lets the devil know where you stand, and it calls in God's heavenly resources, because God and His angelic host watch to act upon our faith.

➤ Look up and record the main idea from each of the following scriptures. You can use any or all of these to worship the Lord and to declare His presence, authority, provision and protection over your life.

Jeremiah 32:17

1 John 4:9,10

Romans 11:33-36

Hebrews 6:16-19

Deuteronomy 31:6

Exodus 34:5-7

1 Corinthians 1:30

John 14:27

Philippians 4:19

Isaiah 54:17

Meditating on such verses greatly strengthens faith.

- **Close doors to the devil.**
  Ask the Lord to bring to your mind anything that you have
  done or said that would allow the enemy access to your
  life. If He shows you anything, confess it as sin and receive
  forgiveness. Keeping your heart pure before God is one of
  your best defenses against the whiles of the enemy.

  1 John 1:9

  2 Corinthians 5:21

- **Declare who you are and what you have in Jesus.**
  If you did the Ephesians exercise from Chapter 2, you
  already have many of these scriptures. I will include a

few here that have been especially meaningful in my fight for identity.

John 14:27

Ephesians 2:6

Ephesians 3:16-19

Romans 8:37

1 Corinthians 2:16

2 Corinthians 3:17

1 Peter 2:24

- **Consecrate every part of you to the Lord.**
Pray something like this, adding the things that come to your mind. Customize it to fit your needs and desires:

"Heavenly Father, I consecrate my body to you today. May everything I do with my body be pleasing in your sight.

"I consecrate my soul to You. I place my thought life in your hands, and I ask you to protect me from thoughts that the enemy would like to insert. I declare that I am your sheep. I will only listen to the voice of my Shepherd. I do not receive the voice of the enemy.

"I consecrate my emotions to You. May I love what You love and hate the things You hate. I trust you to protect my emotions from any attack of the enemy. I consecrate my imagination to You. I invite the Holy Spirit to use my imagination as a screen for things He wants to show me and to protect me from imaginings that would lead me astray.

"I consecrate my will to You and set it in agreement with Your will for my life. I choose to align the desires of my heart with the desires of Your heart.

"I consecrate my spirit to Your Spirit that I may be led in the paths of righteousness and peace."

2 Timothy 1:12 . . for I know whom I have believed and am persuaded that He is able to keep what I have committed to Him until that Day.

As you consecrate yourself to God, you can trust Him to protect you, and you will be freer to follow the impressions you receive. The Lord is faithful to protect that which truly belongs to Him.

- **Take time to listen.**
  Spend some time each day simply relaxing into God's presence. Completely relax and quiet your mind. Making your noisy thought life be still is easier said than done. To start with, it may help to focus on some aspect of God or a portion of scripture. You aren't trying to empty your mind in the way that the Transcendental Meditation people do it. You are simply trying to quiet your own thoughts to make room for God to speak to you or show you something if He wants to. Don't be concerned if you don't receive anything. If you give Him the opportunity and then follow any impressions you do receive, you have done your part.

I WANT TO CLIMB HIGHER – 12
Walking in Obedience

Do the consecration exercises in the "I Want to Learn More" part of this chapter each day this week. Ask the Lord to make you sensitive to the impressions He gives you. When you receive such impressions, choose to act on them.

For example, the Lord has taught me quite a bit about listening just by letting me know when I should quit eating. When I sense that impression that I have had enough, I stop eating. Sometimes I am impressed to fast certain types of food for a time, but for the most part, I eat what I want to eat and stop when God says to stop, and I have never had to go on a diet.

You may be impressed that you should call someone. Just do it.

Usually, an instant after receiving such impressions, your head will kick in with the logical "reasons" why you shouldn't do the thing. Just learn that you don't have to understand why God asks you to do something. Just be obedient. Sometimes you understand later. Sometimes you don't. It doesn't matter. Sometimes you may make a mistake, and it really wasn't God. That's okay. You are learning. God would rather you make a mistake trying to obey Him than to do nothing. He is big enough to take care of your mistakes, and He will work them for good by teaching you something that you need to know. God has often used my mistakes to teach me something I didn't understand about His character or to show me a place where I am still operating out of bondage that needs to be dealt with. He can turn even our errors into blessings.

Chapter 13

MONCLOVA – THE KIDS

—

WE DID A LITTLE BIT OF EVERYTHING IN MONCLOVA, but our main responsibility was to provide training for the children and the youth. We had arrived prepared. We had constructed a large puppet stage with PVC pipe and curtains. We had hired a lady to make some cute hand puppets, and I had written teachings where someone talked to the puppets. It was great stuff, but we had one problem. The kids couldn't understand our Spanish very well.

The youth were a different story. They could understand us, and they loved the special attention we gave them. In those days, young people in Mexico didn't have televisions or cell phones or computer games. They didn't have a whole lot in the way of material goods, at least not in the part of town where we were working, so they were glad for entertainment and community. The youth soon became our assistant leaders for the children. They ran the puppets. They did the skits. They did just about everything, but we still needed that front person who could communicate with the kids and had the maturity to be comfortable there.

That's when we thought of Rafael, the same Rafael that received the baptism of the Holy Spirit in our trailer. Rafael ran a little grocery store, located on the street on the way to the church. He owned an old beat-up pickup that looked like it had been assembled many times over from parts of various colors or lack thereof. The most interesting thing about Rafael's pickup was the black dog that rode on top of the cab everyplace he went. On Saturday mornings, when we had kids' church, Rafael became our self-appointed bus driver. He would pull up near the church, where we had the puppet tent set up in the yard, with kids hanging out of every corner of his pickup and the dog on top.

He loved what we were doing, so he was always there, doing whatever he could to help. He was good with the kids, so we enlisted him to be the front man. It was not unusual to have between fifty to seventy children show up for children's church.

Meanwhile, along with having the youth do skits and run puppets, we began to train them to do a lot of other things. We established a set of goals that included some basic things like attendance and memorizing scripture and some more powerful things like giving testimonies and leading people to Jesus. The prize, if they reached the goal, was a Bible of their very own. As I remember, they all earned their Bibles. And they got to practice by ministering for real to the children.

One night at the youth meeting, I asked a question about what they thought they received when they received Jesus. One of the boys immediately rattled off, "healing, prosperity, well-being, forgiveness, freedom, and victory." I was puzzled. I couldn't remember talking about what I call "The Great Exchange" with the youth. The Great Exchange is a skit we did based on what the words *save* and *salvation* mean in the Hebrew and Greek. I asked the boy how he knew all that, and he reminded me of the skit we had done for the children where we had a cross with those words on it. We had given some of the children articles to bring up and exchange for the words. They had brought up a chain to trade for freedom, a crutch to exchange for healing, etc. That had been weeks before.

That taught us a lesson we never forgot. From that time on we used illustrations even with adults whenever we could. One of the favorites was our teaching on spiritual authority. For the armor of God, I would put a colander on my head for the helmet of salvation, a pair of Dick's old boots for shoes of peace, and take a real machete for the sword of the spirit. When it came time to teach how you bind up the devil, we emphasized that you address the devil directly in the name of Jesus. Dick would pretend to be the devil. He would torment me with words and throw paper wads at me while I prayed to God to remove him. Then I would realize God had already given me the authority to deal with the devil, so I would take the name of Jesus and my machete sword and take after him directly. The people loved it. Better yet, they remembered it.

The other thing we learned was that kids can do spiritually anything adults can do. We took that understanding to whole different levels in Saltillo, but we got our start in Monclova.

Henry, the pastor we were working with, arranged to take our youth to a mountain village near Victoria, most of a day's drive from Monclova. Our arrival was an excuse for a real event. People came from three villages to take part in the party. During the day, our youth helped the village youth carry water—maybe an eighth of a mile—for bathing, washing dishes, etc. Our city youth, who came from homes that would be a culture shock for most American youth, experienced their own culture shock in that little village. They went home realizing how easy they had it.

In the evening we presented some puppet skits and did "The Great Exchange." When the kids finished the skit and gave an altar call, an old man came into the center where the cross was set up and fell on his knees, crying. Dick was puzzled. He was pretty sure the man was saved. He went to talk to him. With tears running down his cheeks, the man explained that he had known Jesus most of his life, but he didn't know until that night what belonged to him through the price Jesus had paid for him. It was a precious sight. Long after we were through with our part—indeed, long after we had gone to bed in sleeping bags on the floor in the little church, we could still hear preaching and worship continuing under the stars.

God used our time in Monclova in many ways in our lives. He continued to teach us about serving under another man's authority.

He expanded our thinking and helped us separate the cultural dressing from the reality of who God is. God doesn't change, but our concept of Him gets a lot broader when we realize He doesn't have to do things the "American way."

For me personally, I learned a whole new level of God's faithfulness. When we went to Monclova all of our daughters were married, but they were young marriages. Sometimes the girls still depended more on us than on their husbands. When they needed us, they had always been able to call us, but now they couldn't. We didn't have a telephone. In an emergency they would have to go through a Spanish-speaking person, and that wouldn't be easy. We would go to a central place and call them every week or so, but my fear was that they wouldn't be able to reach us if they needed us. One day, when I was complaining about that to God, He simply said, "Thana, My umbrella is bigger than yours." I knew it was God, and I knew it was right. I've hung onto that truth for over a quarter of a century. It has never failed to be true.

I WANT TO KNOW MORE – 13
Authority

You were created in the image of God Almighty in order that you might fellowship with Him and that you might extend His authority in the earth and take dominion over the works of the enemy. Just as Adam was given dominion over the earth that he was to protect and care for, you have been given dominion over the things for which you have responsibility. There are stages and levels of authority, both in God's kingdom and in the enemy's realm. Among the enemy's forces there are demons that attack and harass individuals, and there are principalities that rule over territories and realms.

Levels of Authority
God has angels with greater and lesser authority. One of the clearest scriptural pictures we have of the authority clash in the

spirit realm is found in Daniel 10. In that chapter we find Daniel fasting and praying, for understanding of a vision he had received from God, when a messenger arrives. Read verses 12 and 13.

Daniel 10:12-13 Then he said to me ,"Do not fear, Daniel, for from the first day that you set your heart to understand, and to humble yourself before your God, your words were heard; and I have come because of your words. 13 But the prince of the kingdom of Persia withstood me twenty-one days; and behold, Michael, one of the chief princes, came to help me, for I had been left alone there with the kings of Persia.

In several places in the Bible, we find demonic principalities referred to as princes or kings of a certain locality. Here we have reference to the "prince of the kingdom of Persia" and to "kings of Persia." We are getting a glimpse of the top of the devil's hierarchy withstanding God's messenger for twenty-one days, the entire time of Daniel's fast, until the Arch Angel Michael came to help him break through. I don't want to focus in this lesson on heavenly hierarchies, but I do want you to understand that they exist.

Ephesians 6:10-12 Finally, be strong in the Lord and in his mighty power. 11 Put on the full armor of God so that you can take your stand against the devil's schemes. 12 For our struggle is not against flesh and blood, but against the rulers, against the authorities, against the powers of this dark world and against the spiritual forces of evil in the heavenly realms. (from New International Version)

God's kingdom and His ways are full of paradoxes. We have a big one in the verse below. Just as God told Joshua that He had given him the land and to possess it, Jesus gave us similar instructions.

Matthew 28:18-20 And Jesus came and spoke to them, saying, "All authority has been given to Me in heaven and on earth. 19 Go therefore and make disciples of all the nations, baptizing them in the name of the Father and of the Son and of the Holy Spirit, 20 teaching them to observe all things that I have commanded you; and lo, I am with you always, even to the end of the age."

He is saying that all authority belongs to Him, and we, as His body, must possess it. It's purchased. The deed is back in the hands of mankind, but the squatter has to be removed, and he has to be removed through the authority that belongs to Jesus. To dispossess the enemy from the land for which we are to take responsibility, we must step into the authority of Jesus by the force of faith. The amount of His authority we carry depends on the depth of our relationship with Him and the degree to which we trust and obey Him. It also is relevant to the responsibility He has given us to carry. We are to represent Him and extend His authority in the earth realm. We can only do that to the extent that we know His heart and set our hearts in agreement with His. Actually, it's probably more accurate to say that through the power of the Holy Spirit within us, we have authority over all the works of the devil. That's what Jesus said: *Luke 10:19 Behold, I give you the authority to trample on serpents and scorpions, and over all the power of the enemy, and nothing shall by any means hurt you.* However, since everything in God's kingdom works by faith, there is a growing into authority as we grow in faith.

> ➤ Why do you think it is important that we be in agreement with God before we have the ability to release His authority?

> ➤ Can you think of times that if you had been able to use God's authority to impose <u>your will</u>, you would have caused more problems?

God doesn't expect you to have the faith of an apostle, when you haven't yet gone through the life experiences that teach you His faithfulness, any more than He expects a child to have the maturity to do a man's work. So, He has a growth system for growing into authority, and He will give you as much authority as you have the maturity and faith to handle.

God delegates authority anyplace He has given us responsibility. That means that, at the beginning place of authority, we are responsible for our own lives. <u>You have authority over every demon that is assigned to harass and hinder you personally.</u> You don't necessarily have to have won in all the personal areas to have larger realms of authority. I dare say very few parents have won all their personal battles before they receive the responsibility to watch over and protect their family, but the more you enter into those battles and win over your own fears, lusts, insecurities, resentments, and other issues, the more your faith and authority will grow. So, let's look at the ground school of authority.

➤ Look up the following verses and write what each one tells you as to why the devil has no place or authority in your life.

• **Satan has NO authority over your life.**

Colossians 2:13-15

Hebrews 2:14-15

1 Peter 3:21-22

Matthew 28:18-20

If the devil has no authority in your life, why do you listen to his lies?

• *We as believers have been commissioned to take authority over the works of the devil and remove him from our lives, our families, and every place where we carry responsibility.*

Mark 16:15-18

Luke 10:19

1 John 4:4

2 Corinthians 2:14

Galatians 3:13-14

The Galatians passage says that we get the blessing of the Old Covenant without the curses, so I am including a couple of really neat passages from the Old Testament. Isaiah 54:17

Deuteronomy 28:1-14

In verse 11 the New American Standard Bible says we are blessed in the offspring of our bodies and the offspring of our beasts. When we had the hog farm, Dick would walk through the buildings every day claiming that we were blessed in the offspring of our beasts, and God honored it even though swine weren't acceptable under the Old Covenant.

Be sure and note what it says about what's to happen when your enemies rise up against you (and remember your enemies aren't people.)

• *We have been given supernatural weapons to protect us and to break the devil's power.*

2 Corinthians 10:3-6

We will talk more about spiritual weapons in the next chapter, but this passage is so important that I want to take some extra time with it.

2 Corinthians 10:3 For though we live in the world, we do not wage war as the world does. (from New International Version)

2 Corinthians 10:3 For though we walk in the flesh, we do not war according to the flesh. NKJB

This verse is one of the reasons I use the New King James Bible even though it's a little harder to understand. <u>The word in the original Greek should be translated *flesh,* and it is used symbolically of our natural nature or carnal nature, as opposed to our spirit.</u> It has everything to do with depending on our body and soul—what we think, what we want, what we feel, on our ability—as opposed to depending on God and His ability. The devil is a supernatural enemy. If we try to fight him in the natural, we'll end up using his methods and giving him more room to attack us and to attack others. If someone attacks your character and you respond by attacking their character, you've taken God out of the battle and handed both sides to the enemy.

2 Corinthians 10:4-5 For the weapons of our warfare are not carnal but mighty in God for pulling down strongholds, 5 casting down arguments and every high thing that exalts itself against the knowledge of God, bringing every thought into captivity to the obedience of Christ,

➤ Carefully consider what verse 5 is saying, and then tell me what the strongholds of verse 4 refer to. Where are these strongholds located?

The word translated *arguments* is *logismos*, 3053 in Strong's Concordance. That's where our word *logic* comes from. It refers to the reasoning of the mind. The supernatural weapons we need are to protect us from the enemy's assaults on our minds. If we don't receive his lies, he has no power over us. He has no authority of his own. He only has authority in our lives if we give it to him. We'll talk about our weapons and how to use them in the next chapter.

I WANT TO GO HIGHER – 13
Responsibility

List the areas in your life where you have responsibility. Start with your personal life. Are you a parent? Do you have areas of responsibility at work? Church? Clubs?

For each area where you carry responsibility, begin to prayerfully ask God to show you where the enemy is encroaching. Start with your own personal life. When He shows you a place where the enemy is camping, ask the Lord for a strategy to remove him. Don't try to do everything at once. Just let the Lord pick one area to work on at a time. There will be more help in how to do warfare against the enemy in upcoming lessons and in the Appendix.

What you are actually doing with this and other exercises is beginning to form a battle plan for your life. This exercise, along with many of the others, is simply a starting place. If you will actually put them to work in your life for starters, and then follow up as the Lord leads you, you will build your house on The Rock, and it will withstand any storm life can throw at you. But remember, the foundations of life aren't based on knowledge in your head. If you memorize the whole book, but don't put it to work in your life, it will be of no value. The only foundation that stands is the one that is built on actual relationship with the Lord

Chapter 14

THE DARK NIGHT OF THE SOUL

—

THE FINAL MONCLOVA STORY IS DICK'S STORY. WE had been home to Kansas. On our way back to Mexico, we stopped in Austin to visit Cindy. While we were in Kansas, Cheri had called to tell us about a job she had been asked to apply for. When she prayed about whether to pursue the job, the Lord told her He wanted her to have a baby. Cheri had asked Stewart to pray about it, and he received confirmation that it was time to start a family. Cindy, our firstborn, had been trying to get pregnant for several years. It was already a sore point before she heard that God wanted Cheri to have a baby. She was hurt, frustrated, and angry with God. Her pain and her anger with God hurt Dick so deeply that he cried—one of only two times I ever saw my husband cry.

When we arrived home in Mexico, he entered a prayer crusade such as he has never done before or since. By that time, we had moved our trailer to a lot we rented very cheaply from an elderly lady. We were parked beside a house that hadn't been lived in for years. Our landlady described it as being like the destruction in *Gone with the Wind*. Our deal with her was that we would fix up the house for the use of it. We hired men from the church to do repairs. We didn't ever live in the house, but we used it to entertain and minister, and we set up my computer over there, so I didn't have to move it every time we ate.

There was a big room in the front of the house that we didn't repair. Dick made that room his walk-and-pray room. After breakfast he would go over to the house to pace and pray in the Spirit. He

138

would come back to the trailer to eat lunch and then return to pray until it was time to go to the church in the evening. He would cry out to God for mercy for Cindy, that she, too, might have a baby. There was such a passion and so much anointing to pray, so we knew God had ordained the prayer. It's impossible to maintain that level of prayer without the Holy Spirit's help, but it was easy for him to pray those hours on end.

Why was Cheri caught in the midst of her busy life and simply handed the gift of a child while we had to war for a baby for Cindy? I don't know. <u>But I do know that some things in life that God wants us to have, still must be possessed</u>. When God led the Israelites to the bank of the Jordan River, He told them in essence, "I have given you the land. Possess it." Things happen within us in the midst of a battle that would never happen if a thing were easy. A maturing takes place, an understanding of who we are and the authority we carry that is necessary for the next battle. I guess it comes under the heading of warrior training. God has high ground for each of us to take for His kingdom. <u>The higher our mountain to possess, the greater the need for spiritual muscle</u>.

In Dick's case, there was more happening than just muscle building. There was a whole inner shift in the works. He prayed that way for days. Sometime during the second week, He knew in his spirit that Cindy was pregnant. He just kept on praying. A few days, maybe a week after he knew she was pregnant, Cindy, Debra, and three of their cousins came down to visit us. We were having a retreat for our youth in our Gone-with-the-Wind house, and our natural kids were coming to help with and check out what we were doing with our spiritual kids. When they got out of the car, Cindy ran to her dad, hugged him, and joyfully announced, "I'm pregnant." He said, "I know."

The following November, Rikki, Cindy's first-born, was born three weeks early, five days ahead of her cousin, Curtis.

The Dark Night of the Soul

It would seem that the prayer siege might have been over after the announcement of Cindy's pregnancy, but something else was happening. Dick was experiencing a strange phenomenon. It seemed like his emotions were shutting down. It was another time when Henry and Josie were out of the country, so Dick was preaching at church. People were getting saved and baptized in the Holy Spirit, but Dick didn't seem to care. None of the things that normally brought him pleasure or excitement seemed to touch him. I was concerned, and so was he. We simply couldn't understand what was happening to him.

After a couple of days of rebuking the devil and warring on Dick's behalf, I decided maybe this was something God was doing. I remembered a chapter from Richard Foster's book, *Celebration of Discipline,* entitled "The Discipline of Solitude." In that chapter Foster describes an experience called the dark night of the soul. I found the book, and had Dick read this:

"The 'dark night' to which he calls us is not something bad or destructive. On the contrary, it is an experience to be welcomed as a sick person might welcome a surgery that promises health and well-being. The purpose of the darkness is not to punish or afflict us. It is to set us free. ....What is involved in entering the dark night of the soul? It may be a sense of dryness, depression, even lostness. It strips us of overdependence on the emotional life."[1]

Foster went on to quote St. John of the Cross, a mystic from the sixteenth century, who said the experience "puts the sensory and spiritual appetites to sleep, deadens them, and deprives them of the ability to find pleasure in anything."[2] That's what Dick was experiencing. It was not a very pleasant experience for either of us, but the fruit was wonderful. The result of that period in Dick's life was that he was enabled to shut down his mind and emotions

---

[1] Foster, *Celebration of Discipline,* pp. 89,90.

[2] Foster, *Celebration of Discipline,* p. 90.

and become very quiet inside. In that stillness within, he learned to hear the Spirit of God within his spirit at an entirely different level. That was essential preparation for the next assignment that took us to Saltillo.

I WANT TO KNOW MORE − 14
The Armor of God

Because the main battlefield is in the soul, God has given us armor to protect our souls.

Eph 6:10-20 Finally, my brethren, be strong in the Lord and in the power of His might. 11 Put on the whole armor of God, that you may be able to stand against the wiles of the devil. 12 For we do not wrestle against flesh and blood, but against principalities, against powers, against the rulers of the darkness of this age, against spiritual hosts of wickedness in the heavenly places. 13 Therefore take up the whole armor of God, that you may be able to withstand in the evil day, and having done all, to stand.
14 Stand therefore, having girded your waist with truth, having put on the breastplate of righteousness, 15 and having shod your feet with the preparation of the gospel of peace; 16 above all, taking the shield of faith with which you will be able to quench all the fiery darts of the wicked one. 17 And take the helmet of salvation, and the sword of the Spirit, which is the word of God; 18 praying always with all prayer and supplication in the Spirit, being watchful to this end with all perseverance and supplication for all the saints— 19 and for me, that utterance may be given to me, that I may open my mouth boldly to make known the mystery of the gospel, 20 for which I am an ambassador in chains; that in it I may speak boldly, as I ought to speak.

Verse 10 gives us the source of the power we are to use to stand. Give an example from your life of what it looks like to stand in the Lord's power rather than in your own ability.

For me, a simple example has to do with eating habits. I don't try to keep a strict control over what I eat all the time, but sometimes I feel led to give up a certain type of food for a time. Once I was led to give up sweets entirely until a certain issue I was praying for was resolved. It was more than a year before the resolution came. Normally, my mind would fix itself on the "huge sacrifice" I was making whenever I fasted, and that would lead to self-pity, which usually led to self-indulgence, which would lead to guilt for breaking my fast. So, I asked the Holy Spirit for His help. What He showed me to do was to change my focus. Instead of focusing on what I was giving up, I was to focus on the importance of my purpose and on the Lord's ability to help me. In comparison to the freedom that I wanted to see accomplished in the lives of people I loved, my piddling little sacrifice seemed like nothing. And the bonus was that it broke my addiction to sweets!

The Belt of Truth
14 Stand therefore, having girded your waist with truth,

In verse 14 the word translated waist, is more accurately translated loins. The definition from Strong's:

> NT:3751 osphus (os-foos'); of uncertain affinity; the loin (externally), i.e. the hip; intern. (by extension) procreative power:[1]

In other words, the seat of procreation in our physical bodies, which is the also the place within us from which the spirit functions, is to be encompassed with truth. The ancient Romans wore a belt around their hips, which carried their weapons. We are to fill our spirits with truth, so that when our minds are under attack, we can turn to that haven of truth deep within and draw on the revelation we need to withstand the lies of the enemy.

---

[1] *Biblesoft's New Exhaustive Strong's Numbers and Concordance with Expanded Greek-Hebrew Dictionary,* (Biblesoft and International Bible Translators, Inc., 1994).

How can you fill your spirit with truth?

The Breastplate of Righteousness
What does a breastplate cover?

In scripture the heart refers to the control center. I believe it actually encompasses both your soul and spirit. What is the source of your righteousness?

2 Corinthians 5:21 For He made Him who knew no sin to be sin for us, that we might become the righteousness of God in Him.

1 John 1:9 If we confess our sins, He is faithful and just to forgive us our sins and to cleanse us from all unrighteousness.

You cannot stand firm against the attacks of the devil if you are hanging onto sin in your life. You must be willing to confess it and turn loose of it. But once you do that, you can forget it. Jesus already paid for your sin. Sin enslaves us in two major ways. The first is in thinking we have to have it, do it, etc. We don't. Jesus broke the power of sin. We simply have to repent by changing who we agree with, and ask God for the revelation we need to see it His way. If your sin has given place to a demonic stronghold, it can be broken. For further information on deliverance, see the Appendix.

The second way sin enslaves us is by convincing us that, even after we have confessed it, we are still unacceptable.

Colossians 2:13-14 And you, being dead in your trespasses and the uncircumcision of your flesh, He has made alive together with Him, having forgiven you all trespasses, 14 having wiped out the handwriting of requirements that was against us, which was contrary to us. And He has taken it out of the way, having nailed it to the cross.

What does this passage say about your sin?

If you have trouble believing you can be forgiven, get in a relaxed place, alone with God. Ask the Holy Spirit to help you envision the cross. See yourself nailing the sins of your past on the cross. Allow the Holy Spirit to show you anything He wants to about it.

As you deal with the sins of your past and are consistent about confessing the mistakes you make currently, you will establish and keep polished your breastplate of righteousness, and the enemy will not be able to attack your heart.

Shoes of Peace
15 and having shod your feet with the preparation of the gospel of peace;

We know that "gospel" means good news. The word "preparation" here is an interesting word. It means readiness and preparation. It also means firm footing or foundation. This would indicate to me that our feet are to be planted in the firm foundation of peace. If we don't have peace, we aren't trusting God with whatever the situation is.

Think back over past lessons, especially lessons six through eight. How can we come to the place of trust and peace in the midst of unsettling circumstances?

Give an example of what that looks like in real life.

Shield of Faith
16 above all, taking the shield of faith with which you will be able to quench all the fiery darts of the wicked one.

What might be some examples of the enemy's darts?

From past lessons, especially eleven and twelve, and from anything else life has taught you, how can you keep your shield of faith polished and in place?

Helmet of Salvation

17 And take the helmet of salvation, and the sword of the Spirit, which is the word of God;

In the beginning, I said that the main battlefield is the mind, but this is the first piece of armor that actually covers the seat of our mind. It is interesting that every other piece of armor mentioned so far gives us the position or stance from which to fight. If we are firmly grounded in truth, have an understanding of our righteousness, peace, and faith, it doesn't leave a lot of room for the enemy to attack us. It's also interesting that this says the helmet of salvation. We have to be saved to have any of the armor. The word translated salvation here means defender or defense. It is also sometimes translated as deliverance, health, and save. If we fill our mind with an understanding of what we have been saved from and what is ours because of that salvation, we have a full range of answers for the enemy's lies. He tries to plant in our mind, "I don't feel well today. I think I'm catching a cold." From our salvation arsenal, we pull out, "I don't receive that. I don't have to be sick because the word says that by His stripes (or wounds) I am healed." (1 Peter 2:24)

What you are doing in that kind of situation is taking the truth of what belongs to you, because of your salvation, and turning it into the sword of the spirit, which is an offensive weapon. You can say, "Devil, I don't receive your lies because God says _____." Fill in the blank with the promise you need.

The confessions I have been scattering through these lessons or suggesting you write from God's word are swords that you can use against the enemy. We will talk more about that and other weapons in the next lesson.

I WANT TO CLIMB HIGHER – 14
Breaking the Soul's Power

Most of the exercises in this book are things you can choose to do most any time. This one is not. In fact, this is more of an explanation than an exercise.

The dark-night-of-the-soul experience that I described in this chapter is not something that you choose to enter into. But should you find yourself in a place like that someday, there is a scripture that helps:

Isaiah 50:10-11 Who among you fears the LORD and obeys the word of his servant? Let him who walks in the dark, who has no light, trust in the name of the LORD and rely on his God. 11 But now, all you who light fires and provide yourselves with flaming torches, go, walk in the light of your fires and of the torches you have set ablaze. This is what you shall receive from my hand: You will lie down in torment. NIV

The first test as to whether that is what you are going through or not is: <u>Are you walking in obedience</u>? If you are in a depressed place because you are in rebellion against God, your answer is to repent.

But if you are serving God to the best of your ability, the next thing to check is: <u>Are you under attack from the enemy</u>? Is there a sense of fear, condemnation, anxiety, or torment? Or do you simply feel shut off from your emotions? The former is quite likely an attack. Just rebuke the enemy and choose to look to and worship God.

But if you feel shut down inside and spiritual warfare doesn't help, then it's time to consider the next part of the verse above. Just be at peace walking in the darkness and trusting God. I love Proverbs 3:5, which says: *"Trust in the Lord with all your heart, and lean not on your own understanding; in all your ways acknowledge*

Him, and He shall direct your paths." Just choose to rest in Him and trust Him to lead you through the dark time.

What you do not want to do is what is being described in verse 11. Creating your own fire has to do with seeking your own way out of the darkness. That might be seeking entertainment or physical gratification—seeking a shallow substitute for the life of God. These times are dangerous, because it's easy to believe that God has deserted you, so you need to find another means of comfort. But the dark night of the soul is to set you free from shallow substitutes. If you will simply trust God in the darkness, and allow Him to do the work that needs to be done inside of you, you will come out with a spiritual depth and satisfaction that far surpasses anything your soul could come up with.

Your spiritual walk will go through many paths that your mind can't understand. Sometimes it is time to fight through and possess things. Sometimes you must simply be at peace and trust God. Only the Lord can teach you which is which, and He will be faithful to do so.

Chapter 15

SALTILLO

—

IN AUGUST 1986 WE MOVED TO SALTILLO TO JOIN A teaching ministry headed up by Carl Luepnitz. Carl had a walled compound that had a nice facility for housing groups that would come down from the states. He worked with a number of churches in Saltillo and in the mountains that completely encircled the city. Saltillo was cleaner and cooler than Monclova, a pleasant city about an hour southwest of Monterrey.

Our job was to go into a church for a week at a time, teaching a series of lessons on salvation, forgiveness, and the baptism of the Holy Spirit among other things. We would spend five nights in one church one week, and five nights in another church the next week. Carl set the schedule.

The first two churches he scheduled us in were both Baptist churches on the west side of town. We didn't think much about it at the time, but in retrospect, perhaps Carl was throwing us in the deep end to see if God would bail us out. I think we had some sort of blind assumption that maybe Baptist churches in Mexico were less opposed to the baptism of the Holy Spirit than the Baptist churches we were familiar with in the States. Well, they weren't any different. However, the pastors respected Carl, and we were the experts based on the distance rule. The distance rule is an unspoken law that says the farther you travel to teach a thing, the more you know. So, we just went ahead and taught what we knew. They listened...and they received.

We'd been in Saltillo only a short time when a speaker from the states came in to hold a seminar in a meeting room Carl leased for that purpose. By this time, we had purchased a van to haul people around. In Monclova we had hauled them in the back of our truck that pulled our fifth wheel. In Saltillo we rented a real house (with a real telephone!!!), and we no longer needed the truck. We had purchased a used fifteen-passenger van—that is fifteen gringos. It would hold infinitely more Mexicans. We ran a bus route to haul folks to the seminar. Our bus route included picking up a bunch of youth from one of the Baptist churches.

I don't remember who the speaker was or what he was speaking on. Neither do I remember the purpose of the altar call, but I definitely remember what happened next. One of our Baptist girls threw herself on the floor up in front of God and everybody and began to manifest big time. It took four strong men to hold her down while Dick tried to deliver her. The ensuing battle was epic and not the kind of thing you want happening in front of a group of people. It was absolutely amazing the kind of physical strength that can be manifested, even through one small teenage girl, when a demonic spirit is present, but in the end, the good guys won.

With some trepidation, we took the girl back to the local church where we had picked up the kids. Dick told the pastor what had happened. When we went back to pick up people the next day, we didn't expect anyone to be there, especially not that girl, who actually had bruises on her arms from the encounter. But they were all there. She was bright-eyed, eager to go. She didn't even remember what had happened to her the day before, and she was free!

We learned a lot from that encounter. We learned that a demonically-empowered person has many times the strength of a normal person. We learned that when you are in the midst of such a deliverance, you are dealing with the devil, not the person, and that the person is not responsible for what he or she says and does, and frequently doesn't even remember what happened. We learned that we had a lot to learn about dealing with the devil.

We were in the right place to learn. Carl was well known for his healing and deliverance ministry. Pastors from all over the area called him to come deal with their worst cases. Dick became his number one assistant. Sometimes people came to the compound. Sometimes Dick and Carl went to churches or homes. On one of the more unique occasions, they were asked to go pray for a lady who was blind in one eye. When they arrived at the house, they were greeted by a friendly dog in the yard, and then went on in the house. They discovered the lady had some issues with bitterness toward her husband. They ministered to that first and had to deal with a spirit of bitterness before she could forgive. Then they prayed for her eye, which was restored. As they finished ministering to the woman, they heard a loud bang against the door. They looked out to see the dog gathering itself up. It backed off about twenty feet and ran at the door again, hitting the door with all its strength. It fell whimpering to the ground, only to get up and repeat the process. Dick and Carl actually had to deliver the dog before they could get out to leave. Apparently, the spirit had passed from the woman to the dog just like the spirits that left the Gadarenes man in the Mark 5 story and went into the swine.

We'd been in Saltillo for a while when Carl scheduled us into a little congregation in a village east of Saltillo a few miles. The day we were to give our first teaching, the salvation message, the pastor moved his little flock across the village to a place he had rented from a local woman. Moving a church across town, even a small town, in Mexico is a big deal. Churches are neighborhood affairs because most people walked to church. Moving across town meant that some people wouldn't walk that far and that others might come from the new area. That, in itself, was an issue, but in this case, it wasn't the main issue.

We had no more than walked into the place than we sensed the spirit wasn't right there. When we met the new landlady, we knew why. Dick knew in his spirit that we had entered a witch's property. We watched as the pastor and his wife, sweet, godly young people, tried to involve the congregation in worship. The room was full, but mostly with people the pastor didn't know. When it was our turn, we delivered our salvation teaching, including The Great Exchange. We could see tears in the eyes of some of the people, but no one responded. It was the strangest feeling. People always responded to that teaching, but we stood and looked out at people who seemed to be tied to their seats. There was the pastor and his wife in whose eyes we saw the light of the love of God. There was the witch whose eyes had an entirely different kind of light. And then there were the people. It was like there was no one home behind those eyes.

Outside the church, insult was added to injury when the pastor told us that he had to walk some of the girls from his former congregation home to insure their safety, but that we were to eat with his new landlady, and he'd be back. I could feel the hair standing up on the back of my neck while I forced down the meal she served and tried to remain polite, but in the van on the way home, I exploded. I was furious. "God, why didn't you warn us?" I lamented. I assured the devil and the world in general that our next night would be different.

The next day at the compound, we told Carl what had happened, so we prayed there. I reworked the salvation lesson to come at it a different way, and Dick and I went to war. We bound everything we could think of and then asked the Lord to station angels at the door of the meeting, and to not allow any negative spirit to enter. The witch didn't show up. We presented our lesson to hungry hearts, free to receive, and practically everyone got saved.

We understand a lot more about dealing with the devil now. We've learned that he doesn't have any authority if we don't allow him to use ours. We've learned how to deal with lots of things in less stressful ways, but back then we simply fought until we won.

I WANT TO KNOW MORE – 15
The Weapons of Our Warfare

We have talked about our defensive weapons. Let's look at some offensive weapons.

The Name of Jesus
We know that Jesus has all authority. That authority is passed on to us through a power of attorney to use His name. Sometimes when a person is out of the country for a while or due to health issues or for whatever reason can't conduct their own business affairs, he will give someone else the power of attorney to handle his affairs for him. The Great Commission is our power of attorney to use His name to carry on His ministry on the earth.

Mark 16:17-18 And these signs will follow those who believe: <u>In My name</u> they will cast out demons; they will speak with new tongues; 18 they will take up serpents; and if they drink anything deadly, it will by no means hurt them; they will lay hands on the sick, and they will recover."

Peter used that power of attorney at the Gate Beautiful to heal a lame man. The story is found in Acts 3. Peter used the incident as an occasion to preach, but note especially what he said in verses 12 and 16.

> ➤ Where is he saying the power for the healing came from?

> ➤ How was it activated?

> ➤ Read Philippians 2:5-11. Why is the name of Jesus so powerful?

> ➤ What clues do you see in this passage as to the prerequisites for using it powerfully?

When you are praying, when you are ministering, when you are dealing with the devil—do all of it in the name of Jesus. It is His name that carries the authority. But you also need to understand that, while it is right to say, "in the name of Jesus," the authority doesn't come simply from you speaking those words. Yes, they must be spoken, but the thing you are saying and the action you are taking should truly represent the character and heart of the Master. <u>It is in saying what He would say and doing what He would do that brings the alignment of the power and authority of heaven to bear.</u> When your heart is aligned with His heart, your mouth is simply the lever that releases the power.

The Blood of Jesus
Revelation 12:10-11 Then I heard a loud voice saying in heaven, "Now salvation, and strength, and the kingdom of our God, and the power of His Christ have come, for the accuser of our brethren, who accused them before our God day and night, has been cast down. 11 And they <u>overcame him by the blood of the Lamb</u> and by the word of their testimony, and they did not love their lives to the death.

Blood is an ancient covenant symbol. We'll save the study of covenant for another lesson, but the bottom line is that God said the life is in the blood (Genesis 9:4). When a covenant was formed with blood, a sharing of life took place. The covenant partners became responsible to care for and protect one another. When Jesus made a new covenant in His blood (Matthew 26:28), He became our covenant partner. When we declare to the devil that we are covered by the blood of Jesus, we are reminding him of the power force that stands behind us. That's a really good thing to declare when you sense that you are in danger.

Binding and Loosing
Matthew 18:18 "Assuredly, I say to you, whatever you bind on earth will be bound in heaven, and whatever you loose on earth will be loosed in heaven.

If the enemy is harassing you or someone you care about, espe-cially if that someone is within the realm of your responsibility, you have the authority to bind up his works. For example, if you are feeling rejected or left out, you may sense that there's a spirit of rejection operating against you. You can say, "Spirit of rejec-tion, I take authority over you in the name of the Lord Jesus Christ, and I bind up all your works against me." Actually, if it is you the spirit is hindering, you can tell it you don't want it anymore and can cast it out in the name of Jesus. If it is someone else—a family member or a co-worker—you don't really have the authority to cast it out unless that person agrees he or she doesn't want it. Since asking a person if they want deliverance can get kind of messy, you can simply bind the spirit, which gives the other person more freedom to make right choices.

Again, when you are dealing with a demon, talk directly to the demon in the authority of the name of Jesus. Be firm and author-itative. You don't have to be in the presence of the person to bind the spirit. You can do it from your own prayer closet. You aren't dealing with time and distance, as we know it, when you are dealing with the spirit realm.

When you bind something negative, loose something positive. If you bind the spirit of rejection, loose the acceptance of the Lord over their lives.

Binding and loosing are effective, but they aren't a quick fix. Things can happen rapidly, but don't be surprised if you have to keep at it for quite some time before you actually see a difference in the behavior of the person. In fact, it may get worse before it gets better as changes begin to take place that the person doesn't understand.

Praise and Worship
Praise and worship are very powerful weapons against the enemy. In fact, when we seem to be stuck in a spiritual battle, sometimes we will just stop and begin worshipping God and declaring truth

about who He is. For one thing, the enemy knows he isn't getting to you if you can still worship God. He hates worship and usually won't hang around very long where real worship is going on.

Secondly, praise and worship straighten out our perspective. It makes our God bigger in our eyes and shrinks the enemy.

Most importantly, Psalms 22:3 says that God inhabits the praises of His people. It's the quickest way to bring God onto the battlefield.

The Sword of the Spirit – the Word of God
Ephesians 6:17And take . . .. the sword of the Spirit, which is the word of God.

Hebrews 4:12 For the word of God is living and powerful, and sharper than any two-edged sword, piercing even to the division of soul and spirit, and of joints and marrow, and is a discerner of the thoughts and intents of the heart.

The sword of the Spirit is a two-edged sword. One edge separates and clarifies the thoughts and intents of our own hearts. In that sense it is a defensive weapon, once again protecting us from the enemy's lies and deceits.

On the other side you have an offensive weapon that you can use to directly attack the enemy. There is a section in the Appendix called "Standing on the Word of God." It is full of promises on all sorts of topics. You use your word-sword to declare truth into heavenly realms. Remember Jeremiah 1:12 quotes God as saying He watches over His word to perform it. The word of God, declared boldly, draws God and His angelic forces onto the scene. It also boosts your faith because faith comes by hearing the word of God (Romans 10:17). And finally, spoken truth blasts holes in the devil's lies.

Very early in our time in Monclova, Mexico, the youth had invited us to go on a "dia del campo" which means day in the country, or a picnic. Of course, there could be no getting to the country unless we all went in our truck. So actually, it was an invitation for us to pick them up and take them out of town for a picnic. During the night before the event, I woke up feeling very sick to my stomach. My first thought was of what a disappointment it would be to those kids who seldom got out of their own neighborhood, much less out to the country, if we couldn't go.

I drug myself out of bed and found my notebook of promises. Huddled in the corner of the couch, I began to weakly read and put me into the scripture: " Surely Jesus bore my griefs and carried my sorrows. He was wounded for my transgressions, He was bruised for my iniquities; the chastisement for my peace was upon Him, and by His stripes I am healed. (Isaiah 53:4-5) Behold, I will bring it health and healing; I will heal Thana and reveal to Thana the abundance of peace and truth. (Jeremiah 32:44) (Jesus) healed all who were sick, that it might be fulfilled which was spoken by Isaiah the prophet, saying: "He Himself took Thana's infirmities and bore Thana's sicknesses." (Matthew 8:16-17) who Himself bore my sins in His own body on the tree, that I, having died to sins, might live for righteousness—by whose stripes I am healed. (1 Peter 2:24)"

As I read these and other promises concerning healing, my voice got stronger. About the third time through, I got up and started pacing around the tiny living area of our 5th wheel trailer as I declared truth over my body. After a while, my body didn't feel that much better, but my soul was in agreement with my spirit that sickness couldn't stick on me, so I went back to bed and slept. The next morning, I was fine, and we had a great trip to the country.

You can declare the word of God over your own life, over your family, over your church and nation. You will seldom go wrong proclaiming what the Bible says. It is the most powerful, however, when you sense that it is a word that God is quickening to you right then for the situation you are praying about. That's called a *rhema* word. There are essentially two Greek words translated "word" in the New Testament. *Logos* means the spoken or written word. Jesus is referred to as the *Logos* of God, and it is *logos* that is used in Hebrews 4:12. *Rhema* means the word God is speaking now. It can be a verse from the Bible or it can something He is currently speaking to your spirit, but it's more like God is selecting that particular word for you for the current situation you are facing as opposed to scripture which is always true. *Rhema* is used in Romans 10:17 as the basis on which faith comes. It is good to meditate on all the scriptures that pertain to a problem you are dealing with, such as fear or anger. You can proclaim all that seem applicable over your life, but also listen for what God has to say about it. He may quicken a particular passage that will be the most helpful, or He might show you something entirely different. The Bible is a wonderful book no matter how you deal with it. With the Holy Spirit as your guide, it becomes life and strength and a powerful sword.

I WANT TO CLIMB HIGHER − 15
Using Your Weapons

This week ask the Holy Spirit to train you to use the weapons we have been talking about. Watch for places that they apply as you intercede for friends and family and over the situations you face. Expect object lessons. Record what you learn.

Chapter 16

SALTILLO – THE STAFF

As we visited church after church, we were especially attracted to the youth. We would see sharp youth with a hunger for God, and we finally yielded to God's nudging to collect a group of the most promising of them from all over the city and put them in training. Over the years in Saltillo, we did a number of these groups, but the first three held the kids that we handpicked to become our staff. There was **Miguel**, whose gifting as a teacher made him a natural for our teaching ministry. Miguel, who came from a very simple background, is now a neurosurgeon. He still teaches strong faith concepts in his brother-in-law's church.

His brother-in-law and Miguel's sister, **Natan and Dora**, already had a small church when we connected with them. They wanted the training we were giving the youth, so they came, and they too became part of our teaching staff on a part-time basis. Their church is now one of the more powerful churches in Saltillo. The last I heard, several years ago, Natan was overseeing fourteen churches and functioning as a one of a three-pastor team that shared leadership for a large group of the pastors in the city.

Miguel married **Pita**, who was also one of our first youth. Pita has been teaching God's word ever since we got her started. When we were last in Mexico, she had become ordained and functioned as Natan's main associate pastor. She has learned English, so we still send her good books from time to time.

Yolanda was also in our first class. She was a little fireball that caught onto the concept that she had authority very early. She quit law school to go to seminary, where she met her husband. They have a large church in Chetumal, which is down on the Yucatan Peninsula.

Sarah was our bilingual secretary. After the first few years, I quit writing in Spanish. I'd write the lessons in English, and Sarah would translate. That really speeded things up when we started our full-time Bible school. Sarah and her husband have worked in a church in their neighborhood for years and now lead a church of their own.

Last, but certainly not least, was **Cristy**. She was our youngest, joining our staff when she was only sixteen, but she absorbed everything and became one of our most affective teachers. She married another of our students, and they have a strong church in Queretaro, which is a couple of hours north of Mexico City. At last count they were overseeing five churches.

Each of those young people was handpicked. Only Natan and Dora were in their early twenties. The rest were teenagers. I think Yolanda was the only one who had finished what would be equivalent to high school here. Kids only went to *preparatorio* (high school) if they were going on to college. College wasn't something kids in our neighborhoods considered. But God gave Dick prophetic vision to see the potential in each of them. He spotted Christy at one of Carl's seminars, and before he had even met her, God said, "Put her on staff." I don't know how many of the others who weren't on staff could have gone on to achieve all that these did, but I know of several. Our students are pastoring and teaching all over Mexico, and we only know about a small percentage of them.

I don't think it had to do so much with our "great teaching" or even with the fact that God helped us pick them. I think the biggest thing was that we didn't see them as poor Mexican kids. We saw them the way God showed them to us, as young men and women of God who could do anything, because the Spirit of the Living God dwelled in them. Because we believed in them and treated them like we saw them, they saw themselves that way to, and they have grown into the destiny God had for them.

Perhaps an even more important thing was that God revealed Himself to them in personal ways. They came to know Him for real. Frequently, I would ask the kids to share the most important thing they'd learned that week. I would usually expect it to be some revelation from our teaching, but it never was. It was always something that God Himself had revealed to them. That's so much better.

For our staff to teach and to minister, they had to know what God was saying to do. For the most part the staff taught the things I had written, but as Pita once said, "It doesn't matter how many times I've taught a lesson, I have to seek God for fresh revelation on it every time if I want it to be anointed." So, they taught our material, but they put in their own examples and revelation.

We also took them with us to minister. If we were teaching in a church, we'd take some of them with us to minister to people afterward. One night, near the beginning, Carl was teaching in Natan's church about the baptism of the Holy Spirit. He asked us to bring some of our kids to minister the baptism when he did the altar call. As we sat and listened to him teach, he went into something about demonic activity picking up after you have the baptism. I thought, "Oh, oh, he just gave an invitation for trouble."

Sure enough, five people responded to the call to receive, and four of them started doing strange things. One was hopping around like a kangaroo. One was slithering on the floor like a snake. Our kids looked at Dick as if to say, "What do I do now?" Dick just said, "Deliver them." So, our fledgling recruits got deliverance practice before they got Holy Spirit baptism practice. But they did it and came out asking for more.

One of our early students, Leobardo, wasn't on staff, but he often went along to minister. He loved it! He was never ready to go home. After running around with us for a while, he decided to go to an Assemblies of God Bible School where he could get credentials his church would recognize. During some class, he got a fellow student baptized in the Holy Spirit. His instructor came by and told him he couldn't do it that way. Leobardo, who had used an informal, laid-back Dick-style to minister, just looked at the instructor and said, "But he's speaking in tongues." Leobardo married another of our students, and they also have a church in Saltillo.

Ana Ruth was another early student who was part of our staff for a while. She wasn't a teacher, but she was a people person, and she loved to minister. She would haul us to some of the strangest places to minister to people she had discovered. And she would come with some of the wildest stories. One day she had ridden the bus to get to our place. There was a mother and child on the bus, and the child was screaming constantly. Ana Ruth went back and asked the mother if she could pray for the child. The woman agreed, so Ana Ruth delivered the child of some kind of demon. Then the child was absolutely peaceful and the rest of the people on the bus were amazed.

God sees the potential He has placed in each individual. He doesn't look at financial status or physical ability. He doesn't look at education or clothing. He looks at the heart, and He calls forth the person He created that person to be. If his heart is open and he answers the call, God will enable him to grow into that person.

I WANT TO KNOW MORE – 16
Motivational Gifts

Each of us is a unique creation with our own personal mix of gifts and potential. There are several different gift mixes mentioned in the Bible. It gets a little messy trying to separate them because some words, like prophecy, seem to carry different meanings in different contexts. Prophecy is mentioned in every list. In the Ephesians 4 lists of gifts, it is an office that carries the responsibility of equipping others. In 1 Corinthians 12 it is a declaration spoken at the urging of the Holy Spirit for the immediate situation. In Romans 12 it is a grace in a person's life that can be developed by faith. In all cases, it is a gift a person carries to edify and serve others in the Body of Christ.

For right now we are only going to study the gifts found in Romans 12:3-8. The word for gifts in this passage is *diakonia*, from which comes our word deacon. It refers to one who serves. This passage is speaking of gifts that God has given to each of us in order that we might be of service to others. The emphasis is, that while we are all members of the same body, we do not have the same function. Paul says the same thing in 1 Corinthians 12:14-31, but he uses a different gift set to illustrate in that passage.

In Romans 12 he is talking about a grace that rests upon our lives. I personally believe that these gifts were built in before we were born and that everyone has one or more of them, probably one that is predominant. I am calling them motivational gifts because I learned about them from teachers who called them that. It isn't a scriptural term, but they seem to be gifts that are built into the fiber of our lives that motivate us and add definition to our character.

We are going to start this lesson with a list of statements. Check the ones that seem to be the most true about you. There are many things that have become part of our lives because we have been disciplined in them. For example, you may have servant characteristics because your parents taught you to serve. That's great, but that's not what we're looking for. Check the ones that register the most real with how you look at life. One gift set is not better than another, so don't try to figure out what is what. Just follow your gut level impressions. I am not a qualified test creator, so there is nothing definitive about this, but I believe it will help you see things you haven't seen about yourself and about others.

162

➢ Statements. Place a check beside the ones that are most true of you.

1. I really like and enjoy people.
2. I see the best in people and desire to see them become all they can be.
3. I like to see specific achievement, and I can give clear steps for getting there.
4. When someone has a problem, I often search for an experience to use to relate the answer.
5. I can see how going through hard times can produce maturity.
6. I don't like teaching that isn't practical.
7. I like to use experiences to teach or to illustrate a point.
8. I enjoy counseling and relating directly with people.
9. I rely a lot on the response I see visually in people to determine how I'm doing in speaking to people.
10. It is more important to me that other people get the point from scripture than it is to keep the text in strict Biblical context.
11. It is important to me that scripture stays in context.
12. Truth is very important to me. I don't like to hear stories stretched.
13. I enjoy doing research and discovering the truth about things.
14. I am more interested in understanding the truth than in finding ways for people to apply it.
15. I sometimes feel like people think I'm somewhat cold or impersonal.
16. When someone has a problem, I look for a scriptural answer.
17. It's important to me to understand what's really going on.
18. I tend to not trust advice based on experience only.
19. I tend to test the knowledge of those who teach me.
20. I tend to like a lot of detail to back up my position.
21. I have a lot of insight into people and situations. I frequently have a deeper grasp of what is really going on than most people.

22. I see things pretty black and white. I don't like the compromise of gray areas.
23. I tend to see through people's motives.
24. I am usually aware of when things aren't right, and I won't put up with it.
25. If someone is messing up, I tend to be pretty direct in telling them about it.
26. I am sometimes viewed as being judgmental or harsh.
27. I want to know when I'm wrong.
28. I am more concerned with what God thinks of me than what people think of me.
29. I am direct, frank, and persuasive in my speaking.
30. When someone has a problem, I go for the heart of the issue. I have no patience with pity parties.
31. I see what needs to be done and I do it.
32. When someone has a problem or need, I look for practical ways to help.
33. I tend to remember what people like. I'm a good host or hostess.
34. I like to see needs met as quickly as possible.
35. I am not very comfortable in the limelight.
36. I like it when people notice what I do to help, but I want the appreciation to be real.
37. I have a hard time saying no when I'm asked to do something.
38. I prefer short-term projects to long-term goals.
39. I like the hands-on stuff. I don't like to organize and delegate responsibility.
40. Sometimes I tend to get so involved in helping other people that I neglect my own family.
41. I tend to see the big picture. I don't enjoy getting bogged down in details.
42. I am good at seeing what needs to be done and at delegating the responsibility to get it done.
43. I don't enjoy the hands-on, practical steps so much.
44. I am uncomfortable with disorganization.

45. I'm fine with letting someone else be in charge, but if there seems to be no one in charge, I will step in and take leadership.
46. I can handle criticism. Getting the job done is more important to me than everyone being happy in doing it.
47. I feel fulfilled when the pieces come together and everyone can enjoy the finished product.
48. It seems like I have an innate ability see what needs to be done.
49. I also seem to know who the right person is to do it.
50. I don't procrastinate. I like to see things done as quickly and efficiently as possible.
51. I seem to have an ability to make wise purchases and investments.
52. I like to give but I don't like to make a big deal of it.
53. I tend to see needs that other people don't seem to see.
54. When someone is in trouble, I look for a physical or financial need I can fill.
55. I don't like to be pressured to give. I prefer to see where the need is for myself.
56. It really blesses me to find out that my gift was an answer to a specific prayer.
57. I want to give quality gifts. I get no pleasure from giving inferior things.
58. I take care of my money. I don't spend money on frivolous things.
59. I like to feel like my gifts are significant and strategic in the work that God is doing.
60. Sometimes my motivation for giving is misunderstood.
61. I am drawn to people in distress.
62. I have a deep desire to remove hurts and bring healing.
63. I am very careful not to use words or actions that hurt others.
64. People sometimes see me as a soft touch.
65. I am uncomfortable with insensitive people.
66. I tend to handle things with gentleness. I avoid firmness unless I can see it is necessary.
67. I tend to know when people are not sincere.

68. I tend to see things from the viewpoint of the fragile and wounded, and I try to protect them.
69. Sometimes I feel like people take advantage of my desire to help them.
70. Sometimes I am misunderstood as being weak or indecisive.[1]

Now go back and draw a line after the 10's – after 10, 20, 30, etc. No doubt you have already figured out that each ten statements represent a different motivational gift. Count your check marks in each group of ten and see which group best represents you. Again, I'm not claiming that these questions are scientifically accurate. They just help you get the idea.

- 1-10 Exhorter
- 11-20 Teacher
- 21-30 Prophecy
- 31-40 Serving
- 41-50 Administration or organization
- 51-60 Giving
- 61-70 Mercy

All the gifts are needed in the body. Each gift has strengths and weaknesses. Understanding your gifting frees you from expectations that you be something you were never meant to be. Understanding the gifting of others will help you realize why they react as they do.

Administrator or Organizer
These are the ones who are capable of running the show, seeing the big picture, and being able to delegate the responsibility to make the thing work. They may appear to be somewhat lazy when it comes to the hands-on stuff. They can organize the event, but they probably won't hang around to do the dishes.

---

[1] Marilyn Hickey, *Motivational Gifts,* (Dallas, TX: Word of Faith Publishing, 1983).

Teacher

Here's the detail people. The teacher depends on and builds foundational truth. They keep people grounded. They enjoy study and research. They may be more truth-oriented than people-oriented, so they may be less comfortable in positions that demand people skills. They are usually pretty good at systematic organization and enjoy bringing things into order. A teacher may show less compassion for another person's pain, but quite likely can give the person a logical program to bring him out of it.

Prophecy

These are the seers for the Body of Christ. Prophetic people are good at discerning what the problem is, what the motives are, and in general seeing through people and situations. They tend to put their fingers on sin and have little tolerance for it. They are more likely to be considered critical or judgmental. They are usually direct and forceful. They aren't the people to go to if you're looking for pity, but they are the people to go to if you want to know what the real issues are so they can be dealt with. They tend to see things more from God's perspective than from people's perspective.

Exhorter

Exhorters are a gift of encouragement to other people. They tend to see the best in others and call it forth. They enjoy involvement with people, and are usually well-liked. They are usually good in things that require people skills. They lean more on experience than on facts. They may not be as comfortable in positions that require close attention to detail.

Serving or Ministry

Those with a servant's motivation are very practical. Servants see what needs to be done and do it. They are better at hands-on, short-term things than big-picture, long-term projects. They are better at doing things themselves than at delegating responsibility. Servants aren't vision people, so don't expect them to run the show, but they are the hands and feet that make the show run.

Giver
These people see needs in a financial way. Givers seem to have a gift for handling money. They usually use it wisely in their own lives, and they have a sense of how to give wisely to meet the real need. They don't like to be pressured into giving. They prefer giving where they see the need, and they usually do so inconspicuously. They are more interested in seeing positive results for their money well-used than in receiving accolades for being the donors.

Mercy
Folks gifted with mercy are known for their compassion. They tend to relate with the suffering of others, and are willing to champion their causes. They are very careful not to say things that would offend or cause mental stress. They want to protect and remove pain. They are frequently the one the wounded person will turn to. A mature mercy gift will press people through to the resolution of the problems. An immature mercy person may enable the weakness of another.[1]

Maturity is a factor in all the gifts, and so we are to take our gifts to God and ask Him to teach us how to use them well. For this lesson, the issue is more beginning to see how your motivational gift can help you see the type of thing you are gifted to do. It will also help you understand why your friends and loved ones don't always see things the way you do.

I WANT TO CLIMB HIGHER – 16
Gifts and Desires

Take the information from this lesson, and ask God to give you more clarity on how your motivational gift or gifts affect your life. You may rate rather high in more than one gift.

---

[1] Hickey, *Motivational Gifts.*

Then go back and consider the Climb Higher exercise in Lesson 1 concerning the desires of your heart. If you didn't do it to start with, do it now. Begin to record how your gifting and your desires fit together or relate. Do you find they complement one another or clash with one another?

Record what God shows you.

Chapter 17

AFRICA

—

ONE OF THE NEAT THINGS ABOUT WORKING WITH
Carl was the interesting people he brought into Mexico to teach
the Mexican pastors. One such person was David Keyser who
spent quite a bit of time with our staff teaching about spiritual gifts
and how they function together. We really connected with David,
so much so that he wanted to come visit with us the next time we
were home in Kansas. He spent several days on the hog farm with
us, and the result was that David invited us to join him in Kenya
later in the year. As it turned out, David not only had connections
in Mexico, he also had them in Africa. His plan was to have a
thousand copies of our book, *Fundamentals of Faith,* printed and
shipped ahead of us to Kenya. Then he set up seminars with two
missionaries stationed in Kenya.

In August of 1987, we found ourselves whirling around traffic circles on the wrong side of the street and somehow trusting David,
who's from Alabama, to drive like an Englishman, or worse yet,
a Kenyan. It was better than riding a bus in China though, so I
didn't feel it necessary to pray in tongues every time we hit the
streets of Nairobi.

Our first seminar was in Meru located in the northern part of
Kenya. David stayed in the home of our host. Dick and I stayed
in a bunkhouse-type building just beyond the banana tree. There
were three bedrooms in the bunkhouse. Our host's brother-in-law,
whom we never saw, inhabited one. The other two were just barely
large enough for a single bed, so Dick got one and I got the other.

170

I was okay with the arrangement in the daytime, but at night I would drag my mattress into Dick's room and sleep on the floor beside his bed.

If the accommodations left something to be desired, the seminar didn't. The Kenyan pastors were hungry to learn. We packed as much of our basic course into a week's time as we could. I helped with the teaching in the daytime, and Dick and David did some evening duty. Much to our surprise, the lesson that caused the biggest stir was the one on forgiveness. They simply had never heard that they were to forgive one another. They were still functioning on the eye for an eye principle. There was much crying and asking one another's forgiveness—a very special time.

Back in Nairobi, we taught in a large building instead of a courtyard. One Bishop attended both seminars. Another man had a Bible school a little way outside of Nairobi. He walked for over an hour before daylight to catch a bus to come to the meetings. At night he walked the same distance home after dark. He did that every day and was never late. We marveled at the price he would pay to learn. One day David drove us out to that man's school, and we gave him a stack of the manuals for his students.

One day I stayed at the meeting place at noon while all the rest of the white folks went to lunch. I wanted to visit with the men and learn about their ministries and what was important to them. That didn't work out very well. I think they were uncomfortable visiting with a white woman, and I'm not that great at starting conversations.

One of the very special things about our time with the Kenyan pastors was listening to them worship. While Mexicans worship with guitars, Kenyans use drums. They sang in amazing harmony. It was beautiful.

Dick's request for the trip was to go on safari to shoot with a camera, not a gun. He had in mind at least a couple of days.

171

Unfortunately, it turned out to be only half a day, but he still got a lot of great pictures.

While we were there, the pastors asked us to come back and teach for a month the next summer. We agreed to do it and took names of those who would want to attend. We were going to hold that school in Meru. Then shortly after Christmas, Dick said, "I don't think we are supposed to go to Kenya next summer." I really wasn't that excited about going back to Kenya, but we had a lot of pastors signed up. It was just too great of an opportunity to touch a lot of people. I just couldn't believe God wouldn't want us to go back and do that.

Dick said we needed to be in agreement. We both needed to hear God, so he proposed that we both set our minds for one week as if we were for sure going, and see whether we felt peace in our spirits. Then we would set our minds the other way the second week. We didn't need two weeks. Once I did what Dick suggested, it didn't take long to recognize an uneasy feeling down in the pit of my stomach. I quickly became convinced that Dick was right, that we weren't supposed to go, but I certainly didn't understand why. The next summer, just days before we would have arrived in Kenya, the missionary in Meru was kicked out of the country over some issue with his visa. Had we gone, we would have been on our own with no place to stay or meet.

Since then, we have often used that method of prayer in big decisions. Peace is the ultimate stamp of the Holy Spirit's approval. If you don't have it, you need to take time to find out why.

I WANT TO KNOW MORE – 17
God's Ways

Psalm 86:11
Teach me Your way, O LORD;
I will walk in Your truth;
Unite my heart to fear Your name.

That verse is my hope and my prayer. It's tacked up on the front of our refrigerator, and it's painted upon my heart. I'm an enrollee in the God's Way School, and although I feel I'm still in kindergarten, I've spent a lot of years getting that far, so I'm going to share some of the things I've learned. Of course, that's what I've been doing for sixteen chapters, but I intend to be more direct and less sneaky in this chapter.

God wants relationship. He wants to be known.
He wants friends and lovers and partners, not robots, slaves, or acquaintances with their own agendas. He wants us to know Him and love Him for who He is. He doesn't want us to obey out of fear, nor does He want us to draw close because of what He can do for us. He wants partners with whom He can share destiny. That's why He hides things <u>for</u> us. We have to want the thing enough to really seek it. We have to want it enough to allow God to change us to the place of purity that He can give it to us without hurting us. We will only allow that when we know Him well enough to know we can truly trust Him.

Jeremiah 29:13 And you will seek Me and find Me, when you search for Me with all your heart.

> ➤ Think about the things that are important to you. Which of those things are you willing to put in God's hands and trust Him to work out His way? Which are you not?

> You don't have to feel guilty about areas you can't trust to God. Just tell Him you want to know Him better so you

can trust Him more. If your heart is sincere, He'll show you the way.

The basis for our relationship with God is covenant. There is a whole lesson on covenant in Chapter 21.

God speaks through mysteries, parables and puzzles. He hides things for us. He delights in our pursuing Him to unravel what He wants us to know.

Unraveling God's mysteries includes growth and understanding on several levels. He doesn't simply reveal His purpose to us. He also reveals things about us. He doesn't get in a hurry. Forming the vessel is as much a part of the process as completing the task. I believe that's because each assignment is also preparation for the next assignment. We take the kingdom line upon line, step by step.

Gaining a position has to do with several things:

> Receiving a call or assignment.
> Seeing what is lacking in our own ability to be able to do it.
> Obeying what God is saying when we can't see what He is doing.
> Allowing God to change our belief system and desires to agree with His.
> Coming to a place of truly believing that God is able and willing to do the thing.
> Coming into agreement that He is willing and able to do it THROUGH US.

If we know too much too fast, we will try to do the thing in our strength, our understanding, and our ability, and we'll short circuit the supernatural power of God to do the thing through us.

➤ Meditate on the ideas I set forth above. React to them with your own thoughts. What have you experienced that would cause you to agree or disagree?

God's word is set into motion when man receives and agrees with what God says. It takes God's power and man's agreement to bring God's word into our realm.

Deuteronomy 29:29 "The secret things belong to the LORD our God, but those things which are revealed belong to us and to our children forever, that we may do all the words of this law.

The things we know to be God's will are already established in the eternal realm. This verse says if they have been revealed to us, they belong to us and to those who follow us. We have the right, perhaps even the obligation, to use our power of agreement to draw them from the heavenly realm and establish them on earth. We do that through the faith in our heart and the confession of our mouth.

Isaiah 51:16 And I have put My words in your mouth; I have covered you with the shadow of My hand, that I may plant the heavens, lay the foundations of the earth, and say to Zion, 'You are My people.'

➤ What is this verse saying about our part in establishing God's word?

Luke 1:37 says that nothing will be impossible with God. But the literal translation of the Greek would be better translated: "No freshly spoken word (rhema) from God is without the power to complete itself." The word that God is quickening to you now, whether it is written in the Bible or coming by revelation, is a *rhema* word. Matthew 4:4 says that man is to live by God's rhema, His freshly spoken word.

God watches over His word to perform it (Jeremiah 1:12). Our part is to be the partner who agrees with His word and speaks it back into the heavenlies, thereby giving Him the earth connection to act through.

God operates by faith. To access His kingdom, we must operate by faith.
The principle of faith is that first you believe, and later you receive understanding. Our minds want to understand before they believe. That comes from the tree of the knowledge of good and evil and focuses on circumstances. Faith focuses on God. It grows as relationship grows. It is based entirely on what we know of God—His word, His character, and His ways.

God's revelation and preparation are progressive and cyclical.
This is true on the personal level and on the Body-of-Christ level. For the individual, He reveals something on one level. When the person has progressed sufficiently on that level and his hunger grows sufficiently to desire the next level, He reveals more. You get stuck at any point you choose not to push on.

This is also true in the Body of Christ. He uses forerunners to break into new levels of understanding. John the Baptist (Luke 3) was a forerunner to prepare the way of the Lord—to prepare people for the next level of growth and understanding. What Jesus would bring would be so different from what they had known that they would only be able to hear if their hearts were turned to God in humility. We can't receive a new thing as long as we hold onto an old thing that blocks the new truth. Religious structures must be broken off. Old truths are important. They are the foundation that new truths are built on. It is the structure that men build around them that must be broken off. Religious structures deify the particular truth and stop there, as opposed to keeping the Living God the center of focus. The truth must not be capped as being final. It must be treated as an open door to lead to more truth. It must be stewarded as a treasure that has within it the map to greater treasure. People who prepare the way for the Lord must break the religious structures off the present truth so that the hearts and minds of the people will be free to step to the next level of truth when it comes.

When I go through dry periods after experiencing periods of revelation, it is because God doesn't want me to build a shrine around a method of experiencing Him. He may let me go back to it later, but in the dry place I am seeking a new aspect of the revelation of God. That keeps relationship fresh and real instead of it becoming a religious form.

God has anointings and/or mantles that have been opened by someone who was obedient. Once they have been opened, they are available for others to walk in and build upon.

God gives, but man must possess.
In Joshua 1:3 God says, *"Every place that the sole of your foot will tread upon I have given you."* Verse 11 says, *"possess the land which the Lord your God is giving you to possess."*

➤ Why must we possess what belongs to us?

Phil 3:12...but I press on, that I may lay hold of that for which Christ Jesus has also laid hold of me.

Gen 22:17...and your descendants shall possess the gate of their enemies.

Deut.2:31 "And the LORD said to me, 'See, I have begun to give Sihon and his land over to you. Begin to possess it, that you may inherit his land.'

Possessing is a process. In the process we are trained and prepared and matured to be able to maintain what we possess.

Deut 4:5-6 "Surely I have taught you statutes and judgments, just as the LORD my God commanded me, that you should act according to them in the land which you go to possess. 6 Therefore be careful to observe them;

Our land, like the land of Canaan, must be possessed God's way. Just as David could not take the Ark of the Covenant into Jerusalem on a new cart (representing the best of man's understanding), we cannot possess the land by our logic and our ways.

There is infinitely more to be known about the ways of God. Don't ever stop seeking to know Him better. He will reward your efforts.

I WANT TO CLIMB HIGHER −17
Learning the Ways of God

Choose something from the lesson above to meditate on and to ask God to teach you His ways. Be open to any way He wants to do it. Be alert to the circumstances of life. Look for God in the midst of them. Ask Him questions and expect answers.

There are enough idea doors in the pages above that you could explore their paths for years, and yet they are a drop in the ocean of the revelation of God. We will spend eternity discovering new and wonderful things about Him. The more we know Him, the more we will be able to trust every circumstance of our lives into His care, and the more His peace will fill our lives. You get to that place by walking with Him through every circumstance in life and asking Him to teach you His ways in the midst of it.

Philippians 4:6-7 Do not be anxious about anything, but in every-thing, by prayer and petition, with thanksgiving, present your requests to God. 7 And the peace of God, which transcends all understanding, will guard your hearts and your minds in Christ Jesus. (NIV)

Isaiah 26:3 You will keep him in perfect peace, whose mind is stayed on You, because he trusts in You. NKJV

Chapter 18

BORN TO BE A LIFE GIVER

As I prepared the courses we taught in Saltillo, I did a lot of study on the meaning of the Hebrew and Greek languages from which the Bible was translated. I had always enjoyed digging for deeper meanings hidden in the ancient languages. But it was far from enjoyable to realize that my name means death in Greek. It wasn't exactly a new discovery. From the time I read "Thanatopsis" in high school lit, I had known about my name. But one early morning in Saltillo, it hit me like a ton of bricks. I considered changing my name, but my father had made it up, and I didn't want to hurt him. I finally asked God if I should change my name. He simply replied, "I bring life out of death." That was good enough for me for a long time.

Back when I was teaching, I had a student we'll call Ben. Ben was very quiet—didn't mix with the other kids or offer anything unless he was called on directly. One day Ben asked to talk to me after school. I was delighted at the possibility of helping him; however, my delight came to an abrupt halt when the first thing that Ben confided to me was that his hero was Charles Manson, a mass murderer. Ben dreamed of killing his family. I spent several sessions trying to minister to Ben until it got to the point that I feared for the safety of my own family and drew the principal into the situation. I knew I couldn't help Ben, but the cry of my heart was to be able to help people like Ben who had wounded hearts. I told God that I thought it would be wonderful to heal people's bodies but even more wonderful to heal their hearts.

Somehow, God led me to a book called *The Healing Light* by Agnes Sanford. I was delighted to know that what I dreamed of doing could actually be done. I got hold of every book I could find on inner healing and healing of the memories. Then when we were in language school, I had the opportunity to put into practice what I had read. God anointed my efforts, and I began to sense His heart for the pain people suffer in their lives. When I ministered to people, I would feel His compassion flowing through me. Even people whose stories appalled my mind, drew only loving compassion from my heart.

While I was growing in my ability to minister inner healing, Dick was growing in his ability to perceive and identify the demonic. His forte was deliverance. When we put our giftings together, we were amazed at how God used us to set people free and bring healing into their lives.

One day, early in our time in Saltillo, as we were growing in this, Ana Ruth showed up asking for deliverance. At that time, Dick had ministered with Carl quite a bit, but we hadn't done hard core deliverance on our own. We had just barely started ministering to Ana Ruth when she became paralyzed from the neck down. She couldn't feel it if we touched her body, and she began to have trouble breathing. We hadn't bargained for that! I ran to the phone and tried to call Carl, but he wasn't home. We were on our own. You don't tell someone who is paralyzed and gasping for breath that she'll have to wait for better help.

<u>One of the saving graces of our lives is simply knowing that God is bigger than the devil and that He won't forsake us</u>. When we have to win, we just keep fighting until we do, no matter how long it takes. This one took quite a while. We did everything we could think of and then listened with all our hearts to hear what else we could do. Finally, the demonic spirit left, and Ana Ruth just went out under the power of God. We carried her to our bed. When she woke up, she was full of joy and freedom, and we were full of awe at what God can do, even through inadequate vessels.

As our staff grew spiritually, we began pulling them in to help with ministry sessions. We would have them listening for what the Lord was saying to do. As time passed, we let them lead, and we'd assist them. The last year or so we were in Mexico, it wasn't unusual to have three ministry sessions going on in our home at one time. I would help with one of the sessions, but Dick would "float." He would go from room to room, sticking his head in, and the Lord would show him what was needed if they were stuck. He operated in amazing discernment during that time. A lot of life and freedom happened in our house in those days.

It seems that all of my life has been a quest for identity. The enemy has worked hard to keep me from knowing who I am. Even when God told me clearly, I still didn't really get it. From my journal on February 3, 1990, I recorded this word God had given me:

"I want to produce life through you. The books we have written produce life. You and Dick and I have produced life in the staff and students. I greatly desire that union, that blending of your life, your character, and your personality with Mine. Together we produce life — life that can be manifested to and in others. The blending of your personality with Dick's, and Mine in both of you makes a more complete whole. It produces more complete life in you and in others."

Several years ago, since we've been living in Austin, I found out that in Anglo-Saxon *Thana* or more precisely a *Thane* is a "warrior who serves the king." I latched right onto that. My grandfather came from Norway, so the Anglo-Saxon heritage should be better than Greek for me anyway. Then a few months ago, as I was walking, the Lord spoke to my heart and said that He had named me Thana. Daddy didn't come up with that name on his own. The Lord said that before I was even born, I was a warrior destined to serve The King, and that it was also my destiny to bring life out of death.

So, there's the destiny trail again. My name wasn't a mistake. It was God's declaration of who He created me to be. Ben's place in my life wasn't a mistake. He was a God prod to purpose. I couldn't help Ben, but my time with him wasn't a failure; it was an invitation to go higher, to learn more, to find the path into God's great compassionate heart. In finding it, there has been great healing in my own heart as well. It has been my path from death to life to purpose. God has a similar path for you.

I WANT TO KNOW MORE – 18
What's in a Name?

It's pretty clear in the Bible that God considers names to be important. Sometimes He even changed people's names to call forth the changes He was ordaining in their lives. Abram, Exalted Father, became Abraham, Father of a Multitude. His wife Sarai, one who dominates, to Sarah, a princess. Simon, which means hearing, became Peter, a rock, and Saul, whose name had a Hebrew origin, became Paul, which was of Latin origin, perhaps more fitting for the Apostle to the Gentiles.

The names God applies to Himself are even more significant because they help us understand the attributes and character of God. For this study we are going to concentrate on who God says He is.

Jehovah
> ➤ Read Exodus 3:13-15. How does God identify Himself in these verses?

"I Am that I Am" is translated from the Hebrew word *hayah* that means to exist. The word implies self-existence. He is the Self-existent One, the Eternal One, who always has been and always will be.

Read Exodus 6:1,2. Here the Lord defines Himself by another word which is actually a derivative of *hayah*. The Hebrew word here translated Lord is *Yahweh* which the Hebrew people considered to be a name too sacred to be said or written. They would write it YHWH. Strong's dictionary also has it written as *Yehovah* which we translate into Jehovah. This word also means Self-existent One.

The name Jehovah, which is used in conjunction with a number of other names defines God as one who has life within Himself. He is indeed the source of life, and the life within Him cannot cease to exist. With that in mind let's look at the words that He Himself attaches to His name.

Jehovah-Tsidkenu – The Lord, Our Righteousness
For each of what is called the redemptive names of God (because they describe how He redeems us), I am going to list several scriptures that pertain to the meaning and benefits of that name. Beside each scripture write the key thought of the passage. At the end of each scripture set, write a prayer of worship that magnifies the Lord for that particular aspect. I have done the first one for you to give you an example to work from.

Jeremiah 23:5,6 God will (He has already done it in Jesus) raise to David a Branch of righteousness who will bring judgment and righteousness in the earth. He will be called Jehovah-Tsidkenu— the Lord, Our Righteousness. (This is where God introduced this name.)

Jeremiah 33:15,16 This is a similar verse. It adds, "In those days Judah will be saved."

The fulfillment of these promises is met in the life, death and resurrection of Jesus.

2 Corinthians 5:21 He made Jesus to be sin for us that we might be the righteousness of God in Him.

Romans 5:17 Righteousness is a gift. I don't have to earn it.

Philippians 3:9 My righteousness is by faith in Christ.

Isaiah 64:6 My own righteousness is like a filthy rag, so I don't depend on my righteousness, but on the righteousness of Jesus in me.

Once you have looked up and meditated on the scriptures, write a confession that reflects your gratefulness to God for who He is and what He has done for you.

Example:
Father, I worship You as Jehovah-Tsidkenu, the one who provides my righteousness. Lord, without Your provision of righteousness, all my good works and efforts to be righteous are like filthy rags. I am so grateful that I don't have to work to earn righteousness. I am so thankful that Jesus took all my sin and gave me His righteousness. What an incredible concept! What an incredible gift! I release and turn away from all thoughts of condemnation and my fear of not measuring up. I gratefully receive the price Jesus paid for me. Thank you, Lord, for such freedom!

> ➢ Now it's your turn. Use my pattern and do a similar thing with the other names of God.

Jehovah-M'Kaddesh – The Lord that Sanctifies
Sanctification means separated from the world, useful to God.

Leviticus 20:6-8

1 Corinthians 1:30

Galatians 6:14

Romans 6:14

1 Corinthians 6:11

2 Timothy 2:21

Your prayer:

Jehovah-Shalom – The Lord Is Peace

Judges 6:23,24

Isaiah 26:3

John 14:27

Philippians 4:6,7

What is the foundation of our peace?

How can we maintain peace?

Your prayer:

Jehovah-Shammah – The Lord Is Here

Ezekiel 48:35

Matthew 28:20

John 14:16,17

Hebrews 13:5

Your prayer:

Jehovah-Rapha – The Lord Heals

Exodus 15:26

Matthew 8:17

1 Peter 2:24

Why is healing and health your right?

Your prayer:

Jehovah-Jireh – The Lord Provides

Genesis 22:1-14

Deuteronomy 28:1-14

2 Corinthians 8:9

Philippians 4:19

Your prayer:

Jehovah-Nissi – The Lord Is My Banner
Here banner refers to the flag that flies over a military unit. It represents covering or protection.

Exodus 17:8-16

Isaiah 54:17

1 Corinthians 15:57

Romans 8:37

2 Corinthians 2:14

Deuteronomy 28:13

Matthew 28:18

Your prayer:

Jehovah-Rohi – The Lord Is My Shepherd

Psalm 23 (There are 7 of the names of God represented in this Psalm. Can you find them?)

Proverbs 3:5,6

John 16:13

Your prayer:

I WANT TO CLIMB HIGHER – 18
Worship with the Names of God

Use your prayers, together or separately, to worship God for who He is. With each name take the time to really meditate on what it means in your life, on the price Jesus paid for you to illustrate who God really is. Let the Holy Spirit guide you. The prayers you have written are only your starting point. Don't limit yourself to simply reading that. Let it be a time of true worship. You may want to add songs that come to mind that relate to the names. The Holy Spirit may give you new songs to sing. He may even say, "Dance it." If so, let your body express your gratitude. God loves your total involvement in worship. If you don't think so, check out 2 Samuel 6.

Another benefit of dancing before the Lord is that it is very liberating. It's a great measure of just how free you are. When you first start dancing before God, every demon in hell will be telling you how ridiculous you look, how foolish you are, and a hundred other things to paralyze you. The more you care what God thinks over what people think, the more you will experience freedom and joy. But you don't have to start in front of a crowd. You can start in the privacy of your own room.

Chapter 19

LIFE PRODUCES LIFE

—

AFTER WE HAD TAUGHT OUR THIRD GROUP OF YOUTH, their parents started requesting classes, so we started having classes in the evenings for adults. We had a wild cross-section that ranged from unskilled workers to doctors. Some pastors wanted to come as well. I remember one particular evening with a class that was meeting in our living room. Cristy was teaching. From our seat behind her, we could see her pastor in the class. It was such a blessing to watch him while the authority and anointing on her held the people in awe. We knew Cristy was anointed, but that was the first night we had seen it so powerfully. When the house was empty, we almost cried from joy. It's really wonderful to feel the anointing of God as you teach or minister. Dick and I both love that feeling, but we agreed that it's much more satisfying to see it on one of your spiritual kids.

Carl arranged for a week's seminar with pastors from rural areas around Saltillo. That was the first live-in seminar we had done. Because our teaching had to do with faith, relationship with God, and freedom, it flew in the face of religious custom. Most of these guys ate and breathed religion. God had to have prepared their hearts, because the truth set so many of them free at whole new levels. Many of them sent their own children and the most promising of their congregations back to us later when we did our longer live-in schools.

We were invited to one of those villages to teach in the local church. We turned it into a lab for our staff. Dick and I didn't teach.

The kids did everything. They taught at night and had a great time with the villagers in the daytime. Somewhere we probably still have a picture of Ana Ruth on a donkey. She had a blast.

One day we took our young staff to a nearby village where there wasn't a church. We took the puppet stage to draw a crowd, and the kids did "The Great Exchange." I specifically remember Yolanda, sitting on the dirt in a circle of tough-looking young men in straw hats, earnestly explaining why they needed Jesus. She got several of them saved.

Back in the original village, there was a man who had gone to seminary in his youth. Something had happened to make him bitter toward God. He refused to let his family come to our meetings at first, but later he relented. Dick made him his special project. He talked to him about the crops and about life in general, being very careful not to challenge his beliefs in any way. By the last night the man was in the circle of men who would stand outside in the dark and listen from a safe distance.

Several months later, a knock at our door woke us up one morning. It was that man, who had come in all the way from his village because he wanted to get right with God and to receive the baptism of the Holy Spirit. After Dick was through ministering to him, he took him to his sister's house. His sister just happened to be the mother of one of our staff members. There was great amazement and joy released in that household. That incident was one of the very special blessings God gave Dick while we were in Mexico.

As the demand grew, we planned a five-month live-in school. We got kids from the mountain villages, a few from Monterrey, and one young man from as far away as Guadalajara. By this time, we had three houses rented. The boys lived in one house, and the cooks prepared meals there. The girls had the other house, and we held classes there. Our house was the one that felt like it had a revolving door as the staff ran in and out for supplies, and the students came day and night for ministry.

Natan led praise and worship first thing every morning. The students would worship God, and Dick would watch and listen. Sometimes he would say, "Someone has a word from God." Dick would usually know who it was, and sometimes he'd have to encourage them further. Sometimes one of the kids would give something that wasn't from God. Dick would encourage and correct and then encourage some more. The kids learned to operate in the gifts of the spirit in those morning worship times.

By the time the five-month school ended, we had connected with Bob Nichols of Redeemed Christian Fellowship in Austin, where Cindy and Dennis attended church. Bob had come down and held a pastors' seminar in our facilities. He brought some Hispanic men from El Paso to minister to the pastors. Redeemed had a whole core of people trained to minister in the area of breaking vows, judgments, curses, dealing with iniquities, etc. That turned lights on for me. Another way to set people free! I pumped him and took notes as fast as I could during all his spare moments. He responded by giving me a set of tapes that he and his ministry pastor had made, which gave the scriptural background for all he was teaching me.

By late summer, shortly before our next class came in, we had a whole new aspect of freedom to teach. We invited our last year's students back to be our guinea pigs. They arrived on a day that I had gone to the hospital to sit with an American lady who had to be rushed in for emergency treatment. I spent most of the day in the hospital and left more convinced than ever that, at least as long as I was in Mexico, God would be my healer.

It was late afternoon when her husband picked me up to take me home. It was pouring down rain. Our house was built on a slope, so we had one step down from the bedrooms to the kitchen and dining room level, and another step down to the living room and front door. When it rained hard, the water would run in from the back yard (a small concrete area which shared a common wall with neighbors on all sides), across the kitchen, and out the opposite door which led to another even smaller concrete area with a small room on the far end. If it rained really hard, the water swirled through the kitchen and down over the step into the living room. Most of the floors were the famous Saltillo tile, but the living room had a carpet.

When I walked in the front door, I found our former students dancing on towels all over my carpet while one of them strummed a guitar, and everyone was singing praise songs. About that time, we got a call from the young couple who had just moved down from Bob's church in Austin to help us that fall. Their furniture was stuck at the border, and their house was also flooding. We moved our party to their house, where a young mom, in a foreign place with four small children and no furniture, huddled in a dry room trying to figure out what was so joyous.

But it was joyous. Our scattered kids were back together, delighted to see each other, and ready to learn more. We taught them what we'd learned from Bob. With the new understanding we'd received, we even water baptized them again in our huge tile bathtub, which was on the second floor of our house. We had never used it. We actually carried water to fill it because there wasn't enough water pressure upstairs to do the job. Then we discovered something else about that bathtub. It leaked. Water ran down through the ceiling dangerously close to Sarah's computer, but we just set down a bucket to catch it and had a glorious time reaching new levels of freedom.

I WANT TO KNOW MORE – 19
A Deeper Look at Water Baptism

When Adam and Eve sinned, they broke man's spiritual connection with God. From that time until Jesus died on the cross, man was limited to living by his own understanding—by his self-nature that the Bible refers to as his flesh. Our flesh is primarily concerned with number one—what I think, what I want, what makes

me look good, etc. One of the biggest challenges in growing in our relationship with God is in overcoming our own self-centered flesh. Years ago, there was a cartoon character called Pogo. My favorite Pogo quote (the only one I remember, actually) is, "We have met the enemy, and he is us."

Our own flesh is self-centered and fights against obedience to God. God provided a way to break the power of the flesh by dealing with it in the spirit realm. There is still a walking it out in obedience that has to take place in our personal lives, but that is not usually possible until the spiritual hold is broken.

Read Deuteronomy 10:10-16 and Colossians 2:11-12. An accurate translation of Deuteronomy 10:16 says, *"Therefore circumcise the foreskin of your heart, and be stiff-necked no longer."*

➢ What is circumcision?

➢ What would it mean to circumcise your heart in order to not be stiff necked (stubborn or rebellious)?

➢ Why does the Colossians passage say you do that?

The Bible gives two strong visual images of how to break the power of sin and of the flesh in our lives. They are both images of what takes place in the spirit realm when we are baptized in water. The first is of circumcision. The people of Jesus' day understood that image very well because circumcision was a very important part of their religious tradition. All Hebrew males were circumcised on the eighth day after birth.

The second image is of dying.
➢ Read Romans 6:1-10. What does this passage say happens when you are baptized in water?

➢ Read 1 Peter 3:21 and Hebrews 10:22. What are the benefits of baptism discussed in these verses?

- ➤ Look again at Colossians 2:11:12. What is the benefit of baptism mentioned here and what do you think it would look like in your life?

- ➤ Read Matthew, chapter 3. John the Baptist baptized people by immersing them in the River Jordan. From verse 11, what does John say is the purpose of the baptism he did?

- ➤ Jesus asked John to baptize Him. Why didn't John want to?

- ➤ What was Jesus' response?

- ➤ Read Matthew 28:18-20 and Mark 16:15-16. What is Jesus' command concerning baptism and new believers?

Some churches baptize people by sprinkling water on their heads, and some churches call their baby dedications a baptism. <u>We believe that the Biblical picture of baptism is total immersion because that is a picture of dying and being buried with Christ.</u> Going under the water symbolizes dying. (You may want to review the Romans 6 verses.) What are we dying to when we are baptized?

Coming up from the water symbolizes being raised with Jesus, being resurrected into new life with Him.

<u>We also believe that a person must be old enough to have an understanding of the sin in his life and to make a conscious decision to die to that sin and live for God.</u> A baby cannot make such a decision, so instead of baptizing babies, we dedicate them to God. Parents take their babies before the congregation and ask God to guide and protect their children. They pledge to do their part in raising them to become godly men and women. Thus, they put a protective hedge about their babies until they grow to the place where they can understand for themselves what it means to receive Jesus as their personal Savior.

Dick and I were both sprinkled in the Methodist Church as children. When we learned more about what the Bible has to say about baptism we each chose to be immersed. Then when we heard Bob's teaching about spiritual bondages and about water baptism having a part in breaking those bondages, we decided we wanted to be baptized again with our new understanding. I don't think it hurts to be baptized more than once, but neither do I know that it's necessary if you have already been immersed. I believe this is a very personal decision that you should talk to God about, and do as you feel led. Either way, doing the study on bondages in the next chapter is useful. Its purpose is to help you find the things of the flesh that you want to cut off and the sin that you want to die to. After doing that, you can decide about baptism. If you have never been immersed, you definitely should be baptized.

I WANT TO CLIMB HIGHER – 19
What I Need to Die to

Look over past lessons and journal entries.

Begin to define more clearly who you are and where you are going. State as clearly and concisely as you can:

- The desires of your heart

- The prophetic words, scriptures, personal insights that give hints or clarity about who you are and the purpose or purposes of your life

- Motivational and other gifts that you can see in your life

Now think about and ask the Lord to reveal to you anything that is still in your life that would hinder you becoming all that God created you to be. List anything that comes to mind, even if it seems like it's part of your character and you're stuck with it. It's important to get rid of hindrances to God's plans; HOWEVER, you don't need to go digging around in stuff you've already dealt with. If it's past and is no longer a hindrance, forget it.

We'll finish this project with next week's "I Want to Know More" lesson.

Chapter 20

THE LAST YEAR

—

THE NEXT AND FINAL SCHOOL WAS THE CROWNING glory. Dick had spotted a pastor at the pastor's seminar Bob had held. Alejandro Villamil was a young pastor from Mexico City. The Lord told Dick that this young man was called to be an apostle to his people. Dick told him that he needed to come to our school the next fall. That would mean seven months away from his church, and he had a wife and little girl. One of his elders was with him. The elder thought they could work out having Alejandro gone for seven months, but Lili, his wife, was a different matter. Dick assured Alejandro that he would talk to his wife, so he did. The results were that both Alejandro and Lili were in school that fall, and we had another pastor and his wife there also.

The latter pastor's brother-in-law, Manny, led our praise and worship for that school. He was a joy to watch. Every morning, after praise and worship, we could see him on his face in the praise area in his own time of rededication making sure there was no pride left from having a prominent place.

We started that school differently. It never took long after starting a school before the demonic bondages in the students would react to the teaching. Usually by the end of the second week, we would have a steady stream of kids wanting ministry. This time we made them wait. We assured them a lot of it would be taken care of in class very soon. Then we did the teaching we had received from Bob, and we'd give them time after each session to get alone with God and deal with the areas that had come up. That saved a lot of ministry time on basic stuff and left the students with tools they could use to help others. (I am putting one of the lessons on bondages in the "I Want to Know More" section of this chapter. The others are in the Appendix.)

They would use it. They used everything. We taught them how to bind up the demonic forces that kept their loved ones from being saved, and how to intercede for their salvation. They would pray in small groups long into the night. Since they didn't pray quietly, we soon got complaints from the neighbors and had to limit the hours they could gather to pray. But their prayer produced results. We heard many glorious stories of fathers and siblings and friends coming to know Jesus.

Dick would go over to the other house when the students were eating breakfast and just look them over. They knew he was reading them. If they weren't where they should be spiritually, they would avoid him, even to the point of walking on the other side of the street. It didn't do any good, of course. He would still nail them. Punishment for such things as being late to class varied. The kids accused him of not being fair because he wasn't consistent in his punishment. He told them he fit the punishment to the person, and the motivation of his or her heart, rather than fitting it to the crime. Even I didn't always understand that at the time, but now I see it had to do with life, not legalism. As time passed, the kids would run to him with their problems, and when graduation day arrived, most of the girls would cling to him like they would cling to their daddy. They didn't want to turn loose. He was the only godly father figure some of them had ever had.

One who considered Dick to be her dad was Cristy. Her own father had abandoned the family when Cristy was just entering adolescence. We helped her work through that step by step to the point where she finally went to see her father and forgave him face to face. But due to her relationship with her father and a few other of life's bumps, Cristy had made some vows that had affected her life. She dealt with most of them as we taught about vows and judgments, but one day Dick realized she had another one she needed to deal with.

It was pretty obvious that Manny really cared about Cristy, and we could see that she was drawn to him too, but she wouldn't let herself be drawn too close. Finally, one day Dick invited her to go with him to get groceries for the school. As they drove, he said, "Cristy, you made a vow that you would never marry a pastor, didn't you?" Cristy thought for a minute and then said she guessed she had. Manny was the son of a pastor and planned to be a pastor. Dick pointed out that this was why she was struggling in her relationship with Manny. Cristy agreed. By that time, they had arrived at the grocery story. Dick said, "You know what to do. You stay here and do it while I get the groceries." She did, and Dick had the privilege of officiating their wedding ceremony the next summer. They now have a church in Queretaro that has given birth to other churches and all sorts of ministries.

There are lots of Mexico stories we could tell. I guess it was the most fruitful time of our lives, but in the midst of making plans for the next year's school, God closed it down. While things had fallen together for six years, all of a sudden nothing fit. So, when Bob Nichols asked us to come out of Mexico and join his staff, it was an easy decision. We would still be working with Mexican pastors, as Bob's liaison among the people we had learned to love. But we would be living in Austin where two of our daughters and three of our grandchildren were. We were moving back home to America, and I was glad.

I WANT TO KNOW MORE–20
Iniquity

Iniquity
Remember in the early lessons where we talked about how Adam's sin passed to all mankind. The type of sin that passes from one generation to the next is called iniquity.

Exodus 34:6-7 And the LORD passed before him and proclaimed, "The LORD, the LORD God, merciful and gracious, longsuffering, and abounding in goodness and truth, keeping mercy for thousands, forgiving iniquity and transgression and sin, by no means clearing the guilty, visiting the iniquity of the fathers upon the children and the children's children to the third and the fourth generation."

Iniquity passes from generation to generation like physical characteristics. A child inherits his mother's eyes, his father's nose, and his grandfather's anger problem. The eyes and nose are physical traits of heredity. The anger problem is a spiritual trait that the devil has attached to the family line because of sin in a previous generation. If we confess that sin and ask God to remove it from our family line, we can be forgiven and can break off that curse from future generations. But if it isn't confessed and dealt with, God allows it to pass from generation to generation.

Deuteronomy 7:9 Therefore know that the LORD your God, He is God, the faithful God who keeps covenant and mercy for a thousand generations with those who love Him and keep His commandments;

> ➤ The good news is that blessings also pass from generation to generation. What does Psalms 37:25 say about the descendants of the righteous?

We receive an inheritance, good and bad, from the generations who have gone before us, and we pass on an inheritance to those who follow. Receive the blessings with thanksgiving, but break off any ungodly heritage so it won't pass on to your children and grandchildren. Begin right now building an inheritance of blessing for your descendants.

> ➤ Make a list of the good things you see in your family line.

Take time to thank God for the good things you see in your inheritance. You may also want to express your gratitude to your parents or grandparents for the blessings they have placed in your inheritance.

Now make a list of the iniquity you see repeating itself in your family. Most of us are accustomed to our hang-ups and issues. They have been part of our lives or our families for so long that we have come to see them as normal. Therefore, I'm going to put in some examples of areas that you might consider.

Anything having to do with fear and rejection, such as: abandonment, timidity, self-hatred, isolation, inferiority, anxiety, and any form of fear—fear of failure, fear of what people think, fear of death, fear of the future, fear of lack, etc.

Issues of sexual immorality: adultery, pornography, masturbation, homosexuality, lust, profanity, premarital sex, etc.

Issues of heaviness or depression: hopelessness, suppressed emotions, stress, excessive daydreaming, unjustified guilt, discouragement, fatalism, shame, despair, sadness, condemnation, self-pity, inability to enjoy life, etc.

Issues of lying or deception: exaggeration, confusion, poor self-image, self-sabotage, doubt/unbelief, intellectualism, legalism, irresponsibility, rebellion, independence, rationalization, manipulation, anything having to do with the occult, witchcraft, horoscopes, etc.

Bondages/addictions: cigarettes, alcohol, drugs, entertainment, the internet, video games, food, work, sex. (Obviously, some things on this list are only bondages if they control you rather than you controlling them. Just be honest with yourself.)

Pride: arrogance, controlling, gossip, prejudice, self-righteousness, self-justification, comparison, perfectionism, attention-seeking, complaining, an accusing nature, self-focus, vanity, defensiveness, love of money/world/social-status, lust for praise/power/control/position, covetousness, jealousy, insecurity, suspicion

Some types of illness can also be linked to iniquity.

> ➤ After you make your list of what you see in your family, put a star beside the iniquitous patterns that are present in your own life. Be as thorough as you can. Ask God to help you be aware of everything that needs to go on this list.

In Exodus 34 it says that iniquity passes to the third and fourth generation. So, the propensity toward a given sin can pass down through the family line, like the color of your eyes, for up to four generations. If one of the people in those four generations participates in the sin, it is set up to pass on to another four generations. And since the devil knows the weaknesses in your family line, you can be sure that he will see to it that each generation gets tested in the weak areas. You can see why it is so hard to get rid of generational sin. But God has a way to deal with sin in any generation. It's called repentance and applying the blood of Jesus. Before we do it, let's look at this from another angle to help you find all the areas of iniquity that you need to deal with.

Wrong Desires
Another aspect of iniquity shows up in wrong desires.

James 1:14-15 But each one is tempted when he is drawn away by his own desires and enticed. Then, when desire has conceived, it gives birth to sin; and sin, when it is full-grown, brings forth death.

Those wrong desires are an expression of iniquity. Every one of us has needs in our lives, real needs connected to legitimate desires. God has a right way to fill each need. When we seek to fill those needs apart from God, they get warped into lust. Iniquity causes us to lean toward filling the need the wrong way. We don't want to wait on God. It is that impatient desire—that iniquity—that the devil uses to grab hold of us. If there is no wrong desire, there is very little to grab hold of. Jesus once said, *"I will not speak much more with you, for the ruler of the world is coming, and he has nothing in me."* (John 14:30) There was no iniquity in Jesus for the devil to grab.

As a Christian you have learned how to receive forgiveness for the sin in your life. You must also learn how to get rid of the wrong desires. If the iniquity is not dealt with, it gives a handle for the devil to use to draw you back into the very thing you left behind.

➢ Make a list of the wrong desires that come up again and again in your life.

These may also be ancestral bondages, or they may have originated in your family with you. But they also need to be dealt with before they pass to your descendants.

Steps to Freedom from Iniquity and Wrong Desires
Take your lists. Take one of the areas of bondage you see in your family. Follow these steps:

1. Confess (simply agree with God) that the anger problem or lust problem, etc. is a sin.
2. Tell the Lord who in your family (as far as you know) participated in that sin.
3. Tell Him that you have also sinned in that area. Confess specific sin as you feel led.
4. Repent (make a choice to turn and go away from that sin).
5. Ask forgiveness for your ancestors. Name the ones you know specifically and then ask Him to also forgive those you may not know, back to the fourth generation.
6. Choose to forgive your ancestors wherever that sin problem in them has hurt you.
7. Ask forgiveness for yourself.
8. Receive forgiveness based on the price Jesus paid for your sin.

9. Ask God to cut off any soul ties or wrong connections between you and the generations before you. Ask Him to also cut off any soul ties between you and your descendents so that this iniquity cannot pass to any more generations in your family line.
10. Put it all under the blood of Jesus, and thank God for your freedom in that area of your life.

Do it something like this:

"Lord, I agree with you that yielding to anger and violence is a sin. It was a sin in Grandpa Joe and in my dad. I confess that the sin of anger has been allowed to enter and pollute my family. I confess that I too have sinned by allowing anger to control me. I have hurt people and caused strife (etc.). That's sin, Lord. I repent. I don't want anger controlling my life. Please forgive me and cleanse me from the sin and the iniquity of anger. Please forgive my father and my grandfather and all who have participated in this sin back to the fourth generation. Lord, I forgive my dad for the times he beat me (etc.). Lord, because of the blood of Jesus, I receive forgiveness on behalf of my family, and I receive forgiveness for myself. I ask you to cut all soul ties connecting me to my father, to my grandfather, and to any other ancestor through which that iniquity could pass. I declare myself free from the ancestral sin of anger. Also, please cut the soul ties between me and my children and all future generations, that anger may not pass to future generations. I put it all under the cleansing blood of Jesus, and I thank you for setting me free from anger."

Do this with each iniquity you find in your family line. Do it with the wrong desires you experience in your own life. If you already have children, the iniquity has already passed. If they are young, pray over them to break these things like you prayed over yourself. If they are older and have already participated in the sin, they will need to do this for themselves.

Water Baptism

How do you get completely free of iniquity and wrong desire?
You do the steps above and you do one more thing—**you die to
it**. <u>Water baptism is an outward sign of dying to sin and iniquity</u>.
If you have never been water baptized you need to be, and when
you are, declare the iniquities you've found to be dead, no longer
active in your life. That will help you. If you already have been
water baptized, declare the same thing on the basis of what you
already received. Then you have to choose to abide in Christ and
depend on His strength to keep you from temptation. When temptation comes, put your focus on the Lord instead of your desires.
Ask Him to help you and focus on His purposes for your life.
Also, ask Him for the revelation that will set you completely free
from the desire. When that comes, it will be much easier. In the
meantime, just remember: <u>that which has already been accomplished for you legally must be appropriated and walked out day
by day</u>. It's the same thing as, "I have given you the land; therefore, possess it.

You will find a study on the other spiritual bondages in the Appendix.

I WANT TO CLIMB HIGHER – 20
Don't Get Stuck in the Garbage Disposal

Take the time with God to do the steps in the "I Want to Learn
More" part of this chapter. Ask Him to help you prepare your list
for what you want to declare yourself dead to when you are baptized—or based on the baptism you already have received. Also
consider the things you want to die to from the last chapter.

Do the steps. Clean out the garbage. You may want to do the stuff
in the study in the Appendix also. Be as thorough as possible. If
you feel you need to, be water baptized again.

BUT THEN WHEN YOU HAVE DONE ALL THAT THE LORD SHOWS YOU TO DO, do what it says in Romans 6:11, *"Count yourself dead to sin, but alive to God in Christ Jesus."*

DON'T continue to search for sin in your life. Trust God that He has taken care of it. Focus on your strengths and on God's ability. Focus on the powerful things God is calling you to do. The pitfall in doing this sort of exercise is that sometimes it causes people to get overly introspective and focused on sin instead of righteousness. If God brings something else to your attention that needs to be dealt with, deal with it, but don't go looking for it anymore. Micah 7:19 says that God will cast all our sins into the depths of the sea. We are not to go fishing there!

Chapter 21

A FORERUNNER CHURCH

—

WE BUILT OUR HOUSE IN AUSTIN THE FALL OF 1990 and moved in a couple of days before Christmas. At the time we were renting the house in Kansas to the couple running the hog farm. It would still be a few years before we sold it, but my heart was no longer attached there. The six years in Mexico had changed me enough that when God told us we wouldn't be going back there, I was actually glad. Family and a good church in Austin were much more attractive to me than Delphos, although I've never stopped loving the peace of the country.

When we moved into our home in Austin, we still had the Bible school going in Saltillo. It wasn't until July that we closed things down and went on staff at Redeemed. We traveled back into Mexico every couple of months ministering to and continuing to train pastors with whom we had relationship, and we'd stay for a week to ten days. Sometimes we set things up for Bob to come in and work with the pastors. Sometimes we were on our own.

The church that we worked the closest with was Alejandro and Lili's church in Mexico City. We had done a lot of ministry to Alejandro and Lili while they were in school. We had a really good relationship, which was a good thing because we were going to need it. Alejandro's church was made up mostly of his peers, buddies he'd known for years. They didn't respect him, and they didn't support him. There wasn't anything there to build a church on. Dick told Alejandro they needed to take the church apart and start with new people. That was hard, incredibly hard. I felt so sorry for him. I don't know how he found the intestinal fortitude to be obedient, but he did. He laid down the law to his lawless friends, and most of them left the church. He started teaching what he'd learned, and new folks came, couples with some stability. They started Sunday school classes and taught *Fundamentals of Faith*. Soon they had their own little Bible school. It's been seventeen years since we closed our Bible school. Now (in 2007) Alejandro and Lili are both in demand as speakers in many places in Mexico and elsewhere. Pastors come to him for help and advice regularly. The apostolic call that Dick saw on him has grown and developed. Some of his old friends have even come back and become faithful members.

The other church that we spent time with was in Pachuca, north of Mexico City. The most memorable experience in Pachuca happened one night at the house where we were staying. The house belonged to a lady from the church. We'd stayed with her before. This particular night we were meeting with the Pastor, his wife, the lady who owned the house, and another lady. Both of the women had cancer. Our hostess confessed to us that she had breast cancer; she had been to numerous doctors. There was nothing they could do. She was in a lot of pain. The Lord gave Dick very specific instructions. He had the pastor's wife pray for her, saying exactly what the Lord instructed him to have her say. Our hostess gasped, said the pain was gone, and excused herself to go check. She came back and announced that the tumor was gone. She was instantly healed!

The other lady was not a Christian. Two young people had practically carried her in. Before praying for her healing, Dick asked the pastor to explain to her about salvation. She received Jesus. Dick didn't receive a specific word for her, so they just prayed in the name of Jesus and ordered the cancer to go. We didn't see any results, and the young people helped her back out. Months later the pastor and his wife came to Austin to a conference Redeemed was hosting, so they stayed with us. We asked about the lady we had stayed with. They said she was just fine, still cancer free. Then the pastor's wife said she had seen the other woman downtown one day, looking fit and healthy. She asked her what had happened. The woman said the cancer had gone away, and she was fine. The pastor's wife said, "Why don't you come to church and share your testimony and give thanks to God?" The woman seemed puzzled. She didn't understand why she should do that.

How often we fail to recognize the blessings of God in our lives! That woman received her healing, but she didn't recognize her Healer. She missed the invitation to relationship that would have healed her heart as well as her body.

We were in and out of Mexico for a couple of years before Bob pulled us in and gave us more responsibility on the home front. From the beginning we had done a lot of personal ministry. At Redeemed the men ministered to men and the women to women, so Dick and I weren't allowed to minister together anymore. However, if I could see that my session was going to require deliverance, I would send someone to find Dick, who was usually in the building. He would come help. Finally, someone told me that I was offending the supervisors by going over their heads to get Dick. So, I followed the rules, but there was no one I trusted to know what to do in deliverance like I trusted my own husband.

One night they actually assigned Dick to partner with a young woman to minister to another young woman. That was pretty much unheard of. I suppose they knew they were going to be dealing with stronger than usual demonic issues. When Dick walked in the door, the woman took one look at him and said, "I don't like you." Dick said, "Good, because I'm going to set you free." That wasn't the first time Dick had received that kind of reaction from the mouth of a demonized person. The demons recognized his authority. When they reacted that way, Dick knew they were afraid, and he would get excited.

This particular evening, among other things, the girl was dyslexic. Before the evening was over, she was free, both of the demons and the dyslexia. Although she was not a member of Redeemed, she came back to the church the next day to say thank you. For the first time she had no problem reading.

Another of my responsibilities was writing what Bob and the ministry director taught. I would listen to tapes of their messages and then put the information in an easily digestible form with specific instructions for ministering to each type of issue. That's the way I wrote the ministry manual and several other things.

Our favorite responsibility was running the youth program. We handpicked about fifteen or sixteen kids to be our leadership team. We called them the Joshua Generation, JGs for short. We met an extra night a week with them and taught them a less intense version of what we'd taught our staff in Mexico. Then at the general youth group meetings, we would lead the big group, and the JGs would lead small group discussion. As they grew spiritually, they took over more and more of the responsibility to run their own youth group. When we had retreats, the JGs would determine the rules, set up work details, and enforce the whole thing. The other kids responded powerfully to the standard the JGs set. The trickle-down effect was more like a flood.

The last full summer we worked with the youth, we took the JGs on tour. We went to churches Bob worked with in El Paso, Arizona, and Colorado. A young woman in the church, who was good with training drama, trained our kids to do a powerful skit and helped them choreograph some songs. Along with the program, the kids gave testimonies and did all of the ministry to those who answered the altar calls. They took turns having a devotional in the vans in the mornings as we traveled from one location to another. A couple of nights there were special things going on. Dick would ask the boy who was our strongest leader what time he would have them head for bed. Then we would leave him in charge and go to bed without a doubt that they would do what they said they'd do. They would never have betrayed the confidence we put in them.

The highlight of our trip was the transformation of a precious African-American girl named Rachel. When we were in Arizona, the pastor of the local church took us up into the mountains for an afternoon of enjoying nature. The other kids poured out of the vans and attacked the nearest incline. Rachel wanted to know if she had to go. Since she was afraid of heights (and a lot of other things, we found out), I sat below with her while the others explored.

The next day we headed for Colorado. The closer we got to the majestic Colorado Rockies, the more uncomfortable Rachel became. Even driving near mountains scared her. We were to spend the night in Buena Vista, and we had reservations to take a white-water raft trip the afternoon we arrived there. When it came time to sign the release before getting on the rafts, Rachel came to us asking if she should sign it. She thought maybe she shouldn't go with us. Dick left no room for doubt. He told her she would sign, and she would go. I told her she could sit right in front of me. I didn't tell her that I'm not a good swimmer.

Fortunately, this was a trip where we had to row. The guide stood in the back of the raft and called out directions. We had to follow his directions in unison if we wanted to arrive where we were going, so Rachel had to concentrate on what she was doing. She didn't have time to worry. The whole group needed her. After the first set of rapids, she relaxed a little. On downstream the rapids got more intense, but by the time we got there, Rachel was looking forward to the next challenge. When we landed, she purchased a T-shirt that boasted of being a whitewater survivor.

That night we all gathered in one motel room to pray. The kids saw many analogies between life and a whitewater raft trip. They likened God to the guiding voice from the back of the raft that kept everyone pulling together.

The next day we stopped for a picnic near a flat-topped mountain that seemed to rise straight up from the forest floor. Several of us were sitting at a picnic table visiting while some of the others tried their hand at climbing the butte. All at once I asked, "Where's Rachel?" I had scarcely more than asked the question when we spotted her waving to us from the crest, and she chose to come down the hard way!

There were lots of wonderful things about that trip. The kids had touched many hearts and lives. We were very proud of all of them, but I will never forget the thrill of watching one young lady discover that if we face our fears, they dissipate.

At Redeemed, we experienced something we hadn't experienced before or since. We got a glimpse of a deeper kind of fellowship. The leadership team was a close-knit unit. We planned together, prayed together, and played together. We even spoke covenant together. I think both God and the devil took that seriously. To the enemy we were a threat—a forerunner church, ahead of the times. God had given Bob so much revelation. He had so many of the pieces, but while he led us into covenant with one another, he didn't realize the depth to which our covenant with God had to be if we were to go where he wanted to take us. If a church is going to aim at the transformation of a city, especially a city like Austin, that prides itself in intellect, independence, and "weirdness," it needs more than revelation. It needs to be rooted in God at the core of its being, not just individually, but also corporately. Leadership and congregation alike need to listen better than we listened, obey better than we obeyed, and have humility worked in at a level that we didn't know existed. Redeemed was wonderful. It was the best church we've ever been a part of, but our mountain was high, and we fell far short.

I WANT TO KNOW MORE–21
The Sure Foundation – Covenant

The foundation of life is our covenant with God. A covenant is a legal agreement. Marriage is a covenant. There are neighborhood covenants that determine rules concerning the community. But a covenant with God is incredibly more powerful than anything we enter into legally in this day and age. God's covenants are blood covenants. They are made with the shedding of blood, and they are never to be broken. Testament is another word for covenant. The Bible is made up of the Old Covenant (Testament) and the New Covenant.

Three Powerful Prayers
Let's look at three powerful prayers. We'll start with Moses. This prayer takes place right after God threatened to destroy the people after the Golden Calf incident. **Read Exodus 32:11-14.**

➢ What arguments does Moses use against the destruction of the people?

➢ For understanding of the argument in verse 13, see **Genesis 17:1-14**. What are the key promises in this covenant that Moses is standing on?

(By the way, it is this piece of the Old Covenant that caused the Jews to be so upset with Paul when he said the Gentiles didn't have to be circumcised to become Christians.)

➢ Now let's look at a prayer we've studied before. See **Nehemiah 1:5-10**. What is the basis for Nehemiah's supplication to God?

➢ Read **Daniel 9:2-19**. Note especially verses 4 and 16. What is the basis for Daniel's request?

➢ What are the common threads in these men's prayers?

➢ Did any of the men base their requests on the actions or worth of the people they were interceding for?

➢ According to these examples, what is the basis for prayer?

The reason God makes covenants with people is so He has the legal right to use His power on their behalf. Since He gave man authority in the earth, He chose to honor that authority and only intervene when man was willing to covenant with Him for that intervention. There is always good reason for man's part of the covenant, but a human being, apart from God's life within, is not capable of keeping a covenant. At best he is capable of agreeing with God to make one. That gives God the legal power to act on his behalf.

Abraham agreed with God by being circumcised—a blood covenant. In turn God agreed to give Abraham's descendants a nation, that they would have the piece of land we now call Israel, and that the covenant they were making would continue to all his descendants.

> ➢ Why are those steps important to God's overall plan for man to have salvation and to receive back his right to dominion?

Abraham's covenant with God was progressive. It started with simply obeying God to leave Ur and go to an unknown land (Genesis 11:31-12:4). It continued with some animal sacrifices in chapter 15 and circumcision in chapter 17. We find the culmination of God's covenant process with Abraham in **Genesis 22** where Abraham shows his faith in God to the point of offering up his own son as a sacrifice to God. With that degree of agreement, God promises to multiply Abraham's descendants as the stars of the sky, but here's the kicker:

Genesis 22:17-18 ...and your descendants shall possess the gate of their enemies. 18 In your seed all the nations of the earth shall be blessed, because you have obeyed My voice."

> ➢ What is the significance of Abraham's descendants possessing the gate of their enemies? Keep in mind that the

gate of a city is where judgments were made. It was the place of rule and where authority sat.

Look at Matthew 16:18: *"And I also say to you that you are Peter, and on this rock I will build My church, and the gates of Hades shall not prevail against it."*

➤ How does this relate to Genesis 22:17-18?

Another man, Peter, agreed with God about the identity of His Son, and a covenant promise to Abraham centuries before was brought into focus. Not only that, but that promised Seed would be the one who would enable the possessing of the gates of the enemy. (Galatians 3:16 identifies Christ as the seed mentioned in Genesis 22:18.) One man, Abraham, agreed with God to sacrifice his son and set up the legal basis of covenant on which God could sacrifice **His Son** and bring about the salvation of mankind. That's the heart of the Old Covenant. The Old Testament is full of the journey of how God brought Israel to the point of obedience to where God could fulfill that ancient promise, but when He did fulfill it, He instigated a whole new covenant.

➤ In the light of this New Testament understanding, write the significance of Genesis 22:17-18 in your own words.

Covenant is such a big topic, and I'm trying to fit it in such a small nutshell, so before we talk about the New Covenant, let's look the steps that seemed to be part of making a covenant among the Hebrew people. There's no single place in the Bible that actually lists all the steps of making a covenant. Perhaps that's because the people were so familiar with covenant that it wasn't necessary. Perhaps it's simply because God hides things for us, and we will have to sincerely seek if we are going to really understand His covenant.

Steps of a Covenant[1]

- **The two parties exchanged robes.** A man's robe represented his life. So, in the exchange, each was saying, "I am yours and you are mine. We are one. What is mine is yours, and what is yours is mine. If you ever need anything that I have, it's yours. Even my very life is in your hands." This step of covenant is shown in 1 Samuel 18:1-4 between Jonathan and David.

- **The participants exchanged belts.** A belt held a man's weapons in place. Giving one's belt to another was like saying, "All my strength and power are yours. If you need protection, I am at your side. I will never use my strength against you, but only on your behalf." These promises of protection not only pertained to the men involved, but also to their families, not only for the present, but also for all generations to come. In 2 Samuel, chapter 9, you'll find the story of David protecting and caring for Jonathan's crippled son, Mephibosheth.

- **Then they took an animal or perhaps several animals and cut them in half.** This is where they actually "cut" the covenant. They placed the two halves side-by-side and stood between them. Then they began to walk through the blood that flowed between the pieces. In this they were saying that they gave up the right to their own life. The two halves represent each person. Genesis 15 has a very interesting picture of this picture of passing between the animal parts, as it appears God passed between the pieces as a smoking oven and a burning torch (verse 17).

- **This part usually also carried an oath.** They would point to the pieces and say something like this: "May the Lord do this and more to me should I ever break this covenant.

---

[1] E.W. Kenyon, *"The Blood Covenant,"* (Kenyon's Gospel Publishing Society, 1999).

Cut me in half and give me to the vultures if I try to break this covenant, which is the most sacred of all covenants." Because of this a blood covenant would carry a curse as to what would happen if it were broken.

- **They would lift their right arms and cut the palms of their hands.** Then they would put them together to mix their blood. It was a symbol of their lives becoming one. The Bible says the life is in the blood. They would rub something in the cuts to make a clear scar. Our tradition of shaking hands comes from this step. In ancient times when people shook hands, they could see whether or not the other person was in covenant with someone. If he was, it would be dangerous to harm him, because his covenant partner was already pledged to defend him. In Genesis 17 God asks for circumcision in place of cutting hands for Abraham's covenant with Him.

- **They exchanged names.** Each took part of the other's name.

- **They would carefully spell out the conditions of the covenant.** There were various reasons for making a covenant. Covenants of war had different rules than marriage covenants.

- **There was a meal to commemorate the covenant.** They would eat bread and drink wine. The bread was a symbol of their own flesh and the wine a symbol of their own blood. It was another way of declaring they were one. In some parts of the world, they would literally drink one another's blood, but the Lord commanded very clearly that His people were not to drink blood, so they used wine as a substitute. Understanding this step will help you understand the very difficult eat-my-flesh-and-drink-my-blood passage in John 6. Jesus was talking about covenant.

- **The final thing they did was leave a physical memorial.**
  They would plant a tree or set up a pillar or make a pile of
  rocks. Genesis 31:43-55 shows this step in the covenant
  between Jacob and his father-in-law, Laban.

With that background as a basic understanding of covenant, let's
look at ours.

On the eve of Passover, Jesus celebrated the Passover meal with
His disciples. Passover is the Old Covenant holiday that commem-
orates the lamb being slain so its blood could atone for the Jewish
people. With the blood over the door, the death angel passed over
that house. This all happened the evening before they left Egypt.
The story is in Exodus 12.

It was no accident that Jesus was crucified at Passover. He was the
Lamb of God that took away the sins of the world. The ancient
Passover was a type of the reality which Jesus fulfilled on the
commemoration of the original event.

**This particular Passover was the fulfilling of the Old Covenant
and the introduction of the New Covenant.**

*Matthew 26:26-28 And as they were eating, Jesus took bread,
blessed and broke it, and gave it to the disciples and said, "Take,
eat; this is My body." 27 Then He took the cup, and gave thanks,
and gave it to them, saying, "Drink from it, all of you. 28 For this
is My blood of the new covenant, which is shed for many for the
remission of sins.*

Here we have the commemorative meal of the new covenant. Jesus
said it was the "new covenant." Chapter 8 of Hebrews goes back
and picks up the prophecies of the new covenant from the Old
Testament. Then it says: *Hebrews 8:13 In that He says, "A new
covenant," He has made the first obsolete. Now what is becoming
obsolete and growing old is ready to vanish away.*

At the Last Supper, Jesus fulfilled the prophecy from the Old Covenant that a New Covenant would be established. The New Covenant superseded the old. There are many Jewish people still living under the Old Covenant, and it is still valid for them. It still has good promises, BUT there is now a better covenant with better promises. That's why Paul said the circumcision was not necessary for the Gentiles. They were entering into their relationship with God under a different covenant.

- Instead of the circumcision of the body, our covenant calls for the circumcision of the heart. Our outward sign is water baptism, but the inward truth is freedom from the tyranny of the flesh so that we can follow the dictates of the Spirit.

  ➢ With what you already studied in the Water Baptism lesson, what does that mean to you?

- Our outward sign of the covenant meal is communion, where the outward action of taking bread and wine represents the inward truth of joining our lives with the powerful, eternal life of our Lord through the presence of His Spirit in our spirits.

  ➢ What understanding do you currently have of God's life in you?

  How have you experienced that practically?
- The blood shed in the making of the Old Covenant was that of an animal, usually a lamb. The blood shed for our covenant was the blood of Jesus that promised, not only to protect us from our enemies, but it actually paid the price for our sin. Sin is what gave Satan legal right to torment mankind in the first place. The Lamb of God took away our sin and gave us His holy life from which to draw strength and power over every attack of the enemy.

➤ We know it is still possible for you to sin, so how does this part of the covenant help you? (Consider both the protection from sin and what you do with sin when you have entered into it.)

• Instead of exchanging physical robes that represented life, we literally receive His life.

➤ What does that mean to you personally? How have you experienced it?

• Instead of a physical belt to hold up physical weapons, we have the belt of truth which guards us from the lies and deceptions of the enemy.

➤ How does the belt of truth work in your life?

• Jesus gave us His name to use against the enemy. Even more important, His name is our key to going before the Father in prayer. Just as Moses, Nehemiah, and Daniel reminded God of the relationship they had with Him by referring to the covenant He had made with their ancestors, we remind God of His relationship to us by taking our position in Jesus with the declaring of His name.

➤ What does that mean to you?

• The rules and conditions of the Old Covenant were spelled out in the Law that God gave to Moses. It included some good promises, but it also included some horrible curses. Paul says in the book of Galatians that we have been redeemed from the curse of the law. *Galatians 3:13-14 Christ has redeemed us from the curse of the law, having become a curse for us (for it is written, "Cursed is everyone who hangs on a tree"), 14 that the blessing of Abraham might come upon the Gentiles in Christ Jesus, that we might receive the promise of the Spirit through faith.*

God has always worked through covenant. The covenant He made with His people in the Old Testament was imperfect because His people had a sin nature and could not keep the covenant. Nevertheless, God worked through that covenant to protect His people and to bring them to the point where a better covenant could be established. This time God Himself came in the form of a man. Jesus, being both God and man, made the covenant through His own blood. He purchased our lives and then placed His very own Spirit within us. Galatians 5:18 says, *"If you are led by the Spirit, you are not under the law."* A couple of verses earlier it says, *"Walk in the Spirit, and you shall not fulfill the lust of the flesh."* <u>God actually made an everlasting covenant with Himself, so that He could keep both sides of it</u>. Then He let us in on it if we would simply receiving what Jesus did for us, <u>AND THEN He put His own Spirit within us so we would be able to walk in freedom from sin and enjoy the benefits of the covenant.</u>

What are the benefits of our covenant? All the blessings of the Old Covenant – Galatians 3 describes how those who are in Christ are free from the curse of the law but are heirs to the blessing of Abraham, PLUS all the blessings and promises you find in the New Testament.

> ➢ List two or three of your favorite promises.

How do you experience them? By growing closer and closer to the Lord and by walking by the guidance of the Holy Spirit—the Tree of Life—rather than by listening to the dictates of your flesh. Instead of the chapters and books of rules and regulations that we find in the Old Testament, the Apostle John sums it up this way: *1 John 3:23 And this is His commandment: that we should believe on the name of His Son Jesus Christ and love one another, as He gave us commandment.*

Too simplistic? Yes and no. The gospel of our Lord is very simple. It only requires the simple faith of a child. Walking it out depends on laying down our legalism, our intellect, our fears, our

220

independence, and anything else that would keep us from being able to walk in that simple faith like a child. The bottom line is that it's easy if you can simply hear and trust God's Spirit in your spirit. It's impossible if you're trying to do it in your own ability.

React to the last two paragraphs. Tell how that works in your life or take the freedom to react in any way you choose.

I WANT TO CLIMB HIGHER − 21
Communion

Spend some time meditating on the above lesson and on what covenant really means. I covered so much so fast that you will need to do some digging for yourself to get the powerful truth of covenant.

When you feel you have a good sense of what it means, and you feel you are ready to enter into covenant with that understanding, take communion as an outward sign of your inward commitment. This isn't to <u>make</u> a covenant with God. <u>You are already sealed in His covenant by your choice to receive Jesus as your Lord and Savior</u>. This is simply an acknowledgement of what you already have. It is good to honor God often with our acknowledgement of the wonderful things He has done for us.

Chapter 22

REDEEMED

—

ATTEMPTING TO WRITE ABOUT OUR TIME WITH Redeemed Christian Fellowship is difficult. It involves trying to capture some of the best and worst memories of my life, and I know that my perspective is clouded and imperfect. Not only do I not fully know nor understand what was going on the in the hearts of other people, I also realize that my particular view was warped by the insecurities and misconceptions of my own heart and mind.

I was delighted to be there. Redeemed was everything I'd ever wanted in a church. When we added our names to the personal ministry team, there were already ninety names of people who had been trained to minister to the wounds and bondages of people. There were multiple ministry sessions every week, and most of them were effective. The Sons Program had classes meeting two mornings a week at 6:00 am. There were several classes each session and around a hundred dedicated people showed up at that hour to take them. That only happens when there's life being released. The leadership team, of which we were a part, met regularly to plan and pray, and we did retreats together that involved fun and fellowship as well as training. The home groups were strong, giving individuals and families a secure support group. In services, the worship was great, and the Spirit moved in prophecy and songs of the Lord. Bob's sermons always had plenty of meat to chew on. Several times a year we hosted what we called City Celebrations, where we would have gifted men come in for a series of meetings and invite other churches to take part. Some of the speakers we had then are big names now: Kim Clement,

Bobby Connors, Joseph Arlington, and Mark Chirona among others. The whole concept of Redeemed was really such a special thing to be part of.

I don't know when it began to change. Maybe it was when Bob started accepting more and more invitations to teach in other places. Maybe it had something to do with some of the influences of the apostolic team that he was part of. Maybe we got too wrapped up in getting the new building right. I dare not judge, but at some point we seemed to be hearing the ideas and strategies of other men in other places rather than from God as to what He had for our fellowship. Little by little, the things we had been doing began to lose life, and in some cases they died altogether.

It's really strange, too, because the last hurrah was a big one. Bob and his wife, Laura, had gone to Toronto, Canada, to Airport Vineyard Church, where revival had broken out. They brought it home with them and then took the whole staff and lots of other people from the church back to experience it for ourselves.

It was an amazing time. There were manifestations of the Spirit that we didn't know existed. There were people from Kentucky who would occasionally bark like dogs. After some research, they had found there had been a revival in their part of Kentucky many decades before that had experienced the same phenomenon. Some folks roared like lions, including one of our own quiet, studious types. We knew <u>he</u> didn't make it up. The spirit of laughter would break out, and people wouldn't be able to stop laughing. Why such strange happenings? I don't know. You'll have to ask God. One thing I do know—God doesn't mind offending our intellect in His quest to set us free from our legalistic bondages.

When the message was over, everyone would just stack all the chairs off to the side and start laying hands on people. People received prophecy and insight. Some people went out under the spirit and were down for a long time. That happened to Dick the first night. He was out for so long that, before he came out of it, the whole building had cleared, except for me and the guy in charge of locking up. God did a lot of direct ministry to people in those times.

The whole experience was transferable. We brought it home to Austin with us. People came from all over and stayed to all hours. The power of the Spirit was intoxicating and wonderful, but we missed something in the stewarding of the experience. Or maybe it simply attracted an attack of the enemy that we weren't prepared to fend off.

Within a year Redeemed had come apart at its seams. The leadership team finally removed Bob for what appeared to be good reasons, but without him, there was no head. People scattered. The remnant sold the big building we had remodeled and bought a smaller building in Round Rock, chose a new name, and Redeemed Christian Fellowship was no more.

How could such a thing happen? What causes people to move away from God? Sometimes it's just the business of life. Things come in and God gets crowded out. Sometimes we simply think we know what we're doing. We've been there; we've done that before; we know the ropes. While we go about doing what we know to do, the cloud moves, and we don't even realize that God went on without us. I don't think it's ever intentional. We just forget what, or more accurately Who, produced the life in the first place. It's like Pita, back in Mexico, saying that no matter how many times she had taught a lesson, she needed fresh revelation every time if there was going to be anointing.

That's true of everything in life. We can do all sorts of things in our own ability and understanding. Most people live their lives that way. I dare say most people don't even know what it feels like to partner with God, and to have His life-giving touch on what they do. But those of us who have experienced it are forever ruined for the natural. We will never again be satisfied with life as usual.

We will never be willing to accept the inadequacy we feel when we are limited to our ability.

There is great pain in watching something you love die, but God is always in the business of bringing life out of death.

I WANT TO KNOW MORE – 22
When the Cloud Moves

Exodus 13:21-22 And the LORD went before them by day in a pillar of cloud to lead the way, and by night in a pillar of fire to give them light, so as to go by day and night. 22 He did not take away the pillar of cloud by day or the pillar of fire by night from before the people.

> ➤ Read Numbers 9:15-23. Think about your life, your family, and/or your church. What would it look like to move only when the cloud moves? What do you think that would mean in the communities of your life?

When the Cloud Moves but You Don't
Let's look at it more closely. *Numbers 9:17 Whenever the cloud was taken up from above the tabernacle, after that the children of Israel would journey;*

> ➤ What does it feel like when the cloud is taken up? What sort of things do you experience when you don't sense the presence of God for a period of time?

For me, it might feel like life is getting boring, or I may just feel dry and kind of empty or like I'm in a rut. Sometimes I feel a little lost or like I just don't fit so well. Those feelings don't always mean that the cloud has moved on without me, but sometimes they do. When you experience that sort of thing for a period of time, say weeks or months, it's time to ask God why.

Sometimes I simply haven't realized that I needed to move. I've been so busy doing life as usually that I just didn't realize God wasn't in the mix anymore. At other times, I've discovered an unwillingness to move. That can happen especially in a church when your friends are there, and you've built your life in that place. If the church gets stuck in its tradition, it may just seem like the right thing to do, but God won't stay limited by man's traditions. Oh, He'll bless the good things that happen there, but if you want to be where His life is flowing, you'll have to be willing to move when the cloud moves. That, of course, means that people won't understand and will be hurt, or they'll think you are a traitor.

That sort of thing doesn't have to be a church situation. As you grow in the Lord and learn more about His ways, you may be called to leave one group of friends, who are holding you back, and find others who are going where you are going. Finding that people you care about won't go on with you is painful.

Another hard thing to get past is false expectations. You may have a dream, or even a word from God of something that you are to do. Sometimes we build expectations of doing the thing we know we are to do, and we try to do it in the wrong place or at the wrong time. In those cases, we have to let the dream die and trust God that if it is really from Him, He will resurrect it in the right place at the right time.

Sometimes we have to turn loose of what we are clinging to before God can give us what He wants us to have. An example is the story of the Rich Young Ruler in Luke 18:18-30. We tend to focus on the sacrifice of that story and to think it's about money. I think it's about priorities and positioning. I think it's saying that if you cling to anything in this life that keeps you from following Jesus, you will miss out on the adventure and the treasures that He has for you.

> ➤ Think about the thing you are hanging on to. It could be a possession, a relationship, an institution or a place, a job,

an identity, an idea—It could be almost anything. Is there anything you are hanging on to that keeps you from something you sense God is wanting you to do? Be honest with yourself. What things in your life fall into that category?

➤ Or you may have experienced this sort of thing and have chosen to move on with God. Do you have something you could share with others that might help them in a similar situation?

I don't suggest that you drop things lightly, but I do suggest, if there is something in your life that is keeping you from following Jesus, that you take it to Him and ask for His wisdom and His enablement to deal with it rightly.

When the Cloud Isn't Moving
Numbers 9:17 and in the place where the cloud settled, there the children of Israel would pitch their tents.

Sometimes God leads us to a place that we know isn't our final destination, but we are to stay there until the cloud moves. That might look like a job that you really don't like very well. It could be a place of service that doesn't utilize your real gifts and talents. It may feel like being camped in the desert. Sometimes God takes us to the desert for a season in order to develop our character and staying power. These are essential places if we are to grow strong enough to possess the land He has for us. Be careful that you don't move on and leave God behind. If you skip a vital step in your journey, you won't be properly prepared when you reach your promised land. Like Israel, you might have to go back to the wilderness to learn what you missed.

➤ Have you experienced those desert places of growth? What did you learn there?

➤ Are you in such a place right now? If so, what do you think you are to learn?

Numbers 9:20-21 So it was, when the cloud was above the tabernacle a few days: according to the command of the LORD they would remain encamped, and according to the command of the LORD they would journey.

When the Cloud Disappears

When it seems like God has simply left us without His presence for a while, there could be various reasons. First of all, it only seems like we're alone, because He promised to never leave us nor forsake us (Hebrews 13:5). If He is hiding and not talking, there's probably a reason.

Sometimes it's because we haven't obeyed the last thing He told us to do. If God talks to us and we ignore Him, He will sometimes allow us to go it on our own for a while until we realize we don't do well without Him. We determine the length of that silence by how long it takes us to decide to deal with the thing He is putting His finger on. It's best to surrender early on this kind of thing. The farther you stray, the harder it is to come back, and besides, it's for your own good and your own freedom.

➢ Have you experienced this sort of thing? If so, what could you share that would help someone else who is in that place now?

Other times a short silence doesn't have anything to do with disobedience. There are times when God simply steps back to see what we will do when we feel alone. Will we continue to trust Him in the silence? The right answer here is to do the things that you know are in agreement with His word, His character, and who HE says you are, believing that He never leaves you or forsakes you. Stay in a place of faith in God while He is demonstrating His faith in you.

When the Cloud Moves too Fast

21 So it was, when the cloud remained only from evening until morning: when the cloud was taken up in the morning, then they would journey; whether by day or by night, whenever the cloud was taken up, they would journey.

Are you struggling with keeping up? Sometimes we just grasp what God is doing, and He moves. Before we can really under-stand that move, something else is falling on our plate. We just want to cry out, "Whoa, God, I need a break. Let me rest a little while." It's always best to take enough time to say, "Okay, Lord, where are You in all this? What is mine to do and what isn't?"

One of the enemy's favorite tricks is to send God's people, the ones who are serving Him well, more than they can handle. He disguises his stuff to look like God's stuff. So, when dozens of people are asking for your help, it's hard to tell which ones God is sending and which ones are the black holes the enemy wants you to pour your life into. One clue here is to discern whether or not the people really want help or whether they just want attention. If they won't do the things you guide them to do, have a serious conversation with the Lord (and then with the person). You may need to deal with them like God deals with our disobedience — pull back and let them try it on their own. That may sound hard, but if you can't say no when it's time to say no, and back off when it's time to back off, your burdens will become such that you won't be able to move when the cloud moves. The Lord promises that His yoke is easy and His burden is light (Matthew 11:30), so if you are sinking under your load, you are either taking on things that God didn't give you or it's time to learn to equip others to help you and learn to delegate.

➢ Are you one who becomes overburdened? If so, talk to the Lord about identity issues. Go back through some of the lessons that deal with identity and see if you can figure out what need you are trying to fill by taking on the world's problems. OR consider that you might not be trusting God to do His part. If you have learned something in this area that would help others, record it here.

God deeply desires to partner with you in the journey of your life. The cloud of His presence is available to protect you, guide you, and enable you. The trick is to learn to move when the cloud moves and stop when the cloud stops. Jesus isn't just your Savior; He's your LORD. That means <u>He</u>'s in charge of the journey. He loves your ideas. He wants your input. But He knows what's best, and He's the one in control. When you get the hang of cooperating with that, you'll find there's joy in the journey.

I WANT TO CLIMB HIGHER − 22
Adjusting to the Cloud

Take some time to look back over this lesson. If there is any place that you saw an issue with your relationship with the Lord, or in your journey with the Him, take some time to talk to Him about it. If you are willing, He will help you work it out.

Chapter 23

LIFE OUT OF DEATH

—

FOR US, FOR EVERYONE I THINK, THE DEATH OF
Redeemed was devastating, kind of what I would imagine it would
be like to go through a divorce.

Redeemed broke up in the summer of 1995. We resigned as elders
of the remnant in September. On October 1, a Sunday, we were
reluctantly getting ready to go to church. Back in May the Lord
had given us a clear word that He was taking us out of Redeemed.
We had been in Colorado on vacation at the time. But, while we
knew we would be leaving, we didn't know when. That Sunday
morning in October I suddenly was doubled over with strong
intercession. I had a message in tongues, which Dick interpreted;
and the gist of it was that we were not to return to that church, not
even that day. Suddenly, I was so relieved that I cried. We spent six
months not going to church anywhere. That didn't affect us from
the standpoint of the services themselves. We had fed ourselves
all the time we were in Mexico, but the pain of what we'd lost
in relationship and vision hurt deeply. It hurt most of all because
we felt partly responsible, and yet we didn't know what we could
have done differently.

For me personally, I felt I'd been benched. Even before the final
stages of the church coming apart, I had had to go back to work
in a secular job. I was working for two of my sons-in-law, and
they were very good to me, so that part of it wasn't bad. The thing
that killed me was that I felt God had benched me. I had so much
of my identity tied up in my teaching gift, and when the church

shut down, so did my gift. Even when I had an opportunity to teach, there was no anointing. Teaching without the anointing was much worse than not teaching at all. My identity simply crashed. I couldn't find my worth.

I was deeply grateful for my family, and I found joy in participating in the lives of my grandchildren, but apart from that, I couldn't see much value in my life. I simply clung to Proverbs 3:5-6, which says: *"Trust in the LORD with all your heart, and lean not on your own understanding; in all your ways acknowledge Him, and He shall direct your paths."* Then, in the midst of a normal day at the office, I heard God speak to me. He said, "There are no limits, absolutely no limits, and you are to have no excuses." At the time all I could see where limits, but I wrote it down and put it on the wall in front of my desk.

One day I picked up Madame Guyon's book, *Experiencing the Depths of Jesus Christ* that had meant so much to Dick in Mexico. I would just read a little bit and then do what she said to do, which was to put everything out of my mind and just relax into God's love. Now to be really honest, I didn't have a clue how to do that, but her directions were simple, and I just kept trying until it happened. Slowly, over a period of months, I began to realize that God doesn't love me for what I can do; He loves me because He is love, and because it's His nature to love me. It's taken years for me to realize that He absolutely delights in me. I've had to experience a lot of deliverance of my own to be able to see God the way I see Him now, but at that time I was simply beginning to realize that my worth didn't lie in my gift. God loved me. Period. I didn't have to earn it and there was nothing I could do to lose it. I quit feeling like I was benched because I had done something wrong. I was in a "time out" in order to be set free from the horrible bondage of performance.

Over the years God had frequently given me dreams and internal visions of my life like a house. The room I was most familiar with was the library, which I identified with my teaching gift. I had seen a worship room, a war room, etc. One evening, during this time, I had a vision of "my house" with most of the walls missing. The back was completely gone. The vestibule, stairs, and at least part of the library were there, and maybe part of the worship room above. Jesus and I sat on the stairs, and He held my hand. I didn't know what to do about my house, but I didn't feel concerned. It was enough that He was with me.

I asked Him to tell me about Him. He said, "Let's go for a walk." We went out front, and He showed me the sky, the stars—infinity. He said, "In Me there are no limits—no limit of time, no limit of space, no limit of power, absolutely no limits."

I said, "But I have limits—of flesh, of soul, of standards I've built." He showed me my house. The walls were out—no limits.

Sometimes we have to die in order to live. God uses people. He delights in partnering with people. He puts desires in our hearts, and He loves to see us grow into them and fulfill them. He's all for us in the truest sense. We were created in His image to take dominion over the enemy and to represent the Lord on the earth, but we were never meant to take His place. The final outcome of things depends on God, not on us. When we take ourselves too seriously, when we think the world hinges on our plans and purposes, when we forget that the vision God gave us will only function as we follow His leading and carry it out His way, when we put our hope and trust in our ability instead of God's ability, we have come to a place where we must die to self. Paul said, *"I have been crucified with Christ; it is no long I who live, but Christ lives in me; and the life which I now live in the flesh, I live by the faith of the Son of God, who loved me and gave Himself for me."* (Galatians 2:20)

Sometimes we come to a place where our best isn't good enough and our wisdom isn't wise enough. In the devastation of that place, He takes our hand and assures us that there are no limits. In Him there are no limits.

I WANT TO KNOW MORE – 23
Rest and Possess

The kingdom of God is made up of many paradoxes. We give to receive. We die to live. We're to love our enemies and to fight from a place of peace. I believe walking in the midst of paradox is a matter of position. Ephesians 2:6 says that we are seated with Christ in heavenly places. It doesn't say that we will be seated with Him sometime in the future. It's a now thing.

> ➤ What does it mean to be seated with Christ in heavenly places? How can you be seated there and in your living room at the same time?

John 15:7-8 If you abide in Me, and My words abide in you, you will ask what you desire, and it shall be done for you. 8 By this My Father is glorified, that you bear much fruit; so you will be My disciples.

> ➤ What do you think it means to abide? How do you do that? What would it look like in your life?

Isaiah 26:3 You will keep him in perfect peace, whose mind is stayed on You, because he trusts in You.

Compare that verse with this one: *Romans 8:5-8 For those who live according to the flesh set their minds on the things of the flesh, but those who live according to the Spirit, the things of the Spirit. 6 For to be carnally minded is death, but to be spiritually minded is life and peace. 7 Because the carnal mind is enmity against God; for it is not subject to the law of God, nor indeed can be.*

> ➤ What do these two verses add to your understanding of being seated with Christ in heavenly places?

There's a story in Numbers 13 and 14 about when the Israelites first reached the promised land. They had sent spies into the land to check it out. Read Numbers 13:27-14:24. This story represents two very different ways of looking at the same situation.

➤ What do you learn from this story about the place of abiding?

➤ Read Hebrews 3:7-4:13. This passage is speaking of the incident you just read about in Numbers. How does it use the Old Testament picture to teach us a new covenant truth about rest?

➤ Why were the Israelites unable to possess the land God had given them?

➤ From the Hebrews scripture, what would you say is the land that we are to possess?

➤ How are we to possess it? Be as specific and practical as possible.

In the midst of the paradox of resting and possessing, let's look a couple of possessing passages. God has given us these two passages repeatedly over the years. The first is *Philippians 3:12 Not that I have already attained, or am already perfected; but I press on, that I may lay hold of that for which Christ Jesus has also laid hold of me*. For years I tried to find ways in the natural to possess the things God has said are ours. God has never allowed me to do that, and I have struggled with the fact that He keeps telling us to lay hold, but when I try to lay hold, the thing I expected to happen elusively slips from my grasp.

The second passage is Matthew 11:12 which the Amplified Bible translates this way: *And from the days of John the Baptist until the present time the kingdom of heaven has endured violent assault, and violent men seize it by force [as a precious prize]—a share in the heavenly kingdom is sought for with most ardent zeal and intense exertion.*

Years ago, I did a word study on that verse and wrote in the margin of my Bible: "Energetic people seize the kingdom of heaven—lay hold and won't let go."

I believe in laying hold of the things of God and not letting go. I believe in a bulldog approach to the things of God. But how do I reconcile that to entering into His rest?

Andrew Murray added another piece to my puzzle in his classic book *Abide in Christ*. Andrew Murray: "But we know that all that God bestows needs time to become fully our own; it must be held fast, and appropriated, and assimilated into our inmost being; without this not even Christ's giving can make it our very own, in full experience and enjoyment."[1]

I began to see again that the battleground is in my own soul and my own flesh. <u>The thing I must first lay hold of is a belief system that is in agreement with the Lord.</u> Murray says: "…when Jesus said, 'My *yoke* is easy,' He spoke truth—that surely *the yoke* gives *the rest*, because the moment the soul yields itself to obey, the Lord Himself gives the strength and joy to do it."[2]

> ➤ Consider and react to what Murray has to say in relationship to the passages above.

Isaiah 40:31 But those who wait on the LORD shall renew their strength; they shall mount up with wings like eagles, they shall run and not be weary, they shall walk and not faint.

The word translated *wait*, literally means to bind together expectantly. It means to entwine yourself with the Lord in expectation of His strength (or wisdom, or enabling, or whatever you need) kicking in. What might that look like?

---

[1] Andrew Murray, *Abide in Christ*, (Fort Washington, PA: CLC Publications, 1997), p. 18.

[2] Murray, *Abide in Christ*, p. 19.

1 John 2:24-27 Therefore let that abide in you which you heard from the beginning. If what you heard from the beginning abides in you, you also will abide in the Son and in the Father. 25 And this is the promise that He has promised us—eternal life.

26 These things I have written to you concerning those who try to deceive you. 27 <u>But the anointing which you have received from Him abides in you, and you do not need that anyone teach you; but as the same anointing teaches you concerning all things, and is true, and is not a lie, and just as it has taught you, you will abide in Him</u>. (emphasis mine)

> ➤ The anointing refers to the Holy Spirit's presence working through your life. How does the anointing teach you? Give an example.

> ➤ How does that relate to waiting on the Lord?

> ➤ What part of you is seated with Christ in heavenly places?

> ➤ Put together the pieces of the above passages. What is the position from which you unravel a paradox?

> ➤ How do you abide in that place?

The more we learn to abide in our place and position in Christ, the more we will have His perspective in each and every situation of life. That place is a place of security, even in the midst of a storm or a demonic attack. It's a place of peace. When we can keep the place of peace another wonderful thing happens:

Romans 16:20 And the God of peace will crush Satan under your feet shortly.

If we stay in peace, we are in a position of faith where God kicks in on our behalf.

If there seems to be a lot missing in this chapter, there is. What you don't understand, you will have to press into God for the answers. I'm going to close this chapter with one last quote from Murray:

"Let it be your first care to abide in Him in undivided fervent devotion of heart; when the heart and the life are right, rooted in Christ, knowledge will come in such measure as Christ's own wisdom sees to be fit. And without such abiding in Christ, the knowledge does not really profit but is often most hurtful. The soul then satisfies itself with thoughts, which are but the forms and images of truth, without receiving the truth itself in its power.

"God's way is always to give us first, even though it be but a seed, the thing itself, the life and the power, and then the knowledge. Man seeks the knowledge first, and often alas, never gets beyond it! God gives us Christ, and in Him He hid the treasures of wisdom and knowledge."[1]

I WANT TO CLIMB HIGHER – 23
Abide in Christ

Find a quiet, relaxed place to be alone with the Lord. Verbally receive the truth that you are seated with Him in heavenly places. I have learned over the years that, when God says a thing is mine, it is better to receive than to ask for it. Continuing to ask for what belongs to us shows a lack of faith. It's better to declare you receive it and thank Him for it, even if it hasn't manifested yet.

Consecrate every part of yourself to Him, especially your imagination, and then ask the Lord to give you a real sense of being seated in His presence. You may actually have a vision of your place with Him, you may simply feel that sweet, deep peace of His presence, or you may not experience anything at all. Don't have any particular expectations. The Lord may do something very

---

[1] Murray, *Abide in Christ*, p. 51.

different with you. He doesn't like being put in a box. Whatever happens or doesn't happen, remain relaxed and at peace.

Sometimes we are blessed with experiences in the Lord's presence that are tangible, but when that doesn't happen, He is still present with you, and He will find a way to show you His perspective in His way and His timing. For me, it always works best to simply seek Him and worship Him and focus on Him rather than on my quest for a particular answer. When I allow the focus to shift to my need, that pulls me back into the soul realm rather than the spirit realm.

Remember spiritual things take practice just like things in the natural. You learn to dribble a basketball or play the piano by spending hours at it. With natural things, you practice mechanically until something inside connects, and suddenly you are doing the thing without thinking about it anymore. In learning a second language, it's when you find yourself thinking in it or dreaming in it that you know it's yours. The same is true of moving in the spirit. It's a second language—even more than that, it's a second lifestyle. Be patient and be faithful. Entwine yourself with the Lord, and it will come.

Chapter 24

MISFITS OR FORERUNNERS?

—

THE NEXT FEW YEARS WERE A SUCCESSION OF DOORS—open doors, closed doors, doors that seemed to lead nowhere. We moved from church to church, looking for what we had found in the early days at Redeemed, but of course, that no longer existed in Austin, Texas. We spent a year at what is now Shoreline back before they moved into their new building. It was a good church—good worship, good messages—but simply not called to the depth we craved. Our next season was at Grace Community Church in Pflugerville, where Dick oversaw a third of the church's home groups for several months. But we didn't have any depth of relationship with the people there, and we felt restrictions on the Holy Spirit that we weren't comfortable with. So, we went to New Hope in Round Rock, which was the church that had been birthed out of Redeemed. We had deep relationships there, and I was allowed to lead a Bible study for a group of women. I discovered the teaching anointing was back, but it was different. God was teaching me that, instead of me doing all the teaching, it was much more affective to hand out assignments and make people dig for their own answers. I became more of a facilitator than a teacher, and we learned from one another.

During this time, the Lord was telling Dick we were to train warriors, so we started a couple of different Bible studies with some young couples who seemed to have more potential than most. The second was more effective and lasted longer than the first, but neither group proved to be the warriors God seemed to be calling us to train.

I also led a Bible study (with a lot of help from the churchwomen I'd been leading) for some women from the Williamson County Crisis Center, a place for abused women. The church did a great job of working to meet as many of the physical needs of those women as they could, and I tried hard to meet spiritual needs, but I could see that what we had to offer wasn't nearly enough. The needs were much deeper and more demanding than we had the capacity or understanding to meet.

During that time, I got deeply involved in trying to help one of the women from the Crisis Center who had drug problems. I found a place to help her get clean, but in spite of all my phone calls and research, I couldn't find any place in the Austin area that could help her rehab back into the community. I found no place that was equipped to provide accountability and fellowship for one with that kind of need. The last I heard of her, she was in jail.

I didn't really look at the situation as failure on my part. I think I did pretty much all I was capable of doing at that point. I wasn't equipped to deal with the drug culture. <u>The big thing that happened in me was it made me take a deep look at the superficiality of church in general and my limitations in particular.</u> I know what I'm about to say is a generalization and that there are notable exceptions, but I have come to see the American church as a holding place for the better-behaved part of society. It provides fellowship, standards, protection, and personal growth for many whose lives fall into the fairly-normal category, and that's incredibly important. <u>But when it comes to those whose bondages and wounds can only be dealt with by the supernatural power of Almighty God, the Church, which is supposed to be the carrier of that power, is sorely lacking</u>. Intellect has replaced spiritual depth, and we deal with people by telling them how they should be instead of taking the power of God into the trenches, where people are suffering, to break the bondages and heal the wounds and give them real answers to life's pain.

Frustrated and disillusioned, Dick and I simply pulled back from church for a while. We knew we would never be able to do at New Hope the things God was putting in our heart to do, so once again, we left. We spent a few more months simply asking God for direction. We didn't go church hunting. We knew there wasn't any point in that. If what we were looking for existed, God would have to show us where. We doubted that it existed at all.

Then through one of those unique, Holy Spirit-designed trails of events, we were led to a relatively new church, Hope in the City, which was meeting in Austin High School at the time. Hope in the City (HITC) was definitely the best fit we'd had since Redeemed days.

The main emphasis of Hope in the City was missions. The pastors, Ron and Janine Parrish, had been missionaries in Indonesia, and their hearts, especially Ron's, never left the mission field. It was logical that one of their main emphases was the School of Church Planting.

We could see a lot of ways that we could fit into that type of emphasis. Over our time at HITC, we taught a lot about spiritual warfare, personal ministry, and prayer. The last year or so we were in charge of the prayer ministry and developed prayer shields for each of the ministries and missionary groups in the church. Ron and Janine made a lot of space for us to do things the way we felt led to do them, for which we are very grateful.

After we'd been at HITC for a while, people began to realize we had done a lot of ministry. Some people sought us out on their own. Others were directed to us by leadership. What we found at Hope in the City was a lot different than ministering in Mexico or even at Redeemed. In Mexico one session seemed to resolve the problem most of the time. I don't know if the anointing was different or if we just didn't recognize continuing issues. At Redeemed people were assigned to various people for ministry, so we didn't usually do more than one session with a given person, but many of the people we dealt with at HITC had issues that you didn't just minister to and walk away. They needed family. We collected a number of young women to walk with and disciple, some of whom we still keep in contact with and minister to from time to time.

But there's a cry in Dick's and my hearts for something that we haven't found in church. Way back in Mexico, God gave us *2 Timothy 2:2 And the things that you have heard from me among many witnesses, commit these to faithful men who will be able to teach others also.* God has repeatedly told us we are to train warriors. We believe He wants warriors who are healed, equipped, and released to, not only fight the battle to establish the kingdom of God, but who will be able to heal and equip others to do the same thing. We've taken part in some churches which have done a piece or two of that, but never a church that had a systematic, God-empowered plan to really build the end-time army that is needed. We feel a bit like Abraham who waited for a city whose builder and maker is God. We can't find such a place, and we have neither the energy, nor the knowledge to build it from scratch, so we do what we can do to equip the young warriors who come to us. Perhaps somewhere among them will be one who can pick up the mantle and take what we have learned to whole new levels.

On September 14, 2007, I was walking in the neighborhood and praying. A beautiful red leaf caught my attention. It was lying on the sidewalk in my path. I picked it up and looked around. The leaf was like the leaves on the trees there, but there was not another leaf anywhere that was even beginning to turn color—all as green as could be. I asked God what it meant—a leaf out of season. He said it was a forerunner. That day I wrote in my journal:

"I believe we are being called into a forerunner season. We are to break open some new places—break through current ceilings—so that our children, our children's children, and our spiritual children have a higher ceiling to make their floor."

Then I had a vision of a large platform or base being erected. It seemed to signify that the Lord is taking the time to prepare a large enough platform from which to launch something significant. God has many anointings and mantles that have been opened by someone who was obedient. Once they have been opened, they are there for others to walk in and build upon.

Dick and I are called to be kingdom builders. The platform God is building in or through us has to do with building the kingdom. What is built on or launched from this platform is going to break through current ceilings into some new levels of understanding. Perhaps what is to be launched from our platform will be launched by someone else or by many others. Perhaps we are only building a small piece of the large platform. I suspect that we are forerunners, and that others will fulfill our vision. <u>My prayer is that we can break some current ceilings so that others, maybe you, can go higher. And I pray that you will make our ceiling your floor</u>.

PART 2

INTRODUCTION TO PART 2

THE FIRST PART OF THIS BOOK, FINISHED IN 2007, ended with the understanding that Dick and I were forerunners, but without clarity concerning where to go from there. While we were at Hope in the City, we had led a small group focused on prayer: Warriors on the Wall. When we left the church, Pastors Ron and Janine graciously allowed us to keep our group. I suppose it was a bit reminiscent of our little group in Delphos that we turned into Living Cornerstone, except this time we didn't pull them out of the local church. In all our church hopping since, we've been very careful not to draw anyone out of a local church. Warriors on the Wall, which met in our family room for over ten years, provided us with fellowship and a prayer group. The group members prayed each other through all sorts of crises and challenges, and we prayed for the issues of our city and nation. It truly was a group of warriors, and they were definitely God's gift to us through those years, but they weren't the kingdom builders to be launched from the platform in my vision.

As I write Part 2, the year is 2020, and a lot has happened in the intervening years. I am sensing the Lord saying that it's time to finish the story.

Chapter 25

THE UPPER LEVEL PLATFORM

—

I THOUGHT ABOUT THAT 2007 PLATFORM VISION FROM time to time, and I still have the red leaf pressed in my Bible. Not until February of 2009 did I have another vision. I saw myself on the corner of a large platform, facing out into space. I thought it might be my launching pad. If so, it was very large now. There was a lot of area behind me, more than I could see, but I was right on the edge with wind blowing in my face. At one point, the wind was so strong that I crouched down and put my head between my legs to protect myself.

I could see that my platform was already large, but I wasn't satisfied. The wind seemed to represent adversity. I didn't mind the adversity. It was more like exhilaration. I was looking for something and was very persistent in my watching. One thing was obvious, there was no more room to build onto my platform. I was on the edge.

Then about three months later, as I prayed in the Spirit, I saw a big load of construction material, which seemed to be there to extend my platform. There was, however, nothing material to build it on, so it would have to be built on something spiritual, unseen by the natural eye.

The Lord likes to work that way with me. He gives me a thought here, a vision there, sometimes a dream, or maybe a scripture, until the pieces start to fit together. I think He does this with me, because I have had a hard time trusting what I'm sensing. I want

248

to know it's from God and not my imagination. When I can see the pieces fitting, I know it's God.

My next piece came on June 28, 2009. From my journal:

> Today I saw an escalator extending into the sky. Jesus seemed to be taking me to a different level. Yesterday, I had lain on the floor and travailed. During the travail, I found myself praying for the fear of God. I desired the fear of God in order not to do something or create something that would not reflect what God wants for His kingdom. It was incredibly strong. Today, I seem to be going to another level. Of what? I don't know. It doesn't matter. I'm with Jesus. One thing though—the escalator ride was quite long. This level must be considerably higher than the last one. The place we left from was my 'platform,' which had grown to look like the deck of an aircraft carrier.

Earlier, I had thought an extended platform would have to be built on a spiritual substance. Now, it appeared that the building was not to take place on the same level as the former platform. We had gone up higher.

Shortly after that last vision, I ran into Janie Fountain, an old friend from Redeemed days.

Janie was now the assistant director for a city nonprofit called Austin Bridge Builders Alliance (ABBA). I learned that ABBA connected pastors, business leaders, nonprofits and government representatives for the betterment of the city. They had been instrumental in coordinating churches to help meet the needs of the people who sought refuge in Austin after Hurricane Katrina devastated New Orleans in 2005. Janie had been tasked with organizing prayer across the city, and she was looking for help. She found me.

The day after Janie asked me to come on board at ABBA and help her with the prayer movement, I took it before the Lord. I sensed Jesus give me a hug, and I heard a phrase that had come up a number of times in the past few days: "For such a time as this."

Then I saw myself before the Father. He reminded me of several things all at once:

> ➢ The leaf out of season—we are forerunners
> ➢ The large platform or launching pad and how He was taking me to a new level above it
> ➢ The truckload of building material I saw to build a new... something. I had seen that we would have to go to a new level to build it, and I came to believe this new level represented the kingdom of God. This was way bigger than me, but apparently, I was to have a part.

In fact, the Lord was showing me that this was that for which I had been in training all those years. This was the thing I'd seen for so long and couldn't fit into a local church. This was the opportunity I'd longed for—or was it?

Chapter 26

BECOMING ONE AT ABBA

───

At ABBA, I was not only to be in charge of organizing hubs of prayer throughout the city, but I was also to write for the EMag, a monthly publication ABBA sent online to all its constituents. Janie introduced me to a number of prayer leaders whom I added to the list of leaders I already knew. As I interviewed people for the articles, I met amazing people with great stories. It was going great! Then I found out I had a whole new paradigm to learn.

Upon leaving the Methodist Church in the 80's, Dick and I had little contact with denominational churches. At ABBA most of the connections were evangelical, with another group who attended denominational churches. We spirit-filled folks were a minority. Some people were a bit shocked by the way I took authority over the devil in my prayers. Most of my stories were okay, but the one where the nurse prayed and brought a dead man back to life got heavily edited. I was frustrated by the level of discomfort about showing the raw power of God.

I'd been on staff a couple years when others began to express frustrations about the role of the Holy Spirit, one way or the other. Some staff members insisted upon the guidance of the Holy Spirit in our activities, while others felt the apostolic/prophetic was becoming too prominent and would drive away denominational people.

The Lord was teaching me that His Body is a lot bigger than my little paradigm. God seemed intent upon showing me the value of ALL His Church. I talked to two ministry leaders who both felt what the world needed was for everyone to get on board with what their ministries were doing. It was called to my attention that the Catholics had preserved the Sacred Canon for centuries and built hospitals and schools all over the place. The Baptists had done an outstanding job of getting people saved and of teaching the Bible. Yes, we needed God's power, and yes, we needed spiritual warriors, but perhaps each of us wrongly saw his or her assignment as the most important.

The Lord wouldn't let me sleep that night, so I got up and told Him I'd like to repent for my arrogance, but that He would have to give me real conviction. What He showed me is that it takes all the giftings and callings to truly represent Him. John 17:21 says, "that they all may be one, as You, Father, are in Me, and I in You; that they may be one in Us, that the world may believe that you sent Me." Ephesians 4:15,16 says, "but, speaking the truth in love, may grow up in all things into Him who is the head, Christ, from whom the whole body, joined and knit together by what every joint supplies, according to the effective working by which every part does its share, causes growth of the body for the edifying of itself in love." If we are going to paint a picture that enables the world to see Jesus, it takes all of us, with all of our gifts and callings, joined together in the way the Holy Spirit directs, and relating to one another in love, appreciation, and honor.

Chapter 27

"DO YOU WANT TO WRITE MY STORY?"

⸺

IN JUNE OF 2011, DICK AND I WERE ON VACATION IN Aspen, Colorado. He had driven up to Maroon Lake early one morning to photograph the beauty of the soft morning light on the mountains. I was enjoying a short hike up the ski slope behind the lodge where we were staying. A small stream and spring flowers seemed to draw the Lord's presence in around me. Then, I sensed his voice within me, "Do you want to write my story?"

The question caught me totally off guard. I didn't know what to do with it. "Your story was written a long time ago," I protested. I was really asking, "What on earth are You talking about?" Over the next few weeks, I began to understand that God's story has no end. He is living and moving through his kids all over the planet all the time. What He was asking of me was to capture a piece of the history of His story in and around Austin, Texas.

Austin is a special city. Maybe that's true of any city, and maybe I'm partial, but there's something special about a city, once known as the atheist capital of the world, that becomes known as the worship capital. It's the city where both *Roe v. Wade* started its march to making abortion legal and where March for Jesus was birthed in the Americas. The motto for the University of Texas is, "What starts here, changes the world." For good and evil, that has proved true any number of times.

For this Kansas girl, writing the God-story of Austin was an amazing adventure. I learned about both racial and church histories and interactions. I was led through the devastation of what the Jim Crow laws did to the black community and found my heart bleeding with them for the inequities that still exist. Having spent six years in Mexico, I had learned a lot of the history and culture there. That taught me nothing about the different issues facing first-generation immigrants to the States, those whose first language is English but who don't really feel accepted. Another group includes those whose ancestors had been here long before white settlers pushed their way across the country to settle in Texas. Of course, all Hispanics are not Mexican, and that has its own nuances. Other stories of Austin that fascinated me were those of church leaders of different races making efforts to move past mistrust and misunderstanding.

I spent the better part of two years listening to the stories and perspectives of dozens of people. By the time I got to the final chapter, I summarized my experience this way:

> As I have gathered information for this book, it has taken me on a journey in perspective. I've looked at the city through the eyes of black pastors and Hispanic pastors. I've seen it through the evangelistic mindset, focused intently on how to reach those who haven't met their Savior. I've seen it through the ministry mindset, geared with equal passion toward meeting the physical and emotional needs of people. I've experienced the hearts of worship leaders who have seen that the presence of God changes everything, and intercessors who understand that change takes place in the heavenlies before it can happen on earth. I've been touched by the deep passions of men and women who carry the burden of God for a particular aspect of His kingdom. Each one believes with all his or her heart that if the church would just get behind

what God has given him/her to do, it would change
the world. Who's right? I believe they all are. They
each carry a unique reflection of the heart of Christ
and of His multi-faceted kingdom. It takes all the
parts to even begin to express God's character and
His immense love.[1]

I have considered that book, *Transforming Austin – a God Story,* to
be the greatest achievement of my nine years on the ABBA staff.
It's certainly the most concrete achievement. Personally, though, I
think God wanted to use those experiences to tear down the walls
of my narrow little world...again.

I remember when He showed me the house of my life with the
walls gone and told me there are no limits. I believe ABBA was
another piece of life's puzzle to help me see how big my God is
and how much He loves and values ALL of His creation.

The pieces to that puzzle have been gathered from an airplane
crash in South Dakota, a hog farm in Kansas, a destiny trip to
China, a stint with Youth with a Mission, and the formation of a
spirit-filled church in North Central Kansas. More pieces were
added from six years of sharing life with our Mexican kids, from
absorbing culture in Kenya, from the rise and fall of Redeemed,
and from seeking a place to fit in a succession of churches.

Then there was ABBA, where I had the privilege of examining
life with an impressive variety of church leaders, businessmen and
women, ministry heads, prayer leaders, and just plain folks. They
came in a variety of ethnic backgrounds and church affiliations,
crossing age and gender barriers, with all sorts of purposes and
ideas. Did I fit there? Well, ultimately almost everyone fit in some
way, because ABBA's purpose is to connect the pieces. I helped
start the ABBA prayer team, and still participate in it. I started the

---

[1] Thana Rolph, *Transforming Austin – A God Story,* (Xulon Press, 2014), p.
119.

Pray the Rock team in Round Rock, which continues to this day. I gained a lot of special friends who come in a variety of types and colors. Those relationships didn't just tear down some narrow walls in my thinking; ABBA gave me the opportunity to leverage them to help makes some holes in the walls of exclusion in the city.

I left the ABBA staff when Dick's health indicated I needed to be home to care for him. A beautiful cross section of friends and family gathered to help me celebrate his homegoing, including Cristy. She came, clear from Mexico, to publicly express her gratitude and love for her American papa, who helped her grow from a bitter teenager to a woman of God.

Losing Dick in July of 2018 definitely sent me back to that old question: Who am I now? Then a world pandemic sent us all on a journey of self-discovery..

Chapter 28

WHO AM I NOW?

—

In March of 2020, the world was shut down by the coronavirus. My initial response was anger and defiance. I saw it as the devil, and I was furious that the whole world was yielding to his fear. But since my family was taking a sensible approach, I bowed to the inevitable. My daughter Debra brought me a mask and visited with me outside from an appropriate six feet distance. I told her, and pretty much anyone who wanted to know, that I was not yielding to fear, that nothing could happen to me that God didn't allow, and if He allowed it, He would work it for good. I also made it clear that I'm not afraid to die. When I die, I get to go home and be with Dick.

Just as we thought things were easing up and life would get back to normal, George Floyd was murdered in Minnesota by a white policeman, who clearly did not have to kill him and clearly did it on purpose. It was televised for the whole world to see and hear, including the pleas of the victim and bystanders to let him up. The past couple years—I suppose you could say the past four hundred years—there has been a series of such unjust killings of black people, but this one could not be ignored. There was no doubt or question that it was unwarranted and unjust, and the whole world was witness. Protest marches filled the streets of cities all over the world. In the U.S., there were many white people who joined the blacks in protest. Everyone was outraged.

At this writing, July 2020, we are still in the midst of both the quarantine and the protests-turned-race-riots. Add to that a bitter election atmosphere with the story of it all told by a media which has lost its regard for truth and justice. The whole world is in chaos. Shut mostly in our homes, we have plenty of time to think about it all and to meditate on that age-old question, "Who am I now?"

I've been bumped around with everyone else: absorbing bad reports, missing hugs from people I love, trying to sort truth from out-and-out lies, watching my black friends suffer yet another hit, trying to comprehend why I'm held accountable for crimes I didn't commit because of the color of my skin, and growing in my understanding of how much more my black friends have suffered because of the color of theirs. I've come to some conclusions. They are my conclusions. No one else has to agree with them, but I have a right to draw them, because I have the right to be who I am.

First and foremost, I am a woman whose foundation for life is built upon God. I know Him to be good. I know He loves me, just the way I am, with all my failures and issues. Because He is who He is, I can be who I am, and you have the right to be who you are. None of life's circumstances change who God created us to be. They merely carve the path through our souls to enable us to get there. I cannot change what is going on around me, but I choose to define it through my lens of a good God.

I still believe this pandemic is the devil's idea, but I can see how God is using it to reset lives, sweep away unhealthy systems, force new ways of thinking, expose corruption, and so much more. I choose to step beyond the battles of who's right and who's wrong, which stem from the tree of the knowledge of good and evil. I prefer to go to the tree of life and ask what will bring life.

Who am I? I'm one who is called to be a life-giver. I choose to look for the men and women, boys and girls who carry God's creativity, who look at problems and see challenges they want to take on, who listen for the voice of the Problem Solver in their hearts, and get excited to do something with what they hear. I'm a woman who is called to find and encourage those people.

That's why I wrote this book. Oh, I started it all those years ago, because Dick wanted me to. He kept bugging me to write our story. I wrote that part for my grandchildren, mostly teenagers at the time. I wanted to give them a vision for who they could be and a challenge to make our ceiling their floor. I'm finishing it because God wants me to, because He's got so many kids down here who need to realize they are Christ-carriers, that He wants very much to partner with them to develop amazing things he's deposited within them—the art, music, literature, scientific discoveries, business and medical solutions, and answers to the world's problems. The Lord wants me to tell my story, so He can get it into the hands of people like you. He wants you to see that a very ordinary person can make a difference in the world if that person is willing to team up with an extraordinary God. He wants you to know He loves you, and He sees you as the person He created you to be, full of potential to change the world.

A couple of days ago, I felt a shift in the spirit. I sensed it is time for God's kids to turn loose of the past and to help design the future. It's time for you to take off whatever is lingering from your past that would limit your future. There are no limits! God is putting out a call for His people to bring their dreams and desires to Him and to help Him design the future. What's that look like to you? I finally know who I am. Now the question is, who are you?

APPENDIX

HOW TO RECEIVE SALVATION

Romans 6:23 For the wages of sin is death, but the gift of God is eternal life in Christ Jesus our Lord.

Romans 10:9-11 If you confess with your mouth the Lord Jesus and believe in your heart that God has raised Him from the dead, you will be saved. 10 For with the heart one believes unto righteousness, and with the mouth confession is made unto salvation.

YOU SIMPLY NEED TO CONFESS WITH YOUR MOUTH that Jesus is Lord and believe in your heart that God raised Him from the dead. Then you invite Him to be the Lord of your life. Pray a prayer similar to the one below, but pray your own words in your own way.

"Heavenly Father, I come to You in the name of Jesus. I want Jesus to be Lord of my life. I confess my sins and receive Your forgiveness. I believe in my heart that Jesus is the Son of God and that You raised Him from the dead. Jesus, come into my heart and be Lord of my life. I receive my salvation. I am a child of God. Thank You, Lord. In the name of Jesus. Amen."

Once you pray your prayer, you may be assured that the Lord has received you into His family.

1 John 5:11-12 And this is the testimony: that God has given us eternal life, and this life is in His Son. 12 He who has the Son has life; he who does not have the Son of God does not have life.

2 Corinthians 5:17 Therefore, if anyone is in Christ, he is a new creation; old things have passed away; behold, all things have become new.

THE BAPTISM OF THE
HOLY SPIRIT

—

DESPITE WHAT IT MIGHT HAVE LOOKED LIKE IN THE third chapter of this book, the baptism of the Holy Spirit isn't principally about speaking in tongues. It's about activating the power of God in your life. The Holy Spirit comes to reside within the believer the minute he receives Jesus as his Savior. The Holy Spirit brings life to the human spirit and reopens a connection to the life of God that was closed when Adam and Eve sinned. When we are "born again," it is our human spirits that gain new life. (John 3:3-6) But receiving the life of the Holy Spirit is not the same as receiving the baptism of the Holy Spirit. To be baptized means "to be fully immersed in." So, let's start our study with John the Baptist speaking about baptism.

Matthew 3:11 I indeed baptize you with water unto repentance, but He who is coming after me is mightier than I, whose sandals I am not worthy to carry. He will baptize you with the Holy Spirit and fire.

How many baptisms does John mention?

What is the purpose of water baptism, according to John?

What other baptism is there?

Read John 20:1, 19-23. Verse 1 tells you what day this is. Verse 19 tells you that it is evening of the same day. What does Jesus do in verse 22, and to whom does He do it?

When Jesus blew on the disciples in John 20, it was the first time He had seen them SINCE HE HAD PAID THE PRICE FOR THEIR SIN. It was the first time they could have received the Holy Spirit in them. This was when the disciples received the very life of God into their human spirits. They were born of the Spirit at that moment, but they weren't baptized in the Spirit. He came to dwell in them to be their teacher, comforter, and helper, but they weren't ready to be the witnesses that were to change the world.

John 3:34 says, *"For the one whom God has sent speaks the words of God, for God gives the Spirit without limit."* (from New International Version)

God's purpose for mankind has never changed. He still wants us to take dominion over that serpent and establish His kingdom on earth. God's kingdom was Jesus' main topic. The word kingdom is used over 120 times in the gospels, most of them printed in red. The Lord's Prayer starts with, "Thy kingdom come, Thy will be done, on earth as it is in heaven." The purpose of the cross was to set mankind free from the bondage of sin and of the devil, so that we can once again carry the dominion we were charged with and establish God's authority on earth.

However, it isn't enough to be free; we must also be empowered. Satan didn't lie down and play dead when he was defeated at the cross.

Read Acts 1:1-8. Note verse 3. What day is this in relation to the day in John 20?
Who is Jesus talking to here?

Read verses 4-8. What is the difference between the receiving of the Holy Spirit in John 20, and what He is telling them to wait for here?

What more did Jesus want them to have before they started their ministries?

Pentecost

So, they waited. For ten days they waited. Imagine what that felt like. I don't think they had a clue what to expect. No one had ever received the baptism of the Holy Spirit before. How were they to know when they got it? During their wait, they chose a replacement for Judas, and they waited some more. Then it happened. When the Holy Spirit finally came, there was no doubt about His presence.

Read Acts 2:1-4. Describe the beyond-the-ordinary things that happened when the Holy Spirit finally showed up.

Consider verse 4 carefully. Who was doing the speaking? Who gave them the sounds they were speaking?

This is important simply because it not only shows how the Spirit works with us in speaking in tongues. It shows how He deals with us in all things. We have to do something; then He adds His part. We have to begin making sounds. That's our faith step. As we begin to make sounds that are not a known language, He gives us the words to speak. In almost anything you ask the Holy Spirit to do in your life, you will have to learn this tandem. You have something that you must do in faith; then He responds to your faith to enable you to do the impossible.

When you receive the baptism of the Holy Spirit, those words coming out your mouth will not make sense. They will sound incredibly strange and silly to your mind. Very quickly the enemy will bring thoughts that say, "You're just making that up. That's silly, it doesn't even make sense. You sound like a fool," etc. I assure you, the devil will do everything he can to steal the experience from you, because he is deathly afraid of Christians who are filled with the Holy Spirit and know how to connect to His power. Part of the Holy Spirit's job is to teach us how to overcome those word attacks the enemy uses to control our lives.

The word *tongues* refers to an "unacquired language," speaking a language the person has never learned. There are cases when what is spoken is an existing language, but one the speaker does not know. There are other times when it is a language that the human race does not know. In 1 Corinthians 13:1 it says, "If I speak with the tongues of men and of angels..." The languages or tongues spoken of in Acts 2:4 are made up of words the Holy Spirit is giving to the person to speak. It doesn't usually make any sense at all to the person speaking or to anyone listening if they are trying to understand it with their natural mind. Spiritual things are spiritually discerned.

The ability to speak in tongues is not strange once you grow accustomed to the way the Holy Spirit operates in and through us. It functions from the tree of life. It cannot be comprehended from the tree of the knowledge of good and evil.

Read Acts 8:9-20. Were the people Philip was ministering to born again/saved before Peter and John came to Samaria?

> Had they been water baptized?
> Why did Peter and John go there?

Read Acts 10:44-48. You may want to review Acts 10 to get the background of how God prepared Peter for this incident. You do need to know that Cornelius was a Gentile and that Jews did not believe that Gentiles could be saved. They believed they themselves would be made unclean, out of favor with God, by even entering the house of a Gentile. Review Acts 11 if you don't remember what a stir this incident caused in the early church.

> This is the only account in the Bible of receiving the baptism of the Holy Spirit at the same time they received Jesus. Why do you suppose God did it that way on this occasion?

> Why did the Jews allow the Gentiles to be water baptized?

Acts 18:24-19:6. In chapter 18, what seems to be missing in Apollos' understanding?

In chapter 19, Paul arrives where Apollos has been. Were the people he encountered there believers?

What did they lack?

Did Paul think it was important that they received the baptism of the Holy Spirit?

You can look at the baptism of the Holy Spirit as being part of a Christian's equipment to do the job God calls him to do. A doctor without his equipment is still a doctor, but he needs his stethoscope and many other tools to do his job well. A Christian without the baptism of the Holy Spirit is still a Christian. He will go to heaven when his body dies, but to do the work God calls us to do here on earth, we need to be fully equipped. The power of the Holy Spirit within us is a major part of our equipping.

Mark 16:15-18. Who did Jesus say would speak with new tongues?

Why Speak in Tongues?
So, what does speaking some words you don't understand have to do with power? A lot more than I want to dump on you in one fell swoop. For now, let's just consider two really important things. Praying in tongues enables you to pray when you don't know how to pray, and praying in tongues builds up your inner man to be able to resist temptation and to know and understand things that you can't understand with your natural mind.

Romans 8:26-27 says, "Likewise the Spirit also helps in our weaknesses. For we do not know what we should pray for as we ought, but the Spirit Himself makes intercession for us with groanings which cannot be uttered. 27 Now He who searches the hearts knows what the mind of the Spirit is, because He makes intercession for the saints according to the will of God."

When you know something is wrong (you get that uneasy feeling inside, but you don't know what it is), how do you pray?

What do these verses say about how you pray when you don't know what to pray?

Sometimes when the Holy Spirit prays through us there are literal groanings. More often we simply pray in tongues and trust Him to pray exactly what needs to be prayed. When our middle daughter, Cheri, was in her last year of college, we were still in Kansas. On a weekend in February she was driving home from the university on roads that were patchy with ice. Cheri had received the baptism of the Holy Spirit a little over a year before this day. She went around a corner and sensed an urgency within that said something was wrong, but she didn't know what was wrong, so she began to pray in tongues. She drove a little farther, went around another corner, and hit a patch of ice, which threw the car into a skid — right into the path of an oncoming semi. At the last minute the semi hit the ice and skidded to the other side of the road. Cheri slid into the ditch, and the semi went on. Neither Cheri nor the car was hurt. The Holy Spirit had warned her, and He gave her the means to pray.

One value of our prayer language is the ability to pray according to the Spirit when our minds don't know how to pray.

Look at Jude 20 for another value of tongues: *"But you, beloved, building yourselves up on your most holy faith, praying in the Holy Spirit..."*

What value do you find in this verse for praying in tongues?

One time, while we were Mexico, Dick's mom called and told him that hog futures had taken a plunge. Since hogs were our living at the time, it meant we would lose thousands of dollars. Dick didn't even tell me what she had said. He just left the house and went for a walk. As he walked, he prayed in tongues. As he prayed, his inner focus changed. He quit focusing on the probable loss and started focusing on our God who is more than enough and forever faithful. By the time he got home from the walk, he was fine. I don't remember how God worked out the situation with the hog prices, but of course He did work it out. The big issue is developing the spiritual maturity to turn to God and to the tree of life when life's circumstances overwhelm us, instead of trying to resolve it in our own minds. I have learned to just tell my mind to be quiet. I say, "Mind, if you had the answer, I would already know it, so just be quiet. I need to hear God."

Situations and circumstances are external things. They only affect us if we see them as bigger than our God. So long as our mind is fixed on God's ability, the enemy can't get us to agree with him. If we don't agree with him, he can't use our authority against us. It's all wrapped up in understanding where power comes from and in connecting to the right Source.

Read Luke 11:9-13. Does the Father want to give you the Holy Spirit?
   Are you ready to receive the baptism of the Holy Spirit?

How to Receive the Baptism of the Holy Spirit
God wants to give good gifts to all of His children. It is not necessary to beg or wait or suffer to receive this gift of the Holy Spirit. Any Christian may receive the baptism of the Holy Spirit easily and quickly. The following steps will guide you in what you need to do. Jesus is actually the one who does the baptizing. Just follow the steps and trust Him to do the rest.

1.   Make sure you have received Jesus as your Savior. If you aren't sure you've done that, do it first. Romans 10:9-10 says that if you confess with your mouth the Lord Jesus and believe in your heart that God has raised Him from the dead, you will be saved. For with the heart one believes unto righteousness, and with the mouth confession is

made unto salvation. Simply confess the truth of what you believe about Jesus and ask Him to come into your heart, take away your sin, and be your own Lord and Savior. All you have to do is ask. He is eager to save you.

2. Jesus is the baptizer (Matthew 3:11), and He wants to baptize you. He said Himself in Luke 11 that the Father always wants to give good gifts to His children. It is your job to receive what He wants to give you.

3. You are going to pray and ask Jesus to baptize you with the Holy Spirit and with the evidence of speaking in tongues. It isn't difficult. It is very easy. After you ask, you only need to take a step of faith and start to speak, but not in a language you know. You need to start making sounds. That is a faith step. Then the Holy Spirit will give you the words. Sometimes people "hear" strange words inside. They only need to speak them. Sometimes their tongue will feel thick or there will be a stirring in their stomach area. But more often none of these things happen, and a person can still receive by starting to make sounds by faith. It's important that you understand that you don't need to try to think what to say. These words don't come from the mind, but from the Spirit, so you can't "think" them up.

4. If you are ready, pray something like this: "Heavenly Father, Jesus is my Savior and my Lord. Now I want Him to baptize me in the Holy Spirit. I want to receive the power of the Holy Spirit and the ability to pray in tongues. Fill me, Lord. I receive all you have for me in the name of Jesus. Amen."

5. Now simply relax, think about anything that makes you feel happy and relaxed, and simply begin to let audible sounds come out of your mouth. It doesn't matter that you don't know what to say. Remember, this isn't a mind

function; it's a faith function. Like the Nike commercial, it's time to just do it.

6. You may receive many words or just a few words. If you only receive a few, use them just as if you had thousands. You will probably receive more in time. But either way, just practice and use your prayer language, and the Holy Spirit will begin to teach you new things and strengthen your inner person.

7. A test that helps people have assurance of what they have is this: while praying in tongues, count to ten in your mind at the same time. Then, with no pauses in either counting or talking, try saying your name and address out loud. You will find that to talk in a known language, you have to stop counting because both the counting and the talking are mind functions. Now, count in your mind and talk in tongues out loud at the same time. You will find you can do it because the tongue comes from the spirit. It is not a mind function. You can actually read or think about other things and pray in tongues at the same time.

8. Usually the above steps will be all that are necessary to receive the baptism of the Holy Spirit. There are a few people who have a problem receiving because of bad religious teaching or blockages due to bitterness or unconfessed sin in their lives. If you do have a problem receiving, find a spirit-filled church and ask for help.

OUR CONFESSION

—

I AM THE RIGHTEOUSNESS OF GOD, FOR JESUS IS MY righteousness, my wisdom, my sanctification, and my redemption. I have the life of God in me. As He is, so am I in the world. The Nature of God is in me. The wisdom of God is in me. I am transformed by the renewing of my mind. God is renewing my mind as the Holy Spirit guides me to all truth.

I am under the counseling eye of God. He instructs me in the way I should go. I hear and know His voice because He is my Shepherd. I have His guard upon my mind, my heart, my mouth, my ears, my thoughts, and my footsteps. His word is a light to my feet. I choose to obey Him in all things.

Sin shall not have dominion over me. I have authority over all the power of the enemy. In all things I am more than a conqueror through Jesus, for I am a fellow heir with Him, seated with Him at the right hand of God to reign over every rule and authority and power and dominion. The works that He did, I do also because He went to the Father. In Jesus' name I put on the full armor of God. I claim the belt of truth to guard me from lies and deception. I put on the breastplate of righteousness to protect me from accusations and condemnation. I wear shoes of peace to guard against inner turmoil, persecution, and against any unloving reactions on my part. I claim the shield of faith to stand against unbelief, doubt, and fear, the helmet of salvation to protect my mind and all my thinking, and the sword of the Spirit to counter all attacks of the enemy. I claim the blood of Jesus as a protective covering for myself and for my family. In the name of Jesus, I bind all the forces of darkness and all the strategies, tricks, and deceits of the enemy from myself, my family, my possessions, my ministry, and all that I put my hand to this day. I ask the Lord to instruct His angels to watch over me, my family, and my possessions to eliminate problems before they have a chance to happen.

I claim the gifts of the Spirit to be manifested in my life whenever they are needed according to 1 Corinthians 12, and the power of the Holy Spirit to back up my authority in Jesus.

The love with which God loved Jesus is in me. Jesus is working through me to be more open and available to love others as He loved me.

I have perfect health because Jesus carried all my sickness and disease to the cross. By His stripes I am healed. My organs function properly; all my systems work properly; my bones, muscles, and tissues are strong and healthy. His words are life and health to my whole body.

I am a cheerful giver, and God makes all grace abound to me, so that I have all I need to abound in every good work. I am rich in every way so I can be generous on every occasion, and my generosity results in thanksgiving to God. God supplies my every need according to His riches in glory in Christ Jesus, exceedingly, abundantly beyond all that I ask or think, according to His power working within me.

The Lord protects, guides and blesses my children. He pours out His Spirit on my offspring and His blessings on my descendants. My children are taught of the Lord, and great is the peace of my children.

I operate in unity and peace with my brothers and sisters in Christ, because Jesus gave me His peace and His love and His wisdom. I am honest, open, transparent and loving.

2 Corinthians 5:21	Psalm 119:105	Ephesians 6:10-17	1 Peter 2:24
1 Corinthians 1:30	Romans 6:14	Revelation 12:11	Proverbs 4:20-23
2 Corinthians 4:10	Luke 10:19	Matthew 18:18	2 Corinthians 9:7-12
1 John 4:17	Romans 8:37	Psalm 91:11	Philippians 4:19
Romans 12:2	Romans 8:17	1 Corinthians 12:1-11	Ephesians 3:20
Psalm 32:8	Ephesians 2:6	Ephesians 3:20	Matthew 18:10
John 10:27	Ephesians 1:20, 21	John 17:26	Isaiah 44:3
Philippians 4:7	John 14:12	Matthew 8:17	Isaiah 54:3

BREAKING BONDAGES

—

Judgments

A JUDGMENT CAN RANGE FROM MAKING A LEGAL DECIsion to forming an opinion. Any time we form an opinion about anyone, ourselves or someone else, we are judging that person in our mind. When we speak that opinion, we are releasing the judgment.

What is the basis you usually use for forming an opinion of someone else, especially someone you don't know very well?

Now think about this, how do you judge your own actions?

We tend to judge other people by what we see them do or hear them say—in other words, by what our senses perceive. However, we judge ourselves by the intent of our heart. If our intentions were good, but the results were not, we give ourselves a break because of our motives, and we expect others to understand our intentions as well.

What problems do you see in the way we usually form opinions and judgments?

1 Samuel 16:7 But the LORD said to Samuel, "Do not look at his appearance or at the height of his stature, because I have refused him. For the LORD does not see as man sees; for man looks at the outward appearance, but the LORD looks at the heart."

According to the above verse, how does God make judgments?

There is a type of judgment based on what we perceive to be right and wrong. That basis of judgment comes from the tree of the knowledge of good and evil. The Bible says that type of judgment is wrong. But there is another type of judgment.

John 7:24 Do not judge according to appearance, but judge with righteous judgment."

The question is, what is righteous judgment?

John 5:30 I can of Myself do nothing. As I hear, I judge; and My judgment is righteous, because I do not seek My own will but the will of the Father who sent Me.

From this verse and the 1 Samuel verse, how would you define "righteous judgment"?

Obviously, there are times we have to make judgments about who we are going to trust, etc. We are going to have to make many of those calls without being able to discern God's under-standing in the matter. BUT YOU DON'T HAVE TO SPEAK YOUR JUDGMENT. There are times when people are in posi-tions of authority that they do have to speak the judgments. That's not the lesson we are working on. This lesson is not about how to make judgments. It's about learning to keep your mouth shut so you won't bring judgment on yourself. There is a Biblical law of sowing and reaping that does apply to us.

Galatians 6:7 Do not be deceived: God cannot be mocked. A man reaps what he sows. NIV

Matthew 7:1-2 "Do not judge, or you too will be judged. For in the same way you judge others, you will be judged, and with the measure you use, it will be measured to you." NIV

Luke 6:37-38 "Do not judge, and you will not be judged. Do not condemn, and you will not be condemned. Forgive, and you will be forgiven. Give, and it will be given to you. A good measure, pressed down, shaken together and running over, will be poured into your lap. For with the measure you use, it will be measured to you." NIV

What do these verses say to you about the results of judging other people?

The sowing and reaping principle says that any seed is going to bear fruit after its kind. If we sow beans, they will produce beans. If we sow love, it will produce love. If we sow judgment, we remove the protection from that area of our lives. Therefore, if the iniquity we are judging is in our heart, there is no grace to stop it or help us hold it back. A child who judges his father for a drinking problem is likely to have that iniquity in his heart, because iniquities pass from generation to generation. He judges his father and removes whatever grace would protect him in that area of his life. The iniquity grows, the temptation comes, and he becomes what he judged.

If we want to stop that crop from bearing fruit, we have to plow up the old crop. God wants us to do that in our hearts. He wants us to plow up the judgments we have made against others and prepare the soil of our hearts for a better kind of crop. We need to break the sowing and reaping principle by breaking the judgments.

How to break judgments:
1. Write down on a piece of paper anyone whom you have judged, especially those who currently have or who have had authority over you. Remember, your opinion may have been accurate ("My dad's an alcoholic."). The issue is your right to release judgment. Ask the Holy Spirit to bring to mind any wrong judgments you have made.

2. Pray through your list. Confess each judgment as sin. "Judging my dad was sin. He was not within my sphere

of authority. I didn't know the intent of his heart or what bondages existed in his life, but I judged him."

3. Confess all bitterness and unforgiveness that brought about the judgment as sin.

4. Confess as sin trying to take God's place as judge.

5. Receive forgiveness. "Lord, I receive Your forgiveness in accordance to 1 John 1:9, and I receive your cleansing from all unrighteousness."

6. Forgive and release the people you have judged. This means to release them from your expectations. Your hope is in the Lord, not in them.

7. Address the enemy and take back any ground given to him because of the above sins. "Devil, I take back all the ground I gave you by judging other people and through bitterness and unforgiveness. You no longer have a place to work in me due to judgment."

8. Break the sowing and reaping principle. Declare that because of repentance, you will not reap what you have sown. Ask for God's grace and mercy.

9. Pray concerning any restitution that the Lord would have you make in the situation, such as asking the person's forgiveness for having judged him.

10. Pray blessings upon the person you judged.

Vows

Vows are closely related to judgments. Where you find a vow, there will also be a judgment. The difference is that judgments are usually turned outward. They judge other people. A vow is turned inward. It is a determination of the heart concerning one's self. A vow is actually saying, "I don't want anyone, not even God, to control this part of my life. I am going to take control of this part myself so that I can guard and protect it." Vows are made because of what someone else has done to us, and that is why they are connected to judgments.

For example, a young girl is mistreated sexually. She not only places her judgment on the person who abused her, but she also vows in her heart that no man is ever going to touch her in a sexual manner again.

What has she done? She has made a determination in her heart. Her purpose was to protect herself from any further hurt and degradation, but in actuality she has taken the authority of that area of her life and removed it from God's authority and, therefore, from His covering. Perhaps she is not even saved at the time she makes the declaration within herself. Perhaps she does not tell anyone else of her determination, and perhaps she forgets she ever made it. Nevertheless, the thing is programmed into her life. She has set the course of her soul and given direction to her mind, will, and emotions in that area of her life. Later she marries, and discovers that she cannot give herself to her husband as she desires to. She just can't release her affections to him fully, especially not physically. Why? Because she has a sexual block programmed into her soul.

Perhaps she is now a Christian and she prays for God's help, but until she breaks that vow and gives that part of her life to God to control, He won't intervene.

Pray and ask the Lord to reveal to you any areas of your life that might be blocked by a vow. If you have any areas where your heart seems to be hardened and you don't know why, look for a vow. If you have any areas where the blockages just won't move, even though you have repented for sin in that area, look for a vow. Wherever you find a vow you will probably also find a judgment. A boy who declares within, "I will never be mean like my father," has not only made a vow, he has also judged his father. You know how to break the judgments, so let's look at how to break the vows.

Steps to breaking a vow:
1. Recognize the vow. Ask the Holy Spirit to reveal to you any vows you have made. Ask Him to bring to your memory any situations that might have led to a vow. You might look over the judgments you wrote down for the last assignment to see if there might have been any vows attached.

2. Confess as sin any sinful reactions that caused you to make the vow—hate, resentment, vengeance, bitterness, fear, shame, etc. Also confess your sin of taking that area of your life out of God's hands by making an unrighteous vow.

3. Repent for what you confessed as sin.

4. Renounce the vow. Take the authority in the name of Jesus to renounce the vow and take back the ground that you gave the enemy through the vow.

5. Give that area of your life to the lordship of Jesus. Put it under the blood and declare Him to be Lord. Determine to do His will.

6. Persevere. Place the word of God, which speaks God's authority concerning the subject of the vow, in your heart. Stand firm on what that word says and in keeping your heart fixed on God.

Not all vows are wrong. There are vows that we make to God and before God which are good vows. Marriage vows are good vows. In this lesson we are only looking for those vows that have taken areas of your life out of God's control. For ministry purposes we want to break all professions of the heart that cut off the glory of God and His working in your life. We want you free from every bondage of the soul in order that you might manifest the life of God to the fullest extent possible.

Offenses

Offenses are closely related to wounds. They can intensify wounds or, if we are wise, they can be used as rays of illumination to point us to old wounds that need to be healed. They can show us where there are still lies concerning identity that need to be dealt with. If our identity is secure in the area of the offense, we won't be offended. It will just wash off. But where identity is not secure, an offense is a stumbling block which creates a trap in people's lives.

One word for offense in the Bible literally means the bait that hangs over a pit to trap animals. We don't have to take the bait, but many times we don't realize it is bait. We have to learn to see how the enemy baits a trap for us.

Usually the reason a person falls over an offense is that he doesn't see it. Something in his life has caused a blind spot. Someone does something that offends him, and all he can see is what the other person did. He can't see that there is something in his own life that causes him to react the way he does.

In Matthew 7, immediately following the verses on judgment, we find an interesting directive:

Matt 7:3-5 And why do you look at the speck in your brother's eye, but do not consider the plank in your own eye? Or how can you say to your brother, 'Let me remove the speck from your eye'; and look, a plank is in your own eye? Hypocrite! First remove the plank from your own eye, and then you will see clearly to remove the speck out of your brother's eye.

What do you think the speck in the brother's eye represents?

Is that speck real (does it exist)? Does it seem to be Jesus' main concern?

Why do you think He is more concerned with the plank?

What does the plank represent?

If we take offense at something someone says or does to us, it is because that circumstance hits something in us that needs to be corrected, our "plank" so to speak. That doesn't mean that what the other person did was right. No, the speck is real, but that speck is the other person's problem. If we allow it to offend us, that shows we have a problem. If we are offended, that indicates we have an identity problem in that area of our lives. We need to ask God to reveal the lie concerning our identity.

Think about the things that offend you. Pick one thing that usually causes offense. What is the lie that you are receiving that causes you to be offended?

How to handle an offense
1. Don't react.
Our natural reaction to any offense is to defend ourselves. We need to learn not to react. If we react before we've had a chance to process it with God, we will say or do something we will regret. So just keep your mouth shut, or say you'll pray about it, or do whatever you have to do to get past the situation without intensifying it.

2. Take it to God with humility.
    a. Pour out your heart. Take the emotion to Him. Don't hold anything back. When you've poured out the hurt or anger, ask Him for revelation.

    b. Be open to truth. Maybe there is something that needs to change in you. If you were offended by the truth, ask God to help you deal with that area of your life.

    c. If the offender was wrong and out of line, forgive him and let it go. In that case it's his problem and not yours. Just release it.

d. Be obedient to do whatever God tells you to do. Pride is the greatest hindrance to handling offenses rightly. You may need to go back and work it out with the offender. If you feel God wants you to do that, get His perspective on how it's to be done, then do it. Don't let your pride keep you from receiving a blessing.

3. Be aware of what offends you.

If you are offended, whether the other person is right or totally wrong, the fact that you feel offended indicates there is something to be dealt with in you. Don't just blame the other person, and don't simply ignore the situation. Ask God to reveal truth as to why that sort of thing offends you. Ask Him to reveal and remove the plank.

Learning to handle offenses properly goes a long way in avoiding wounds that take root and build bitterness and lies into our lives.

SPIRITUAL WARFARE

—

I. Part One – Know your position

If you are going to deal with the devil, you need to know some fundamental things or you won't have the strength to stand when the battle is raging.

1. **You must know the power and authority of the Lord you represent.**

   Matthew 28:18-20 And Jesus came and spoke to them, saying, "All authority has been given to Me in heaven and on earth. 19 Go therefore and make disciples of all the nations, baptizing them in the name of the Father and of the Son and of the Holy Spirit, 20 teaching them to observe all things that I have commanded you; and lo, I am with you always, even to the end of the age." Amen.

   Mark 16:15-18 And He said to them, "Go into all the world and preach the gospel to every creature. 16 He who believes and is baptized will be saved; but he who does not believe will be condemned. 17 And these signs will follow those who believe: In My name they will cast out demons; they will speak with new tongues; 18 they will take up serpents; and if they drink anything deadly, it will by no means hurt them; they will lay hands on the sick, and they will recover."

This is the <u>potential</u> for every believer. There is a potential warrior in every believer just as there is a potential man in every baby boy; however, boys will grow to be men whether they work at it or not. You have to be intentional and dedicated to become a warrior.

Philippians 2:8-11 And being found in appearance as a man, He humbled Himself and became obedient to the point of death, even the death of the cross. 9 Therefore God also has highly exalted Him and given Him the name which is above every name, 10 that at the name of Jesus every knee should bow, of those in heaven, and of those on earth, and of those under the earth, 11 and that every tongue should confess that Jesus Christ is Lord, to the glory of God the Father.

Jesus defeated the devil.

Colossians 2:14-15 Having disarmed principalities and powers, He made a public spectacle of them, triumphing over them in it.

When you represent Jesus, you have the same authority He has against demonic forces. They have to obey you. **Represent** is the key word. You don't confront the devil in the name of your pastor or in your name. You only confront him in the name of Jesus. You have been given the power of attorney to use that name, but you must remember that the one with the power of attorney REPRESENTS the one who gave him the authority. He is bound to do the will of the person he represents—not his own ideas and purposes. So, you represent the One with all power and authority.

2. The amount of His authority you carry will depend on (at least) 4 things.

    a.   **The first thing is the amount of His life that can be manifested through you.**

        1. How well do you know the Master you represent?

- Do you know that He not only saved you but that He has taken responsibility for every area of your life? Have you learned to depend on Him or are you still trying to "earn your own way"?

- You will need to operate from the position of one representing the VICTOR. Never lose sight of His authority and His victory.

- Never get sidetracked into depending on your ability. <u>You</u> are nothing more than a humble servant, and you better remember that...BUT you serve the God of all the universe!

- If you don't have a strong relationship with Jesus, you don't want to get involved in deliverance—but if you don't have a strong relationship with Jesus, you don't want to go to the mission field either.

        2. Are you living your life in obedience to Him?

A private doesn't decide which hill to take.

    b.   **The second is this: are you free from the enemy's bondages, lies and deceptions?**

There is a section called "Breaking Bondages" in the Appendix. It has specific guidelines to get free from your own bondages and to help others get free from theirs. The enemy knows your weaknesses. If you don't deal with them, he'll use them against you. Don't go into battle with holes in your armor.

c.   Number three is the area of responsibility He has given you.

You have authority commensurate to the responsibility God has given you.

Who or what are you responsible for?

- Your personal life.

    Where is your obedience level in the common ordinary things of life?

- Your children.

    Are you seeking God for His will and purposes for your children?

    Are you exercising authority to keep the devil out of their lives AND are you training them to do the same for themselves?

- Your job.

    Do you look to God for His purposes in and through the work you do?

    Do you take authority in the spirit realm concerning situations that affect your workplace?

- Other areas such as organization or church responsibility.

    Are you seeking God for how to minister to the needs of the people in your group?

    Are you doing spiritual warfare for them in your personal times with God?

    Are you training your people to war for themselves (if you're the leader)?

You need to know your authority level. The demons know your authority level. The more you are aware of what the Father is doing, and the more submitted you are to Jesus, the more authority you will carry. And you will move from level to level as you handle authority well on the current level.

d.   And finally, your authority will depend on how you carry the authority you are given.

> Your stance before the devil is very different from your stance before God.
>
> Understand the devil is already defeated.
>
> You are there to enforce the defeat, to call his bluff, to expose his lies, and to command him to go.
>
> You speak to him directly IN THE NAME OF JESUS.

In a nutshell: Jesus defeated the devil on the cross. The devil has no "legal" grounds against Christians AS LONG AS they maintain their place under the blood of Jesus. The problem is that many times demons gained entrance before the person became a Christian, even before he was born. These entry points, or roots, need to be dealt with to make deliverance easier and permanent.

Dealing with the devil is a legal issue before it's a power issue. "Adversary" is a legal term. There are things that give the enemy legal rights to a person and to a territory. We want you to know how to prevent him from gaining legal right to harass you, and later, in the deliverance session, we will talk about taking away his legal right to the people to whom you are ministering. You need to take away his legal right before you exercise the authority and demand him to leave. The bondage section covers a lot of areas where legal ground needs to be taken back to make deliverance much easier. Also, taking away the roots where the bondage came in goes a long way to keep it from coming back. Once his legal right is gone, you still have to take authority and demand him to go. Otherwise he won't, because even though he demands we follow the legal letter, he won't unless he is forced to. To live free, we need to come into agreement with what Jesus did and keep that before the devil's face.

Part Two – Understanding territory and setting your personal shield of protection.

The enemy is territorial. Many times, he has been given authority in areas. Areas where the predominant religion is something other than Christianity will have ruling spirits that oppose Christians. Areas of a city where sin abounds or areas where there has been great injustice done have open doors for demonic activity. Spiritual forces launched against you can be real and deeply entrenched. Even in dark places, Jesus is still Lord. He is still more powerful. He is still greater than all the forces of hell. You should be neither intimidated nor presumptuous. Just stay close to Him and do what He shows you to do. There are ways to set shields of protection around yourself and your family in your home and in the places where you work or study. Again, let's look at where He is giving you authority.

1. **In your home—guard your home**
    An ambassador to any nation has diplomatic immunity on his own grounds. You are ambassadors for Jesus. Your home has diplomatic immunity from the spiritual government over your area. Guard it. Don't give the enemy access.

    a. Be careful about objects of art that you bring into your home, especially those created in foreign cultures. Some carry curses or spiritual significance that is geared to give the enemy access. A good book to read on making sure your home is spiritually clean is *Protecting Your Home from Spiritual Darkness* by Chuck Pierce and Rebecca Wagner Sytsema.

    b. Be careful about people you allow to stay in your home, especially for extended periods of time. Make sure God approves and is saying yes before you bring any person into your home to dwell there. Compassion without wisdom and direction from God can give the enemy open access to your family.

The same is true of your ministry. Be aware that the enemy can and will send "plants" to hinder and disrupt. While you don't want to be overly suspicious, you do want to keep in tune with your spirit concerning the people you are dealing with. If you sense an uneasy feeling deep within about a person, spend some time seeking God as to the reason. Then be obedient to what He shows you. Don't allow logic to overrule your spirit.

c. Learn to set hedges and be faithful in setting protective hedges.
    A resource that you all should have and should take with you and use regularly is *God's Shield of Protection* by Mike Servello. The material below is taken from this book, but he amplifies it so much more.[1]

•   Personalize and pray the 91st Psalm over yourself, your family, and your team.

•   Declare the blood of Jesus as a protective shield over you and your family, team, ministry, etc. (Col. 1:14; Rev. 1:5; Eph. 1:7; Rev. 12:11)

•   Shield of intimacy of relationship with God the Father. In Genesis 15:1 God said to Abraham, "I am your shield, your exceedingly great reward." Galatians 3:29 says that if we belong to Christ then we are Abraham's seed, and heirs according to the promise. So whatever God promised Abraham also belongs to us if we are in Christ. You can pray, "Lord, I am Abraham's seed in Christ. You're my shield and my very great reward."

Psalm 3:3 says, "You, O Lord, are a shield around me..."

---

[1] Mike Servello, *God's Shield of Protection,* (DS Lisi, 2009).

- Pray for God's Angels to protect you, and believe that they are protecting you. Psalm 34:7 says, "The angel of the Lord encamps all around those who fear Him, and delivers them." Other promises of angels: Heb. 1:14; Ex. 23:20; Psalm 91:11.

- Receive and put on the full armor of God from Ephesians 6.

- Faith and truth are strong weapons against the enemy. 1 John 5:4 says, *"this is the victory that has overcome the world – our faith."* Romans 10:17, *"Faith comes by hearing, and hearing by the word of God."* The enemy's chief weapons are lies and deception. If you look at a bad circumstance and choose to believe it and confess it, he will make it worse. If you look at a bad circumstance and choose to believe what God says about it, God will transform it into something good. You choose where your eyes look, and you choose what your mouth speaks. You choose what you agree with.

- The last shield we are going to mention is integrity. Every other shield only works fully as we walk in integrity with a heart fully committed to the Lord. Sin puts a big target on us for the enemy to attack. Keep short accounts. When you mess up, confess it and repent. (See Pr. 28:1; James 4:7; Ps. 25:19-21; Ps. 84:11)

- We build these hedges through declaring the promises and believing that God is faithful to His word.

2. **In your neighborhood, job—areas that you share on a regular basis with unbelievers.**

- Proclaim truth wherever you go. Truth of who God is, what God says, and who you are in Him helps weaken the forces of darkness around you. As you move out onto turf that you are trying to possess for the kingdom, you can take your personal protection with you. If you want to begin trying to break down hindrances to the gospel in neighborhoods, etc., it is good to partner with other believers. Two good books that have useful strategies are *Taking Our Cities for God* by John Dawson and *Possessing the Gates of the Enemy* by Cindy Jacobs.

- The thing to remember is that you are always dealing with two worlds, a natural world where your senses can relate what is going on, and a spiritual world that must be revealed by the Spirit of God through your spirit (not your mind). Of the two worlds, the spiritual one is the one that is the more real and that controls the natural. Many times, we try to fight our battles in the wrong realm.

- If you are part of a ministry or a team of some sort, protect it. Pray the above hedges around your team members also, and realize that team discord needs to be dealt with first and foremost in the spirit realm. If all team members will submit to the Holy Spirit and pray things through, you'll get to the real issues. The enemy will attack your team relationships. If he can divide, he can conquer.

3. Territorial spirits govern over regions and areas of influence.

- There are levels of hierarchy in the devil's kingdom. The spirits over regions are governmental authorities. It takes governmental authority to remove or replace governmental authority. This is the job of mature apostolic networks. Don't try to take out territorial spirits. You may have that sort of anointing someday, but in the meantime:

- Guard yourself, your home, your family and your team ferociously. Set borders. Establish a shield of protection and be faithful in maintaining it. Don't give an inch to the enemy on your turf.

- Where you are infiltrating into the enemy's turf, declare truth and walk in love and righteousness. Trust God to cover you personally and to extend His kingdom through you. Don't try to make anything happen that God isn't doing and inviting you to join Him in doing, but be bold to do what you know He's wanting to do through you.

- STAY CLOSE TO GOD. Don't let any good thing steal from your time with God. Spend quality time with HIM every day. Don't allow the tyranny of the urgent.

STANDING ON THE
WORD OF GOD

—

Authority Over Temptation and the Devil

Faith

Family

Fear/worry

Finances

Forgiveness

Friendship

Healing

Holy Spirit

Joy

Love

Mercy

Obedience

Patience

Peace

Praise & Worship

Prayer

Protection

Righteousness

Salvation

Self-Control

Strength

AUTHORITY OVER TEMPTATION AND OVER THE DEVIL

—

GENESIS 1:26-28 THEN GOD SAID, "LET US MAKE man in Our image, according to Our likeness; let them have dominion over the fish of the sea, over the birds of the air, and over the cattle, over all the earth and over every creeping thing that creeps on the earth." 27 So God created man in His own image; in the image of God He created him; male and female He created them. 28 Then God blessed them, and God said to them, "Be fruitful and multiply; fill the earth and subdue it; have dominion over the fish of the sea, over the birds of the air, and over every living thing that moves on the earth."

Matthew 28:18-20 And Jesus came and spoke to them, saying, "All authority has been given to Me in heaven and on earth. 19 Go therefore and make disciples of all the nations, baptizing them in the name of the Father and of the Son and of the Holy Spirit, 20 teaching them to observe all things that I have commanded you; and lo, I am with you always, even to the end of the age." Amen.

Mark 16:15-18 And He said to them, "Go into all the world and preach the gospel to every creature. 16 He who believes and is baptized will be saved; but he who does not believe will be condemned. 17 And these signs will follow those who believe: In My name they will cast out demons; they will speak with new tongues; 18 they will take up serpents; and if they drink anything deadly, it will by no means hurt them; they will lay hands on the sick, and they will recover."

Luke 10:19 Behold, I give you the authority to trample on serpents and scorpions, and over all the power of the enemy, and nothing shall by any means hurt you.

Romans 8:37-39 Yet in all these things we are more than conquerors through Him who loved us. 38 For I am persuaded that neither death nor life, nor angels nor principalities nor powers, nor things present nor things to come, 39 nor height nor depth, nor any other created thing, shall be able to separate us from the love of God which is in Christ Jesus our Lord.

2 Corinthians 2:14 Now thanks be to God who always leads us in triumph in Christ, and through us diffuses the fragrance of His knowledge in every place.

2 Corinthians 10:3-6 For though we walk in the flesh, we do not war according to the flesh. 4 For the weapons of our warfare are not carnal but mighty in God for pulling down strongholds, 5 casting down arguments and every high thing that exalts itself against the knowledge of God, bringing every thought into captivity to the obedience of Christ, 6 and being ready to punish all disobedience when your obedience is fulfilled.

Ephesians 1:19-23 and what is the exceeding greatness of His power toward us who believe, according to the working of His mighty power 20 which He worked in Christ when He raised Him from the dead and seated Him at His right hand in the heavenly places, 21 far above all principality and power and might and dominion, and every name that is named, not only in this age but also in that which is to come. 22 And He put all things under His feet, and gave Him to be head over all things to the church, 23 which is His body, the fullness of Him who fills all in all.

Ephesians 6:10-18 Finally, my brethren, be strong in the Lord and in the power of His might. 11 Put on the whole armor of God, that you may be able to stand against the wiles of the devil. 12 For we do not wrestle against flesh and blood, but against principalities, against powers, against the rulers of the darkness of this age, against spiritual hosts of wickedness in the heavenly places. 13 Therefore take up the whole armor of God, that you may be able to withstand in the evil day, and having done all, to stand. 14 Stand therefore, having girded your waist with truth, having put on the breastplate of righteousness, 15 and having shod your feet with the preparation of the gospel of peace; 16 above all, taking the shield of faith with which you will be able to quench all the fiery darts of the wicked one. 17 And take the helmet of salvation, and the sword of the Spirit, which is the word of God; 18 praying always with all prayer and supplication in the Spirit, being watchful to this end with all perseverance and supplication for all the saints—

Philippians 2:5-11 Let this mind be in you, which was also in Christ Jesus, 6 who, being in the form of God, did not consider it robbery to be equal with God, 7 but made Himself of no reputation, taking the form of a bondservant, and coming in the likeness of men. 8 And being found in appearance as a man, He humbled Himself and became obedient to the point of death, even the death of the cross. 9 Therefore God also has highly exalted Him and given Him the name which is above every name, 10 that at the name of Jesus every knee should bow, of those in heaven, and of those on earth, and of those under the earth, 11 and that every tongue should confess that Jesus Christ is Lord, to the glory of God the Father.

Colossians 2:9-15 For in Him dwells all the fullness of the Godhead bodily; 10 and you are complete in Him, who is the head of all principality and power. 11 In Him you were also circumcised with the circumcision made without hands, by putting off the body of the sins of the flesh, by the circumcision of Christ, 12 buried with Him in baptism, in which you also were raised with Him through faith in the working of God, who raised Him from the dead. 13 And you, being dead in your trespasses and the uncircumcision of your flesh, He has made alive together with Him, having forgiven you all trespasses, 14 having wiped out the handwriting of requirements that was against us, which was contrary to us. And He has taken it out of the way, having nailed it to the cross. 15 Having disarmed principalities and powers, He made a public spectacle of them, triumphing over them in it.

1 Peter 3:21-22 There is also an antitype which now saves us — baptism (not the removal of the filth of the flesh, but the answer of a good conscience toward God), through the resurrection of Jesus Christ, 22 who has gone into heaven and is at the right hand of God, angels and authorities and powers having been made subject to Him.

1 John 4:4 You are of God, little children, and have overcome them, because He who is in you is greater than he who is in the world.

Revelation 1:17-18 And when I saw Him, I fell at His feet as dead. But He laid His right hand on me, saying to me, "Do not be afraid; I am the First and the Last. 18 I am He who lives, and was dead, and behold, I am alive forevermore. Amen. And I have the keys of Hades and of Death.

Revelation 12:10-11Then I heard a loud voice saying in heaven, "Now salvation, and strength, and the kingdom of our God, and the power of His Christ have come, for the accuser of our brethren, who accused them before our God day and night, has been cast down. 11 And they overcame him by the blood of the Lamb and by the word of their testimony, and they did not love their lives to the death.

Faith

Matthew 17:20-20 So Jesus said to them, "Because of your unbelief; for assuredly, I say to you, if you have faith as a mustard seed, you will say to this mountain, 'Move from here to there,' and it will move; and nothing will be impossible for you.

Mark 9:23 Jesus said to him, "If you can believe, all things are possible to him who believes."

Mark 11:22-24 So Jesus answered and said to them, "Have faith in God. 23 For assuredly, I say to you, whoever says to this mountain, 'Be removed and be cast into the sea,' and does not doubt in his heart, but believes that those things he says will come to pass, he will have whatever he says. 24 Therefore I say to you, whatever things you ask when you pray, believe that you receive them, and you will have them.

John 14:13-14 And whatever you ask in My name, that I will do, that the Father may be glorified in the Son. 14 If you ask anything in My name, I will do it.

John 15:7 If you abide in Me, and My words abide in you, you will ask what you desire, and it shall be done for you.

Romans 4:13 For the promise that he would be the heir of the world was not to Abraham or to his seed through the law, but through the righteousness of faith.

Romans 5:1-2 Therefore, having been justified by faith, we have peace with God through our Lord Jesus Christ, 2 through whom also we have access by faith into this grace in which we stand, and rejoice in hope of the glory of God.

Romans 10:17 So then faith comes by hearing, and hearing by the word of God.

Galatians 5:22-23

22 But the fruit of the Spirit is love, joy, peace, patience, kindness, goodness, faithfulness, 23 gentleness, self-control. Against such there is no law.

Ephesians 2:8 For by grace you have been saved through faith, and that not of yourselves; it is the gift of God,

Ephesians 6:16 above all, taking the shield of faith with which you will be able to quench all the fiery darts of the wicked one.

Hebrews 11:1-3 Now faith is the substance of things hoped for, the evidence of things not seen. 2 For by it the elders obtained a good testimony. 3 By faith we understand that the worlds were framed by the word of God, so that the things which are seen were not made of things which are visible.

Hebrews 11:6 But without faith it is impossible to please Him, for he who comes to God must believe that He is, and that He is a rewarder of those who diligently seek Him.

James 1:2-4 My brethren, count it all joy when you fall into various trials, 3 knowing that the testing of your faith produces patience. 4 But let patience have its perfect work, that you may be perfect and complete, lacking nothing.

1 John 5:4 For whatever is born of God overcomes the world. And this is the victory that has overcome the world—our faith.

Family

Deuteronomy 4:40 You shall therefore keep His statutes and His commandments which I command you today, that it may go well with you and with your children after you, and that you may prolong your days in the land which the LORD your God is giving you for all time."

Psalm 128:1-6 Blessed is everyone who fears the LORD,

Who walks in His ways.
2 When you eat the labor of your hands,
You shall be happy, and it shall be well with you.
3 Your wife shall be like a fruitful vine
In the very heart of your house,
Your children like olive plants
All around your table.
4 Behold, thus shall the man be blessed
Who fears the LORD.
5 The LORD bless you out of Zion,
And may you see the good of Jerusalem
All the days of your life.
6 Yes, may you see your children's children.

Proverbs 20:7 The righteous man walks in his integrity; his children are blessed after him.

Proverbs 22:6 Train up a child in the way he should go, and when he is old he will not depart from it.

Isaiah 44:3 For I will pour water on him who is thirsty, and floods on the dry ground; I will pour My Spirit on your descendants, and My blessing on your offspring;

Isaiah 54:13 All your children shall be taught by the LORD, and great shall be the peace of your children.

Isaiah 59:21 "As for Me," says the LORD, "this is My covenant with them: My Spirit who is upon you, and My words which I have put in your mouth, shall not depart from your mouth, nor from the mouth of your descendants, nor from the mouth of your descendants' descendants," says the LORD, "from this time and forevermore."

Jeremiah 32:38-39 They shall be My people, and I will be their God; 39 then I will give them one heart and one way, that they may fear Me forever, for the good of them and their children after them.

Ephesians 6:1-4 Children, obey your parents in the Lord, for this is right. 2 "Honor your father and mother," which is the first commandment with promise: 3 "that it may be well with you and you may live long on the earth." 4 And you, fathers, do not provoke your children to wrath, but bring them up in the training and admonition of the Lord.

Colossians 3:18-21 Wives, submit to your own husbands, as is fitting in the Lord. 19 Husbands, love your wives and do not be bitter toward them. 20 Children, obey your parents in all things, for this is well pleasing to the Lord. 21 Fathers, do not provoke your children, lest they become discouraged.

Fear/Worry

Deuteronomy 31:6 Be strong and of good courage, do not fear nor be afraid of them; for the LORD your God, He is the One who goes with you. He will not leave you nor forsake you."

Deuteronomy 31:8 And the LORD, He is the one who goes before you. He will be with you, He will not leave you nor forsake you; do not fear nor be dismayed."

Joshua 1:7

7 Only be strong and very courageous, that you may observe to do according to all the law which Moses My servant commanded you; do not turn from it to the right hand or to the left, that you may prosper wherever you go.

Psalm 27:1 The LORD is my light and my salvation; whom shall I fear? The LORD is the strength of my life; of whom shall I be afraid?

Isaiah 41:10 Fear not, for I am with you; be not dismayed, for I am your God. I will strengthen you, yes, I will help you, I will uphold you with My righteous right hand.'

Isaiah 54:4 "Do not fear, for you will not be ashamed; neither be disgraced, for you will not be put to shame; for you will forget the shame of your youth, and will not remember the reproach of your widowhood anymore.

Luke 12:32 Do not fear, little flock, for it is your Father's good pleasure to give you the kingdom.

Romans 8:14-17 For as many as are led by the Spirit of God, these are sons of God. 15 For you did not receive the spirit of bondage again to fear, but you received the Spirit of adoption by whom we cry out, "Abba, Father." 16 The Spirit Himself bears witness with our spirit that we are children of God, 17 and if children, then heirs—heirs of God and joint heirs with Christ, if indeed we suffer with Him, that we may also be glorified together.

Philippians 4:6-8 Don't worry about anything; instead, pray about everything; tell God your needs, and don't forget to thank him for his answers. 7 If you do this, you will experience God's peace, which is far more wonderful than the human mind can understand. His peace will keep your thoughts and your hearts quiet and at rest as you trust in Christ Jesus. TLB

2 Timothy 1:7 For God has not given us a spirit of fear, but of power and of love and of a sound mind.

1 John 4:18 There is no fear in love; but perfect love casts out fear, because fear involves torment. But he who fears has not been made perfect in love.

(There is one kind of fear that the Bible says is good. In fact, it will protect you from all other fear. The Bible speaks often of the "fear" of God. In this case "fear" has the idea of reverence, of deep respect, of such a deep desire to please God and be close to Him that there is fear of anything that would cause separation from Him.)

Psalm 25:12-14 Who is the man that fears the LORD? Him shall He teach in the way He chooses. 13 He himself shall dwell in prosperity, and his descendants shall inherit the earth. 14 The secret of the LORD is with those who fear Him, and He will show them His covenant.

Psalm 34:7-11
7 The angel of the LORD encamps all around those who fear Him,
And delivers them.
8 Oh, taste and see that the LORD is good;
Blessed is the man who trusts in Him!
9 Oh, fear the LORD, you His saints!
There is no want to those who fear Him.
10 The young lions lack and suffer hunger;
But those who seek the LORD shall not lack any good thing.
11 Come, you children, listen to me;
I will teach you the fear of the LORD.

Psalm 111:10
10 The fear of the LORD is the beginning of wisdom;
A good understanding have all those who do His commandments.
His praise endures forever.

Proverbs 1:7

7 The fear of the LORD is the beginning of knowledge, but fools despise wisdom and instruction.

Proverbs 19:23 The fear of the LORD leads to life, and he who has it will abide in satisfaction; He will not be visited with evil.

Proverbs 22:4 By humility and the fear of the LORD are riches and honor and life.

Finances

Proverbs 28:27 He who gives to the poor will not lack, but he who hides his eyes will have many curses.

Ecclesiastes 11:1 Cast your bread upon the waters, for you will find it after many days.

Malachi 3:10-11 Bring all the tithes into the storehouse, that there may be food in My house, and try Me now in this," says the LORD of hosts, "If I will not open for you the windows of heaven and pour out for you such blessing that there will not be room enough to receive it.

11 "And I will rebuke the devourer for your sakes, so that he will not destroy the fruit of your ground, nor shall the vine fail to bear fruit for you in the field," says the LORD of hosts;

Matthew 7:7-11 "Ask, and it will be given to you; seek, and you will find; knock, and it will be opened to you. 8 For everyone who asks receives, and he who seeks finds, and to him who knocks it will be opened. 9 Or what man is there among you who, if his son asks for bread, will give him a stone? 10 Or if he asks for a fish, will he give him a serpent? 11 If you then, being evil, know how to give good gifts to your children, how much more will your Father who is in heaven give good things to those who ask Him!

Matthew 18:19 Again I say to you that if two of you agree on earth concerning anything that they ask, it will be done for them by My Father in heaven.

Mark 11:22-24 So Jesus answered and said to them, "Have faith in God. 23 For assuredly, I say to you, whoever says to this mountain, 'Be removed and be cast into the sea,' and does not doubt in his heart, but believes that those things he says will come to pass, he will have whatever he says. 24 Therefore I say to you, whatever things you ask when you pray, believe that you receive them, and you will have them.

Luke 6:38 Give, and it will be given to you: good measure, pressed down, shaken together, and running over will be put into your bosom. For with the same measure that you use, it will be measured back to you."

John 10:10 The thief does not come except to steal, and to kill, and to destroy. I have come that they may have life, and that they may have it more abundantly.

John 14:12-14 "Most assuredly, I say to you, he who believes in Me, the works that I do he will do also; and greater works than these he will do, because I go to My Father. 13 And whatever you ask in My name, that I will do, that the Father may be glorified in the Son. 14 If you ask anything in My name, I will do it.

John 16:24 Until now you have asked nothing in My name. Ask, and you will receive, that your joy may be full.

2 Corinthians 1:20 For all the promises of God in Him are Yes, and in Him Amen, to the glory of God through us.

Philippians 4:19 And my God shall supply all your need according to His riches in glory by Christ Jesus.

3 John 2 Beloved, I pray that you may prosper in all things and be in health, just as your soul prospers.

Forgiveness

Psalm 103:2-3 Bless the LORD, O my soul, and forget not all His benefits: 3 Who forgives all your iniquities, Who heals all your diseases,

Psalm 103:12 As far as the east is from the west, so far has He removed our transgressions from us.

Jeremiah 31:34 No more shall every man teach his neighbor, and every man his brother, saying, 'Know the LORD,' for they all shall know Me, from the least of them to the greatest of them, says the LORD. For I will forgive their iniquity, and their sin I will remember no more."

Jeremiah 33:8 I will cleanse them from all their iniquity by which they have sinned against Me, and I will pardon all their iniquities by which they have sinned and by which they have transgressed against Me.

Matthew 6:12-15 And forgive us our debts, as we forgive our debtors... 14 "For if you forgive men their trespasses, your heavenly Father will also forgive you. 15 But if you do not forgive men their trespasses, neither will your Father forgive your trespasses.

Mark 11:25-26 "And whenever you stand praying, if you have anything against anyone, forgive him, that your Father in heaven may also forgive you your trespasses. 26 But if you do not forgive, neither will your Father in heaven forgive your trespasses."

Luke 6:37-38 "Judge not, and you shall not be judged. Condemn not, and you shall not be condemned. Forgive, and you will be forgiven. 38 Give, and it will be given to you: good measure, pressed down, shaken together, and running over will be put into your bosom. For with the same measure that you use, it will be measured back to you."

John 1:29 The next day John saw Jesus coming toward him, and said, "Behold! The Lamb of God who takes away the sin of the world!

Romans 5:1 Therefore, having been justified by faith, we have peace with God through our Lord Jesus Christ,

Romans 8:1 There is therefore now no condemnation to those who are in Christ Jesus, who do not walk according to the flesh, but according to the Spirit.

2 Corinthians 5:21 For He made Him who knew no sin to be sin for us, that we might become the righteousness of God in Him.

Colossians 1:13 He has delivered us from the power of darkness and conveyed us into the kingdom of the Son of His love, 14 in whom we have redemption through His blood, the forgiveness of sins.

Colossians 2:9-15 For in Him dwells all the fullness of the Godhead bodily; 10 and you are complete in Him, who is the head of all principality and power.

11 In Him you were also circumcised with the circumcision made without hands, by putting off the body of the sins of the flesh, by the circumcision of Christ, 12 buried with Him in baptism, in which you also were raised with Him through faith in the working of God, who raised Him from the dead. 13 And you, being dead in your trespasses and the uncircumcision of your flesh, He has made alive together with Him, having forgiven you all trespasses, 14 having wiped out the handwriting of requirements that was against us, which was contrary to us. And He has taken it out of the way, having nailed it to the cross. 15 Having disarmed principalities and powers, He made a public spectacle of them, triumphing over them in it.

1 Peter 2:24-25 who Himself bore our sins in His own body on the tree, that we, having died to sins, might live for righteousness—by whose stripes you were healed. 25 For you were like sheep going astray, but have now returned to the Shepherd and Overseer of your souls.

1 John 1:7-9 But if we walk in the light as He is in the light, we have fellowship with one another, and the blood of Jesus Christ

His Son cleanses us from all sin. 8 If we say that we have no sin, we deceive ourselves, and the truth is not in us. **9 If we confess our sins, He is faithful and just to forgive us our sins and to cleanse us from all unrighteousness.**

Friendship

Proverbs 18:24 A man who has friends must himself be friendly, but there is a friend who sticks closer than a brother.

John 15:13-14 Greater love has no one than this, than to lay down one's life for his friends. 14 You are My friends if you do whatever I command you.

1 Corinthians 13:4-8 Love suffers long and is kind; love does not envy; love does not parade itself, is not puffed up; 5 does not behave rudely, does not seek its own, is not provoked, thinks no evil; 6 does not rejoice in iniquity, but rejoices in the truth; 7 bears all things, believes all things, hopes all things, endures all things. 8 Love never fails. But whether there are prophecies, they will fail; whether there are tongues, they will cease; whether there is knowledge, it will vanish away.

2 Corinthians 6:14-15 Do not be unequally yoked together with unbelievers. For what fellowship has righteousness with lawlessness? And what communion has light with darkness? 15 And what accord has Christ with Belial? Or what part has a believer with an unbeliever?

1 John 1:7 But if we walk in the light as He is in the light, we have fellowship with one another, and the blood of Jesus Christ His Son cleanses us from all sin.

Healing

Exodus 23:25 So you shall serve the LORD your God, and He will bless your bread and your water. And I will take sickness away from the midst of you.

Deuteronomy 7:13-15 And He will love you and bless you and multiply you; He will also bless the fruit of your womb and the fruit of your land, your grain and your new wine and your oil, the increase of your cattle and the offspring of your flock, in the land of which He swore to your fathers to give you. 14 You shall be blessed above all peoples; there shall not be a male or female barren among you or among your livestock. 15 And the LORD will take away from you all sickness, and will afflict you with none of the terrible diseases of Egypt which you have known, but will lay them on all those who hate you.

Psalm 103:1-5
Bless the LORD, O my soul;
And all that is within me, bless His holy name!
2 Bless the LORD, O my soul,
And forget not all His benefits:
3 Who forgives all your iniquities,
Who heals all your diseases,
4 Who redeems your life from destruction,
Who crowns you with loving kindness and tender mercies,
5 Who satisfies your mouth with good things,
So that your youth is renewed like the eagle's.

Proverbs 18:20-21 A man's stomach shall be satisfied from the fruit of his mouth, from the produce of his lips he shall be filled. 21 Death and life are in the power of the tongue, and those who love it will eat its fruit.

Isaiah 53:4-5 Surely He has borne our griefs and carried our sorrows; yet we esteemed Him stricken, smitten by God, and afflicted. 5 But He was wounded for our transgressions, He was bruised for our iniquities; the chastisement for our peace was upon Him, and by His stripes we are healed.

Isaiah 61:1-3
"The Spirit of the Lord GOD is upon Me,
Because the LORD has anointed Me
To preach good tidings to the poor;
He has sent Me to heal the brokenhearted,
To proclaim liberty to the captives,
And the opening of the prison to those who are bound;
2 To proclaim the acceptable year of the LORD,
And the day of vengeance of our God;
To comfort all who mourn,
3 To console those who mourn in Zion,
To give them beauty for ashes,
The oil of joy for mourning,
The garment of praise for the spirit of heaviness;
That they may be called trees of righteousness,
The planting of the LORD, that He may be glorified."

Jeremiah 33:6 Behold, I will bring it health and healing; I will heal them and reveal to them the abundance of peace and truth.

Ezekiel 16:6 "And when I passed by you and saw you struggling in your own blood, I said to you in your blood, 'Live!' Yes, I said to you in your blood, 'Live!'

(The above verse has been effective in stopping bleeding.)

Malachi 4:2 But to you who fear My name the Sun of Righteousness shall arise with healing in His wings; and you shall go out and grow fat like stall-fed calves.

Matthew 4:23 And Jesus went about all Galilee, teaching in their synagogues, preaching the gospel of the kingdom, and healing all kinds of sickness and all kinds of disease among the people.

Matthew 7:7-9 "Ask, and it will be given to you; seek, and you will find; knock, and it will be opened to you. 8 For everyone who asks receives, and he who seeks finds, and to him who knocks it will be opened. 9 Or what man is there among you who, if his son asks for bread, will give him a stone?

Matthew 10:1 And when He had called His twelve disciples to Him, He gave them power over unclean spirits, to cast them out, and to heal all kinds of sickness and all kinds of disease.

Matthew 10:8 "Heal the sick, cleanse the lepers, raise the dead, cast out demons. Freely you have received, freely give.

Matthew 15:30-31 Then great multitudes came to Him, having with them the lame, blind, mute, maimed, and many others; and they laid them down at Jesus' feet, and He healed them. 31 So the multitude marveled when they saw the mute speaking, the maimed made whole, the lame walking, and the blind seeing; and they glorified the God of Israel.

Mark 6:56 Wherever He entered, into villages, cities, or the country, they laid the sick in the marketplaces, and begged Him that they might just touch the hem of His garment. And as many as touched Him were made well.

Mark 9:23 Jesus said to him, "If you can believe, all things are possible to him who believes."

Mark 16:17-18 And these signs will follow those who believe: In My name they will cast out demons; they will speak with new tongues; 18 they will take up serpents; and if they drink anything deadly, it will by no means hurt them; they will lay hands on the sick, and they will recover."

John 10:10 The thief does not come except to steal, and to kill, and to destroy. I have come that they may have life, and that they may have it more abundantly.

John 14:12-14 "Most assuredly, I say to you, he who believes in Me, the works that I do he will do also; and greater works than these he will do, because I go to My Father. 13 And whatever you ask in My name, that I will do, that the Father may be glorified in the Son. 14 If you ask anything in My name, I will do it.

John 16:23-24 And in that day you will ask Me nothing. Most assuredly, I say to you, whatever you ask the Father in My name He will give you. 24 Until now you have asked nothing in My name. Ask, and you will receive, that your joy may be full.

Acts 10:38 how God anointed Jesus of Nazareth with the Holy Spirit and with power, who went about doing good and healing all who were oppressed by the devil, for God was with Him.

Romans 8:11 But if the Spirit of Him who raised Jesus from the dead dwells in you, He who raised Christ from the dead will also give life to your mortal bodies through His Spirit who dwells in you.

Hebrews 10:23 Let us hold fast the confession of our hope without wavering, for He who promised is faithful.

James 5:14-16 Is anyone among you sick? Let him call for the elders of the church, and let them pray over him, anointing him with oil in the name of the Lord. 15 And the prayer of faith will save the sick, and the Lord will raise him up. And if he has committed sins, he will be forgiven. 16 Confess your trespasses to one another, and pray for one another, that you may be healed. The effective, fervent prayer of a righteous man avails much.

3 John 2 Beloved, I pray that you may prosper in all things and be in health, just as your soul prospers.

Rev 12:11 And they overcame him by the blood of the Lamb and by the word of their testimony, and they did not love their lives to the death.

Holy Spirit

Genesis 1:1-3 In the beginning God created the heavens and the earth. 2 The earth was without form, and void; and darkness was on the face of the deep. And the Spirit of God was hovering over the face of the waters. 3 Then God said, "Let there be light"; and there was light.

Matthew 3:11 I indeed baptize you with water unto repentance, but He who is coming after me is mightier than I, whose sandals I am not worthy to carry. He will baptize you with the Holy Spirit and fire.

Luke 4:18-19 "The Spirit of the LORD is upon Me, because He has anointed Me to preach the gospel to the poor; He has sent Me to heal the brokenhearted, to proclaim liberty to the captives and recovery of sight to the blind, to set at liberty those who are oppressed; 19 To proclaim the acceptable year of the LORD."

Luke 11:9-13 "So I say to you, ask, and it will be given to you; seek, and you will find; knock, and it will be opened to you. 10 For everyone who asks receives, and he who seeks finds, and to him who knocks it will be opened. 11 If a son asks for bread from any father among you, will he give him a stone? Or if he asks for a fish, will he give him a serpent instead of a fish? 12 Or if he asks for an egg, will he offer him a scorpion? 13 If you then, being evil, know how to give good gifts to your children, how much more will your heavenly Father give the Holy Spirit to those who ask Him!"

John 14:15-17 "If you love Me, keep My commandments. 16 And I will pray the Father, and He will give you another Helper, that He may abide with you forever— 17 the Spirit of truth, whom the world cannot receive, because it neither sees Him nor knows Him; but you know Him, for He dwells with you and will be in you.

John 14:26 But the Helper, the Holy Spirit, whom the Father will send in My name, He will teach you all things, and bring to your remembrance all things that I said to you.

John 20:22-23 And when He had said this, He breathed on them, and said to them, "Receive the Holy Spirit. 23 If you forgive the sins of any, they are forgiven them; if you retain the sins of any, they are retained."

Acts 1:4-5 And being assembled together with them, He commanded them not to depart from Jerusalem, but to wait for the Promise of the Father, "which," He said, "you have heard from Me; 5 for John truly baptized with water, but you shall be baptized with the Holy Spirit not many days from now."

Acts 1:8 But you shall receive power when the Holy Spirit has come upon you; and you shall be witnesses to Me in Jerusalem, and in all Judea and Samaria, and to the end of the earth."

Acts 2:1-4 Now when the Day of Pentecost had fully come, they were all with one accord in one place. 2 And suddenly there came a sound from heaven, as of a rushing mighty wind, and it filled the whole house where they were sitting. 3 Then there appeared to them divided tongues, as of fire, and one sat upon each of them. 4 And they were all filled with the Holy Spirit and began to speak with other tongues, as the Spirit gave them utterance.

Acts 10:44-48 While Peter was still speaking these words, the Holy Spirit fell upon all those who heard the word. 45 And those of the circumcision who believed were astonished, as many as came with Peter, because the gift of the Holy Spirit had been poured out on the Gentiles also. 46 For they heard them speak with tongues and magnify God. Then Peter answered, 47 Can anyone forbid water, that these should not be baptized who have received the Holy Spirit just as we have?" 48 And he commanded them to be baptized in the name of the Lord. Then they asked him to stay a few days.

Romans 8:16-17 The Spirit Himself bears witness with our spirit that we are children of God, 17 and if children, then heirs—heirs of God and joint heirs with Christ, if indeed we suffer with Him, that we may also be glorified together.

Romans 8:26-28 Likewise the Spirit also helps in our weaknesses. For we do not know what we should pray for as we ought, but the Spirit Himself makes intercession for us with groanings which cannot be uttered. 27 Now He who searches the hearts knows what the mind of the Spirit is, because He makes intercession for the saints according to the will of God. 28 And we know that all things work together for good to those who love God, to those who are the called according to His purpose.

Galatians 4:6-7
6 And because you are sons, God has sent forth the Spirit of His Son into your hearts, crying out, "Abba, Father!" 7 Therefore you are no longer a slave but a son, and if a son, then an heir of God through Christ.

Galatians 5:22-23 But the fruit of the Spirit is love, joy, peace, patience, kindness, goodness, faithfulness, 23 gentleness, self-control. Against such there is no law.

1 John 2:27 But the anointing which you have received from Him abides in you, and you do not need that anyone teach you; but as the same anointing teaches you concerning all things, and is true, and is not a lie, and just as it has taught you, you will abide in Him.

Joy

Deuteronomy 12:7 And there you shall eat before the LORD your God, and you shall rejoice in all to which you have put your hand, you and your households, in which the LORD your God has blessed you.

Nehemiah 8:10 Then he said to them, "Go your way, eat the fat, drink the sweet, and send portions to those for whom nothing is prepared; for this day is holy to our LORD. Do not sorrow, for the joy of the LORD is your strength."

Psalm 16:11 You will show me the path of life; in Your presence is fullness of joy; at Your right hand are pleasures forevermore.

Isaiah 51:11 So the ransomed of the LORD shall return, and come to Zion with singing, with everlasting joy on their heads. They shall obtain joy and gladness; sorrow and sighing shall flee away.

Isaiah 61:3 To console those who mourn in Zion, to give them beauty for ashes, the oil of joy for mourning, the garment of praise for the spirit of heaviness; that they may be called trees of righteousness, the planting of the LORD, that He may be glorified."

John 15:11 These things I have spoken to you, that My joy may remain in you, and that your joy may be full.

John 16:22-24 Therefore you now have sorrow; but I will see you again and your heart will rejoice, and your joy no one will take from you. 23 And in that day you will ask Me nothing. Most assuredly, I say to you, whatever you ask the Father in My name He will give you. 24 Until now you have asked nothing in My name. Ask, and you will receive, that your joy may be full.

Romans 14:17 for the kingdom of God is not eating and drinking, but righteousness and peace and joy in the Holy Spirit.

Galatians 5:22-23 But the fruit of the Spirit is love, joy, peace, patience, kindness, goodness, faithfulness, 23 gentleness, self-control. Against such there is no law.

Philippians 4:4-8 Rejoice in the Lord always. Again, I will say, rejoice! 5 Let your gentleness be known to all men. The Lord is at hand. 6 Be anxious for nothing, but in everything by prayer and supplication, with thanksgiving, let your requests be made known to God; 7 and the peace of God, which surpasses all understanding, will guard your hearts and minds through Christ Jesus.

8 Finally, brethren, whatever things are true, whatever things are noble, whatever things are just, whatever things are pure, whatever things are lovely, whatever things are of good report, if there is any virtue and if there is anything praiseworthy—meditate on these things.

James 1:2-4 My brethren, count it all joy when you fall into various trials, 3 knowing that the testing of your faith produces patience. 4 But let patience have its perfect work, that you may be perfect and complete, lacking nothing.

Love

John 3:16 For God so loved the world that He gave His only begotten Son, that whoever believes in Him should not perish but have everlasting life.

John 13:34 A new commandment I give to you, that you love one another; as I have loved you, that you also love one another.

Romans 5:5 Now hope does not disappoint, because the love of God has been poured out in our hearts by the Holy Spirit who was given to us.

Romans 8:37-39 Yet in all these things we are more than conquerors through Him who loved us. 38 For I am persuaded that neither death nor life, nor angels nor principalities nor powers, nor things present nor things to come, 39 nor height nor depth, nor any other created thing, shall be able to separate us from the love of God which is in Christ Jesus our Lord.

1 Corinthians 13:4-8 Love suffers long and is kind; love does not envy; love does not parade itself, is not puffed up; 5 does not

behave rudely, does not seek its own, is not provoked, thinks no evil; 6 does not rejoice in iniquity, but rejoices in the truth; 7 bears all things, believes all things, hopes all things, endures all things. 8 Love never fails.

Galatians 5:22-23 But the fruit of the Spirit is love, joy, peace, patience, kindness, goodness, faithfulness, 23 gentleness, self-control. Against such there is no law.

Ephesians 3:17-19 that Christ may dwell in your hearts through faith; that you, being rooted and grounded in love, 18 may be able to comprehend with all the saints what is the width and length and depth and height— 19 to know the love of Christ which passes knowledge; that you may be filled with all the fullness of God.

1 John 4:7-16 Beloved, let us love one another, for love is of God; and everyone who loves is born of God and knows God. 8 He who does not love does not know God, for God is love. 9 In this the love of God was manifested toward us, that God has sent His only begotten Son into the world, that we might live through Him. 10 In this is love, not that we loved God, but that He loved us and sent His Son to be the propitiation for our sins. 11 Beloved, if God so loved us, we also ought to love one another.

12 No one has seen God at any time. If we love one another, God abides in us, and His love has been perfected in us. 13 By this we know that we abide in Him, and He in us, because He has given us of His Spirit. 14 And we have seen and testify that the Father has sent the Son as Savior of the world. 15 Whoever confesses that Jesus is the Son of God, God abides in him, and he in God. 16 And we have known and believed the love that God has for us. God is love, and he who abides in love abides in God, and God in him.

Mercy

1 Chronicles 16:34 Oh, give thanks to the LORD, for He is good! For His mercy endures forever.

Psalm 23:6 Surely goodness and mercy shall follow me all the days of my life; and I will dwell in the house of the LORD forever.

Psalm 33:18 Behold, the eye of the LORD is on those who fear Him, on those who hope in His mercy,

Psalm 52:8 But I am like a green olive tree in the house of God; I trust in the mercy of God forever and ever.

Psalm 85:10 Mercy and truth have met together; righteousness and peace have kissed.

Proverbs 20:28
28 Mercy and truth preserve the king,

And by lovingkindness he upholds his throne.

Hosea 6:6 For I desire mercy and not sacrifice, and the knowledge of God more than burnt offerings.

Hosea 10:12 Sow for yourselves righteousness; reap in mercy; break up your fallow ground, for it is time to seek the LORD, till He comes and rains righteousness on you.

Micah 6:8 He has shown you, O man, what is good; and what does the LORD require of you but to do justly, to love mercy, and to walk humbly with your God?

Matthew 5:7 Blessed are the merciful, for they shall obtain mercy.

Luke 1:50 And His mercy is on those who fear Him from generation to generation.

Ephesians 2:4-7 But God, who is rich in mercy, because of His great love with which He loved us, 5 even when we were dead in trespasses, made us alive together with Christ (by grace you have been saved), 6 and raised us up together, and made us sit together in the heavenly places in Christ Jesus, 7 that in the ages to come He might show the exceeding riches of His grace in His kindness toward us in Christ Jesus.

Obedience

Acts 5:29 But Peter and the other apostles answered and said: "We ought to obey God rather than men.

Acts 5:32 And we are His witnesses to these things, and so also is the Holy Spirit whom God has given to those who obey Him."

Romans 5:19 For as by one man's disobedience many were made sinners, so also by one Man's obedience many will be made righteous.

2 Corinthians 10:3-6 For though we walk in the flesh, we do not war according to the flesh. 4 For the weapons of our warfare are not carnal but mighty in God for pulling down strongholds, 5 casting down arguments and every high thing that exalts itself against the knowledge of God, bringing every thought into captivity to the obedience of Christ, 6 and being ready to punish all disobedience when your obedience is fulfilled.

Philippians 2:5-13 Let this mind be in you which was also in Christ Jesus, 6 who, being in the form of God, did not consider it robbery to be equal with God, 7 but made Himself of no reputation, taking the form of a bondservant, and coming in the likeness of men. 8 And being found in appearance as a man, He humbled Himself and became obedient to the point of death, even the death of the cross. 9 Therefore God also has highly exalted Him and given Him the name which is above every name, 10 that at the name of Jesus every knee should bow, of those in heaven, and of those on earth, and of those under the earth, 11 and that every tongue should confess that Jesus Christ is Lord, to the glory of God the Father.

12 Therefore, my beloved, as you have always obeyed, not as in my presence only, but now much more in my absence, work out your own salvation with fear and trembling; 13 for it is God who works in you both to will and to do for His good pleasure.

James 1:22-26 But be doers of the word, and not hearers only, deceiving yourselves. 23 For if anyone is a hearer of the word and not a doer, he is like a man observing his natural face in a mirror; 24 for he observes himself, goes away, and immediately forgets what kind of man he was. 25 But he who looks into the perfect law of liberty and continues in it, and is not a forgetful hearer but a doer of the work, this one will be blessed in what he does.

Patience

Psalm 37:7-9 Rest in the LORD, and wait patiently for Him; do not fret because of him who prospers in his way, because of the man who brings wicked schemes to pass. 8 Cease from anger, and forsake wrath; do not fret—It only causes harm. 9 For evildoers shall be cut off; but those who wait on the LORD, they shall inherit the earth.

Isaiah 40:31 But those who wait on the LORD shall renew their strength; they shall mount up with wings like eagles, they shall run and not be weary, they shall walk and not faint.

Luke 21:19 By your patience possess your souls.

Galatians 5:22-23
22 But when the Holy Spirit controls our lives he will produce this kind of fruit in us: love, joy, peace, patience, kindness, goodness, faithfulness, 23 gentleness and self-control; and here there is no conflict with Jewish laws. TLB

Galatians 6:9 And let us not grow weary while doing good, for in due season we shall reap if we do not lose heart.

Ephesians 4:1-3 I beg you—I, a prisoner here in jail for serving the Lord—to live and act in a way worthy of those who have been chosen for such wonderful blessings as these. 2 Be humble and gentle. Be patient with each other, making allowance for each other's faults because of your love. 3 Try always to be led along together by the Holy Spirit and so be at peace with one another. TLB

Colossians 3:12-13
12 Since you have been chosen by God who has given you this new kind of life, and because of his deep love and concern for you, you should practice tenderhearted mercy and kindness to others. Don't worry about making a good impression on them, but be ready to suffer quietly and patiently. 13 Be gentle and ready to forgive; never hold grudges. Remember, the Lord forgave you, so you must forgive others. TLB

Hebrews 6:11-12 And we desire that each one of you show the same diligence to the full assurance of hope until the end, 12 that you do not become sluggish, but imitate those who through faith and patience inherit the promises.

James 1:2-4 My brethren, count it all joy when you fall into various trials, 3 knowing that the testing of your faith produces patience. 4 But let patience have its perfect work, that you may be perfect and complete, lacking nothing.

1 Timothy 6:11 But you, O man of God, flee these things and pursue righteousness, godliness, faith, love, patience, gentleness.

Peace

The Hebrew word for peace is *shalom* (shaw-lome'). It carries a broad range of meaning which pretty well encompasses the whole being. It means safe, well, happy, friendly; also (abstractly) welfare, i.e. health, prosperity, peace. Peace in the Bible sense includes much more that an absence of strife.

Psalm 4:8 I will both lie down in peace, and sleep;
For You alone, O LORD, make me dwell in safety.

Psalm 29:11 The LORD will give strength to His people; the LORD will bless His people with peace.

Psalm 37:11 But the meek shall inherit the earth, and shall delight themselves in the abundance of peace.

Psalm 119:165 Great peace have those who love Your law, and nothing causes them to stumble.

Psalm 122:6-8 Pray for the peace of Jerusalem: "May they prosper who love you. 7 Peace be within your walls, prosperity within your palaces." 8 For the sake of my brethren and companions, I will now say, "Peace be within you."

Isaiah 26:3 You will keep him in perfect peace, whose mind is stayed on You, because he trusts in You.

Isaiah 26:12 LORD, You will establish peace for us, for You have also done all our works in us.

Isaiah 32:17 The work of righteousness will be peace, and the effect of righteousness, quietness and assurance forever.

Isaiah 54:13 All your children shall be taught by the LORD, and great shall be the peace of your children.

Matthew 11:28-30 Come to Me, all you who labor and are heavy laden, and I will give you rest. 29 Take My yoke upon you and learn from Me, for I am gentle and lowly in heart, and you will find rest for your souls. 30 For My yoke is easy and My burden is light."

John 14:27 Peace I leave with you, My peace I give to you; not as the world gives do I give to you. Let not your heart be troubled, neither let it be afraid.

Romans 8:6 For to be carnally minded is death, but to be spiritually minded is life and peace.

Rom 16:20 And the God of peace will crush Satan under your feet shortly. The grace of our Lord Jesus Christ be with you. Amen.

Ephesians 6:14-18 Stand therefore, having girded your waist with truth, having put on the breastplate of righteousness, 15 and having shod your feet with the preparation of the gospel of peace; 16 above all, taking the shield of faith with which you will be able to quench all the fiery darts of the wicked one. 17 And take the helmet of salvation, and the sword of the Spirit, which is the word of God;

Philippians 4:6-7 Be anxious for nothing, but in everything by prayer and supplication, with thanksgiving, let your requests be made known to God; 7 and the peace of God, which surpasses all understanding, will guard your hearts and minds through Christ Jesus.

2 Thessalonians 3:16 Now may the Lord of peace Himself give you peace always in every way. The Lord be with you all.

2 Timothy 1:7 For God has not given us a spirit of fear, but of power and of love and of a sound mind.

Praise & Worship

2 Samuel 6:14-15 Then David danced before the LORD with all his might; and David was wearing a linen ephod. 15 So David and all the house of Israel brought up the ark of the LORD with shouting and with the sound of the trumpet.

Psalm 9:1-2 I will praise You, O LORD, with my whole heart; I will tell of all Your marvelous works. 2 I will be glad and rejoice in You; I will sing praise to Your name, O Most High.

Psalm 28:6-7 Blessed be the LORD, because He has heard the voice of my supplications! 7 The LORD is my strength and my shield; my heart trusted in Him, and I am helped; therefore, my heart greatly rejoices, and with my song I will praise Him.

Psalm 29:2 Give unto the LORD the glory due to His name; worship the LORD in the beauty of holiness.

Psalm 34:1-3 I will bless the LORD at all times; His praise shall continually be in my mouth. 2 My soul shall make its boast in the LORD; the humble shall hear of it and be glad. Oh, magnify the LORD with me, and let us exalt His name together.

Psalm 63:3-4 Because Your lovingkindness is better than life, my lips shall praise You. 4 Thus I will bless You while I live; I will lift up my hands in Your name.

Psalm 66:1-4 Make a joyful shout to God, all the earth! 2 Sing out the honor of His name; make His praise glorious. 3 Say to God, "How awesome are Your works! Through the greatness of Your power Your enemies shall submit themselves to You. 4 All the earth shall worship You and sing praises to You; they shall sing praises to Your name."

Psalm 95:6 Oh come, let us worship and bow down; let us kneel before the LORD our Maker.

Psalm 100 Make a joyful shout to the LORD, all you lands!
2 Serve the LORD with gladness;
Come before His presence with singing.
3 Know that the LORD, He is God;
It is He who has made us, and not we ourselves;
We are His people and the sheep of His pasture.
4 Enter into His gates with thanksgiving,
And into His courts with praise.
Be thankful to Him, and bless His name.
5 For the LORD is good;

His mercy is everlasting,
And His truth endures to all generations.

John 4:23-24 But the hour is coming, and now is, when the true worshipers will worship the Father in spirit and truth; for the Father is seeking such to worship Him. 24 God is Spirit, and those who worship Him must worship in spirit and truth."

1 Corinthians 14:15-16 What is the conclusion then? I will pray with the spirit, and I will also pray with the understanding. I will sing with the spirit, and I will also sing with the understanding.

Ephesians 5:18-20 And do not be drunk with wine, in which is dissipation; but be filled with the Spirit, 19 speaking to one another in psalms and hymns and spiritual songs, singing and making melody in your heart to the Lord, 20 giving thanks always for all things to God the Father in the name of our Lord Jesus Christ,

Philippians 3:3 For we are the circumcision, who worship God in the Spirit, rejoice in Christ Jesus, and have no confidence in the flesh,

Hebrews 13:15 Therefore by Him let us continually offer the sacrifice of praise to God, that is, the fruit of our lips, giving thanks to His name.

Prayer

Prayer is simply talking to God. It doesn't have to be fancy. Just talk to Him like you would to a good friend. One very good way to pray is to pray back to Him what the Bible says. Find scripture that meets your needs and prayer the promises back to God.

Isaiah 43:26 Put Me in remembrance; let us contend together; state your case, that you may be acquitted.

Matthew 18:18-20 Assuredly, I say to you, whatever you bind on earth will be bound in heaven, and whatever you loose on earth will be loosed in heaven. 19 Again I say to you that if two of you agree on earth concerning anything that they ask, it will be done for them by My Father in heaven. 20 For where two or three are gathered together in My name, I am there in the midst of them."

John 4:24 God is Spirit, and those who worship Him must worship in spirit and truth."

John 14:6 Jesus said to him, "I am the way, the truth, and the life. No one comes to the Father except through Me.

John 14:13-14 And whatever you ask in My name, that I will do, that the Father may be glorified in the Son. 14 If you ask anything in My name, I will do it.

John 16:23-24 And in that day you will ask Me nothing. Most assuredly, I say to you, whatever you ask the Father in My name He will give you. 24 Until now you have asked nothing in My name. Ask, and you will receive, that your joy may be full.

2 Corinthians 4:18 while we do not look at the things which are seen, but at the things which are not seen. For the things which are seen are temporary, but the things which are not seen are eternal.

Ephesians 6:17-18 And take the helmet of salvation, and the sword of the Spirit, which is the word of God; 18 praying always with all prayer and supplication in the Spirit, being watchful to this end with all perseverance and supplication for all the saints—

Hebrews 13:15 Therefore, by Him let us continually offer the sacrifice of praise to God, that is, the fruit of our lips, giving thanks to His name.

1 John 5:14-15 Now this is the confidence that we have in Him, that if we ask anything according to His will, He hears us. 15 And

if we know that He hears us, whatever we ask, we know that we have the petitions that we have asked of Him.

Protection

Exodus 14:14 The LORD will fight for you, and you shall hold your peace."

Deuteronomy 3:22
22 You must not fear them, for the LORD your God Himself fights for you.'

Deuteronomy 31:6 Be strong and of good courage, do not fear nor be afraid of them; for the LORD your God, He is the One who goes with you. He will not leave you nor forsake you."

Joshua 1:9 Have I not commanded you? Be strong and of good courage; do not be afraid, nor be dismayed, for the LORD your God is with you wherever you go."

Psalm 18:2-3 The LORD is my rock and my fortress and my deliverer; my God, my strength, in whom I will trust; my shield and the horn of my salvation, my stronghold. 3 I will call upon the LORD, who is worthy to be praised; so shall I be saved from my enemies.

Psalm 28:7-8 The LORD is my strength and my shield; my heart trusted in Him, and I am helped; therefore, my heart greatly rejoices, and with my song I will praise Him.
8 The LORD is their strength, and He is the saving refuge of His anointed.

Psalm 32:7 You are my hiding place; You shall preserve me from trouble; You shall surround me with songs of deliverance.

Psalm 34:7-8 The angel of the LORD encamps all around those who fear Him, and delivers them. 8 Oh, taste and see that the LORD is good; blessed is the man who trusts in Him!

Psalm 46:1-2 God is our refuge and strength, a very present help in trouble. 2 Therefore we will not fear, even though the earth be removed, and though the mountains be carried into the midst of the sea;

(Dick prayed Psalm 91 over our family every day for many years. Now I do. I believe it covers and protects us.)

Psalm 91He who dwells in the secret place of the Most High
Shall abide under the shadow of the Almighty.
2 I will say of the LORD, "He is my refuge and my fortress;
My God, in Him I will trust."
3 Surely He shall deliver you from the snare of the fowler
And from the perilous pestilence.
4 He shall cover you with His feathers,
And under His wings you shall take refuge;
His truth shall be your shield and buckler.
5 You shall not be afraid of the terror by night,
Nor of the arrow that flies by day,
6 Nor of the pestilence that walks in darkness,
Nor of the destruction that lays waste at noonday.
7 A thousand may fall at your side,
And ten thousand at your right hand; But it shall not come near you.
8 Only with your eyes shall you look, And see the reward of the wicked.
9 Because you have made the LORD, who is my refuge, Even the Most High, your dwelling place,
10 No evil shall befall you, Nor shall any plague come near your dwelling;
11 For He shall give His angels charge over you, To keep you in all your ways.
12 In their hands they shall bear you up, Lest you dash your foot against a stone.
13 You shall tread upon the lion and the cobra,
The young lion and the serpent you shall trample underfoot.
14 "Because he has set his love upon Me, therefore I will deliver him;

I will set him on high, because he has known My name.
15 He shall call upon Me, and I will answer him; I will be with him in trouble;
I will deliver him and honor him. 16 With long life I will satisfy him, And show him My salvation."

Psalm 125:2 As the mountains surround Jerusalem, so the LORD surrounds His people from this time forth and forever.

Proverbs 30:5 Every word of God is pure; He is a shield to those who put their trust in Him.

Isaiah 43:2 When you pass through the waters, I will be with you; and through the rivers, they shall not overflow you. When you walk through the fire, you shall not be burned, nor shall the flame scorch you.

Luke 10:19 Behold, I give you the authority to trample on serpents and scorpions, and over all the power of the enemy, and nothing shall by any means hurt you.

2 Thessalonians 3:3 But the Lord is faithful, who will establish you and guard you from the evil one.

Righteousness

Isaiah 32:17 The work of righteousness will be peace, and the effect of righteousness, quietness and assurance forever.

Romans 4:13 For the promise that he would be the heir of the world was not to Abraham or to his seed through the law, but through the righteousness of faith.

2 Corinthians 5:17 Therefore, if anyone is in Christ, he is a new creation; old things have passed away; behold, all things have become new.

2 Corinthians 5:21 For He made Him who knew no sin to be sin for us, that we might become the righteousness of God in Him.

Galatians 2:20-21 I have been crucified with Christ; it is no longer I who live, but Christ lives in me; and the life which I now live in the flesh I live by faith in the Son of God, who loved me and gave Himself for me. 21 I do not set aside the grace of God; for if righteousness comes through the law, then Christ died in vain."

Ephesians 6:13-14 Therefore take up the whole armor of God, that you may be able to withstand in the evil day, and having done all, to stand. 14 Stand therefore, having girded your waist with truth, having put on the breastplate of righteousness,

James 5:16 Confess your trespasses to one another, and pray for one another, that you may be healed. The effective, fervent prayer of a righteous man avails much.

1 John 1:7-9 But if we walk in the light as He is in the light, we have fellowship with one another, and the blood of Jesus Christ His Son cleanses us from all sin. 8 If we say that we have no sin, we deceive ourselves, and the truth is not in us. 9 If we confess our sins, He is faithful and just to forgive us our sins and to cleanse us from all unrighteousness.

Salvation

John 14:6 Jesus said to him, "I am the way, the truth, and the life. No one comes to the Father except through Me.

Romans 6:23 For the wages of sin is death, but the gift of God is eternal life in Christ Jesus our Lord.

Rom 10:8-10 But what does it say? "The word is near you, in your mouth and in your heart" (that is, the word of faith which we preach): 9 that if you confess with your mouth the Lord Jesus and believe in your heart that God has raised Him from the dead, you will be saved. 10 For with the heart one believes unto righteousness, and with the mouth confession is made unto salvation.

2 Corinthians 5:17 Therefore, if anyone is in Christ, he is a new creation; old things have passed away; behold, all things have become new.

1 Timothy 2:3-4 For this is good and acceptable in the sight of God our Savior, 4 who desires all men to be saved and to come to the knowledge of the truth.

1 John 2:2 And He Himself is the propitiation for our sins, and not for ours only but also for the whole world.

Revelation 3:20 Behold, I stand at the door and knock. If anyone hears My voice and opens the door, I will come in to him and dine with him, and he with Me.

Prayer to receive salvation:
Heavenly Father, I come to you in the name of Jesus. I want Jesus to be Lord of my life. I confess my sins and I receive your forgiveness. I believe in my heart that Jesus is the Son of God and that you raised Him from the dead. Jesus, come into my heart and be the Lord of my life. I receive my salvation. I am a child of God. Thank you, Lord. In the name of Jesus. Amen

Self-Control

Psalm 119:89-90 Forever, O Lord, your Word stands firm in heaven. 90 Your faithfulness extends to every generation, like the earth you created; it endures by your decree, for everything serves your plans. TLB

Psalm 119:105 Your word is a lamp to my feet and a light to my path.

Psalm 119:133-134 Direct my steps by Your word, and let no iniquity have dominion over me. 134 Redeem me from the oppression of man, that I may keep Your precepts.

John 15:4-5 Abide in Me, and I in you. As the branch cannot bear fruit of itself, unless it abides in the vine, neither can you, unless you abide in Me. 5 I am the vine, you are the branches. He who abides in Me, and I in him, bears much fruit; for without Me you can do nothing.

Romans 8:1-2 So there is now no condemnation awaiting those who belong to Christ Jesus. 2 For the power of the life-giving Spirit—and this power is mine through Christ Jesus—has freed me from the vicious circle of sin and death. TLB

Galatians 5:22-23 But the fruit of the Spirit is love, joy, peace, patience, kindness, goodness, faithfulness, 23 gentleness, self-control. Against such there is no law.

2 Timothy 1:7 For God has not given us a spirit of fear, but of power and of love and of a sound mind.

Hebrews 10:23 Let us hold fast the confession of our hope without wavering, for He who promised is faithful.

1 John 1:7 But if we walk in the light as He is in the light, we have fellowship with one another, and the blood of Jesus Christ His Son cleanses us from all sin.

Jude 20 But you, beloved, building yourselves up on your most holy faith, praying in the Holy Spirit,

Strength

Nehemiah 8:10 Do not sorrow, for the joy of the LORD is your strength.

Psalm 1:1-3 Blessed is the man who walks not in the counsel of the ungodly, nor stands in the path of sinners, nor sits in the seat of the scornful; 2 But his delight is in the law of the LORD, and in His law he meditates day and night. 3 He shall be like a tree planted by the rivers of water, that brings forth its fruit in its season, whose leaf also shall not wither; and whatever he does shall prosper.

Psalm 27:14 Wait on the LORD; be of good courage, and He shall strengthen your heart; wait, I say, on the LORD!

Psalm 37:3-7 Trust in the LORD, and do good; dwell in the land, and feed on His faithfulness. 4 Delight yourself also in the LORD, and He shall give you the desires of your heart. 5 Commit your way to the LORD, trust also in Him, and He shall bring it to pass. 6 He shall bring forth your righteousness as the light, and your justice as the noonday. 7 Rest in the LORD, and wait patiently for Him; do not fret because of him who prospers in his way, because of the man who brings wicked schemes to pass.

Isaiah 40:31 But those who wait on the LORD shall renew their strength; they shall mount up with wings like eagles, they shall run and not be weary, they shall walk and not faint.

Isaiah 41:10 Fear not, for I am with you; be not dismayed, for I am your God. I will strengthen you, yes, I will help you, I will uphold you with My righteous right hand.'

Romans 8:37 Yet in all these things we are more than conquerors through Him who loved us.

2 Corinthians 3:5 Not that we are sufficient of ourselves to think of anything as being from ourselves, but our sufficiency is from God,

Galatians 2:20 I have been crucified with Christ; it is no longer I who live, but Christ lives in me; and the life which I now live in the flesh I live by faith in the Son of God, who loved me and gave Himself for me.

Philippians 4:13 I can do all things through Christ who strengthens me.

1 Thessalonians 5:24 He who calls you is faithful, who also will do it.

Hebrews 4:16 Let us therefore come boldly to the throne of grace, that we may obtain mercy and find grace to help in time of need.

Hebrews 10:23 Let us hold fast the confession of our hope without wavering, for He who promised is faithful.

REFERENCES

Buonarroti, Michelangelo. http://thinkexist.com/quotes.

Foster, R. (1978). *Celebration of Discipline*. Harper and Row.

Guyon, J. (1981). *Experiencing the Depths of Jesus Christ*. Christian Books Pub House.

Hickey, M. (1983). *Motivational Gifts*. Word of Faith Publishing.

Kenyon, E.W. (1999). *The Blood Covenant,* Kenyon's Gospel Publishing Society.

Murray, A. (1997). *Abide in Christ*. CLC Publications.

Pierce, C., and Wagner Sytsema, R. (2004). *Protecting Your Home from Spiritual Darkness*.

Chosen Books.

Rolph, T. (2014). *Transforming Austin – a God Story*. Xulon Press.

Sanford, A. (1983). *The Healing Light*. Ballantine Books.

Servello, M. (2009). *God's Shield of Protection*. DS Lisi.

Sherill, J. (2018). *They Speak with Other Tongues*. Chosen Books.

Strong, J. (1994). *Biblesoft's New Exhaustive Strong's Numbers and Concordance with*

Expanded Greek-Hebrew Dictionary. Biblesoft and International Bible Translators, Inc.

Wallnau, L. *Doing Business Supernaturally 101*. Lance Wallnau Ministries.

Wallnau, L. (2003). *In a Heartbeat* CD series. Lance Wallnau Ministries.

CPSIA information can be obtained
at www.ICGtesting.com
Printed in the USA
BVHW041153040121
596016BV00010B/7